Praxis Special Education: Foundational Knowledge (5355)

How to *Think Like a Test Maker*™ and pass the Praxis 5355 using effective test prep, relevant practice questions, and proven strategies.

Kathleen Jasper LLC
Estero, FL 33928
http://www.kathleenjasper.com | info@KathleenJasper.com

Praxis Special Education: Foundational Knowledge (5355): *How to Think Like a Test Maker*™ and pass the Praxis 5355 using effective test prep, relevant practice questions, and proven strategies.

Printed in the United States of America
ISBN: 9798878222389

I'm Kathleen Jasper, and for the last decade, I've been helping prospective teachers and school leaders pass their certification exams and get the positions they want in education. To date, I've helped over 80,000 educators through their certification journeys.

I've had many positions in public education. I started off as a substitute teacher and went through the certification process you are going through right now. I was hired as a high school reading and biology teacher, and a couple of years later had the opportunity to work in curriculum at the district office. Finally, I became a high school assistant principal.

I left public education to start my own company, Kathleen Jasper LLC, and now I write study guides, conduct online courses, create content, and more to help you pass your exams and land your desired position.

I am thrilled you're here. Thank you for taking the time to review my content and purchase my products. It means the world to me to help educators all over the country.

Would you mind leaving a review?

Did you purchase this book on Amazon? If so, I would be thrilled if you would leave an unbiased review at your convenience. Did you purchase this book from kathleenjasper.com? If so, you can leave a review on Facebook, Google, or directly on our website on the product page. Thank you so much.

Check out my other products.

I have built several comprehensive, self-paced online courses for many teacher certification exams. I also have other books, webinars, and more. Go to https://kathleenjasper.com/ and use offer code **SPED** for 10% off any of my products.

If you have any questions, don't hesitate to reach out to info@kathleenjasper.com. It will be my pleasure to help. Good luck with your exam.

~Kathleen Jasper, Ed.D.

Follow me on social media.

 @kathleenjasperEdD

 @kathleen_jasper

 KathleenJasperEdD

 @kj_kathleenjasper

 @kathleenjasper

This page intentionally left blank.

Table of Contents

This page intentionally left blank.

About the Praxis Special Education: Foundational Skills (5355) study guide

This study guide is aligned with the test specifications and blueprint of the Praxis Special Education 5355 exam. All the sections of the study guide and content follow the organizational structure of the test specifications for the exam. We recommend downloading the ETS study companion for this test and reviewing its contents. You can do that by googling "Praxis 5355 study companion."

The following is the overall structure of the study guide:

1. Human Development and Individual Learning Differences
2. Effective Planning, Instruction, and Productive Learning Environments
3. Assessment
4. Professional Learning, Practice, and Collaboration

After each content category is a mini practice test with ten test questions and detailed answer explanations. At the end of the study guide are two, full-length practice tests with 120 questions each. These practice tests also contain detailed answer explanations. In total, there are 280 practice tests questions with answer explanations in the study guide. Finally, there is a *Good Words List* in the back of the study guide that details good words and phrases you should look for in the correct answer choices on this exam.

You can learn more about our *good words* strategy and our *Think Like a Test Maker*™ methods by going to the Kathleen Jasper YouTube channel and watching the videos in our *Test Strategy* playlist.

Test Structure

The Praxis Special Education: Foundational Knowledge 5355 examination is crafted to assess the essential knowledge and skills required for the beginning practice of a special education teacher, ensuring they are equipped for a safe and effective teaching career.

The Praxis 5355 test consists of 120 selected-response questions that evaluate the examinee's grasp of special education theories, principles, and application practices. These questions simulate real-world situations that educators will face in classrooms and schools, asking them to apply their specialized knowledge to various teaching scenarios.

A significant portion of the test focuses on instructional situations involving students with mild-to-moderate disabilities, often in a mainstream classroom setting, where they receive support from general and special education teachers through accommodations and/or modifications. The examination also addresses some severe-to-profound disabilities, testing candidates on their understanding of supporting students with these less common disabilities, typically outside the mainstream classroom environment.

The test is aligned with state and national standards for special educators, incorporating the Council for Exceptional Children (CEC) standards for Initial Practice-Based Professional Preparation for Special Educators, ensuring that the test reflects the current best practices and knowledge required in the field. We recommend downloading these standards and becoming familiar with them. The language in these standards will be in the correct answers on the exam.

Test Structure and Content	
Test Name	Praxis Special Education: Foundational Knowledge (5355)
Time	2 hours
Number of Questions	120 selected-response
Test Format	The test consists of only selected-response questions. You may have questions that ask you to choose all or some that apply. Other questions will have only one correct answer. The test is delivered on the computer and may contain some audio and visual elements. You may have additional questions on your exam that do not count toward your score.

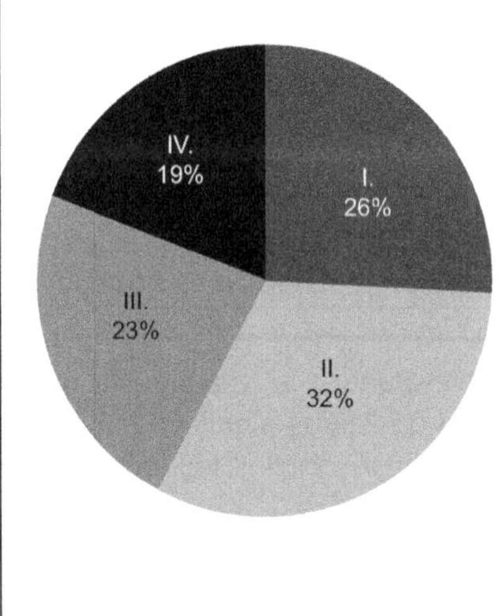

Content Category	Approx. Number of Questions	Approx. Percentage of Exam
I. Human Development and Individual Learning Differences	32	26%
II. Effective Planning and Instruction and Productive Learning Environments	38	32%
III. Assessment	27	23%
IV. Professional Learning, Practice, and Collaboration	23	19%

Things You Should Know

Special education provides support for the individual differences and needs of students with disabilities. It involves customizing instructional methods, educational services, learning environments, and curricular modifications to support students with various challenges, including physical, cognitive, emotional, and social disabilities.

The objective of special education is to provide these students with equitable access to education, often through the development of Individualized Education Programs (IEPs), ensuring they receive a free and appropriate public education (FAPE) in the least restrictive environment (LRE). Special education emphasizes inclusive practices, specialized interventions, and assistive technologies to enhance educational opportunities and facilitate the fullest possible integration of students with disabilities into mainstream education and society.

Before digging into this study guide, you'll need to be able to answer the following frequently asked questions regarding special education.

What is an IEP?

An Individualized Education Program (IEP) is a critical document for children with disabilities and is a cornerstone of special education services in the United States. Mandated by the Individuals with Disabilities Education Act (IDEA), the IEP is both a process and a product that ensures a child with a recognized disability receives personalized instruction and services tailored to their unique learning needs.

The IEP is developed by a team that typically includes:

- The child's parents or guardians
- At least one of the child's general education teachers (if applicable)
- At least one special education teacher or provider
- A representative of the school system who is knowledgeable about the general curriculum and the availability of resources
- An individual who can interpret the instructional implications of evaluation results (this can be a team member already mentioned)
- Others at the discretion of the parents or school
- The child, when appropriate, especially when transition services are being discussed

The IEP outlines the following:

1. **Current Performance**: A detailed description of the child's current academic and functional performance, which includes how the child's disability affects their involvement and progress in the general education curriculum.
2. **Annual Goals**: Specific, measurable educational goals for the child to achieve in the academic year, which are designed to meet their needs that result from the disability and to enable them to make progress in the general education curriculum.
3. **Special Education and Related Services**: The specific special education and related services that will be provided to the child, including supplementary aids and services, modifications, or accommodations that will be provided in the classroom or other settings.
4. **Participation with Non-Disabled Children**: An explanation of the extent to which the child will not participate with non-disabled children in the regular class and other school activities.

5. **Participation in State and District-Wide Assessments**: The accommodations that are necessary for the child to participate in state or district-wide assessments, or the justification for why a separate assessment is needed.
6. **Dates and Places**: When services and modifications will begin, how often they will be provided, where they will be provided, and their duration.
7. **Transition Services**: For students who will reach the age of transition during the IEP period, a plan for transition services to post-school activities, including post-secondary education, vocational education, integrated employment, continuing and adult education, adult services, independent living, or community participation.
8. **Progress Measurement**: How the child's progress toward meeting the annual goals will be measured and how the child's parents will be informed of that progress.

The IEP is a legally binding document, and schools are required to implement all components of the IEP as it is written. The IEP is developed in an IEP meeting and must be reviewed at least annually to determine if the annual goals are being achieved and to revise the IEP as appropriate to address any lack of expected progress.

What is IDEA?

The Individuals with Disabilities Education Act (IDEA) is a federal law in the United States that mandates the provision of free and appropriate public education (FAPE) to children with disabilities. IDEA ensures that children with disabilities have the same opportunities for education as those children who do not have disabilities.

Key components of IDEA include:

1. **Individualized Education Program (IEP)**: IDEA requires the creation of an IEP for each child with a disability, which is tailored to their individual needs and outlines specific educational goals, services, and accommodations.
2. **Free and Appropriate Public Education (FAPE)**: Schools must provide students with disabilities a free education that is tailored to their individual needs as outlined in their IEP, at no cost to the family.
3. **Least Restrictive Environment (LRE)**: IDEA stipulates that children with disabilities should be educated to the greatest extent appropriate with peers who do not have disabilities. This principle promotes inclusion and access to general education classrooms and curricula.
4. **Appropriate Evaluation**: Before providing special education, schools must conduct comprehensive evaluations to determine if a child has a disability and what their educational needs are.
5. **Parent and Teacher Participation**: IDEA ensures that parents and teachers are involved in the decision-making process regarding the child's education. This includes participation in the development of the IEP and decisions about placement.
6. **Procedural Safeguards**: The law provides a set of procedural safeguards designed to protect the rights of children with disabilities and their families. This includes the right to confidentiality, the right to review educational records, and the right to dispute resolutions such as mediation and due process hearings.
7. **Early Intervention**: IDEA Part C covers early intervention services for infants and toddlers with disabilities, which includes services from birth through age two. This is followed by transition to preschool services.

IDEA is central to special education in the U.S. and has undergone several updates since its initial passage in 1975 (originally named the Education for All Handicapped Children Act). These updates have continued to refine and expand the scope of services and protections to ensure an inclusive and equitable education for all children with disabilities.

What are the main terms/acronyms in special education?

For those seeking certification in special education, familiarity with a range of terms and acronyms is essential. These terms will be further explored in the study guide with scenarios and test questions. However, it is important that you look over this list while you study for the exam. Here is a selection of key terms and acronyms that are commonly used in the special education field:

- **IEP (Individualized Education Program)**: A document that is developed for each public-school child who needs special education. It is created through a team effort and reviewed periodically.
- **IFSP (Individualized Family Service Plan)**: A plan for special services for young children with developmental delays. It is designed for children from birth to three years old.
- **IDEA (Individuals with Disabilities Education Act)**: A federal law that requires schools to provide special education and related services to eligible students with disabilities.
- **FAPE (Free Appropriate Public Education)**: An educational right of children with disabilities in the United States that is guaranteed by the IDEA.
- **LRE (Least Restrictive Environment)**: The requirement in federal law that students with disabilities receive their education, to the maximum extent appropriate, with nondisabled peers and that special classes, separate schooling, or other removal of students with disabilities from the regular educational environment occurs only when the nature or severity of the disability is such that education in regular classes with the use of supplementary aids and services cannot be achieved satisfactorily.
- **504 Plan**: A plan developed to ensure that a child who has a disability identified under the law and is attending an elementary or secondary educational institution receives accommodations that will ensure their academic success and access to the learning environment.
- **ADA (Americans with Disabilities Act)**: A civil rights law that prohibits discrimination against individuals with disabilities in all areas of public life, including jobs, schools, transportation, and all public and private places that are open to the public.
- **FBA (Functional Behavioral Assessment)**: A process that identifies a specific target behavior, the purposes of the behavior, and the intervention strategies that directly address the behavior.
- **BIP (Behavior Intervention Plan)**: A plan incorporating the insights gained from an FBA to outline a coherent strategy for dealing with a student's behavioral problems.
- **ESY (Extended School Year)**: Special education and related services that are provided to a child with a disability beyond the normal school year, in accordance with the child's IEP, and at no cost to the parents.
- **AT (Assistive Technology)**: Any item, piece of equipment, or product system, whether acquired commercially off the shelf, modified, or customized, that is used to increase, maintain, or improve the functional capabilities of children with disabilities.
- **RTI (Response to Intervention)**: A multi-tier approach to the early identification and support of students with learning and behavior needs.
- **MTSS (Multi-Tiered System of Supports):** A mechanism of providing tiered supports to students during the prereferral stage of special education. MTSS is used to intervene before students are designated as needing special education services.
- **SLD (Specific Learning Disability)**: A disorder in one or more of the basic psychological processes involved in understanding or in using language, spoken or written, that may manifest in the imperfect ability to listen, think, speak, read, write, spell, or to do mathematical calculations.
- **EI (Early Intervention)**: Services provided to very young children with special needs, generally from birth until the child turns three.
- **PLOP (Present Level of Performance)**: Describes a student's current achievement in the areas of need as determined by an evaluation.

These terms and acronyms form the bedrock of the special education vocabulary and are crucial for effective communication and understanding within the field. Mastery of these concepts is vital for educators to navigate the special education landscape effectively, advocate for their students, and collaborate with families and other educators.

This page intentionally left blank.

Human Development and Individual Learning Differences

In this segment of the examination, candidates must demonstrate an understanding of the following key areas:

A. Human Development

B. Individualized Learning Differences

These core concepts encompass an array of more intricate aspects of special education, which demand an in-depth comprehension of developmental benchmarks and the variances found in typical versus atypical development. Such knowledge is crucial for educators to design and implement educational experiences that are meticulously tailored to the distinct strengths and challenges of students, particularly those enrolled in special education programs.

A proficient special education teacher is one who understands the various etiologies that may affect growth and development, recognizing that developmental milestones can exhibit considerable variability among individuals with exceptionalities. These differences may be observed across linguistic, physical, cognitive, and social/emotional domains.

To achieve success in this portion of the exam, it is also imperative to have a grasp of the adaptive behavioral needs of individuals with exceptionalities. Candidates should be able to identify how environmental and biological factors influence students with exceptionalities. Moreover, an effective educator should be adept at modifying instruction and curriculum to accommodate the unique learning requirements of each student.

Human Development

As children mature, they progress through distinct developmental phases. It is imperative for special education instructors to possess a comprehensive understanding of these phases to discern both conventional and anomalous patterns in the cognitive, physical, and emotional growth of their students.

Piaget – Stages of Cognitive Development

Perhaps the most widely used framework when analyzing child development is Piaget's stages of cognitive development. Piaget asserted that cognitive development was a reorganization of mental processes resulting from biological maturation and environmental experience.

Piaget's 4 Stages of Cognitive Development		
Sensorimotor	0–2 years	In this initial phase, infants learn about the world through their senses and motor activities. Intelligence is demonstrated through motor activity without the use of symbols, such as language. Knowledge of the world is limited because it's based on physical interactions and experiences. The key achievement of this stage is object permanence—understanding that objects continue to exist even when they cannot be seen, heard, or touched.
Pre-operational	2–6 years	During this stage, children begin to engage in symbolic play and learn to manipulate symbols but do not yet understand concrete logic. They are egocentric, meaning they cannot perceive the world from others' viewpoints. The preoperational stage is split into two sub-stages: the symbolic function sub-stage (2-4 years), where the child learns to formulate designs in their mind, and the intuitive thought sub-stage (4-7 years), where the child moves toward understanding the logic of numbers and categories.

Piaget's 4 Stages of Cognitive Development		
Concrete operational	7–12 years	At this point, children start to think logically about concrete events. They gain a better understanding of the concept of conservation (the understanding that quantity does not change even when its shape does). Children at this stage are less egocentric and begin to think about how other people might think and feel. They also understand the concept of reversibility, which enables them to reverse their thinking.
Formal operational	12 years–adult	The final stage of Piaget's theory involves an increase in logic, the ability to use deductive reasoning, and an understanding of abstract ideas. At this point, people become capable of seeing multiple potential solutions to problems and think more scientifically about the world around them. Adolescents who reach this stage can process hypothetical situations and reason about consequences and possibilities.

(Piaget, 1972)

Atypical Child Development

Atypical development means a child does not develop normally. This can result in developmental disabilities—a group of conditions due to a physical, neurological, learning, language, or behavioral impairment. These conditions impact day-to-day functioning and usually last throughout a person's lifetime.

Key characteristics of developmental disabilities include:

- **Onset**: Disabilities manifest early in development, typically before a child enters grade school, and are often identified when a child fails to meet expected developmental milestones.
- **Long-term implications**: These disabilities persist throughout an individual's lifespan. The impact of the disability can vary significantly, with some individuals requiring lifelong care and assistance.
- **Impact on life activities**: Developmental disabilities can affect various aspects of life, including educational performance, personal care, language and communication, mobility, self-direction, and independent living.
- **Variability**: The nature and severity of the disability can vary widely among individuals. Some common developmental disabilities include autism spectrum disorder (ASD), cerebral palsy (CP), Down syndrome (DS), and intellectual disabilities.

Etiology

Etiology examines the myriad of causes and factors that contribute to the diverse patterns and outcomes in human development and individual differences. Etiology is the study of causation or origination. In medicine, psychology, or special education, etiology refers to the investigation and understanding of the causes or reasons for certain conditions or disorders. This can include a wide range of factors, such as genetic, neurobiological, environmental, and psychological causes that contribute to developing a condition or behavior. Understanding etiology is crucial for developing effective treatments, interventions, and support mechanisms for individuals with various conditions or learning differences.

Common etiologies related to growth and development in special education are varied and encompass a range of biological, environmental, and genetic factors that can influence a child's developmental trajectory. Understanding these etiologies is crucial for educators in special education to effectively address and support the diverse needs of their students.

Key etiologies include:

1. **Genetic factors**: Certain genetic conditions, such as Down syndrome, Fragile X syndrome, and other chromosomal abnormalities can impact cognitive, physical, and social-emotional development.
2. **Prenatal influences**: Factors such as maternal health, substance use during pregnancy (e.g., alcohol, drugs), and prenatal exposure to toxins can affect the neurological development of the fetus, leading to conditions like fetal alcohol spectrum disorders.
3. **Perinatal factors**: Complications during birth, such as lack of oxygen (hypoxia) or premature birth can lead to developmental challenges, including cerebral palsy or cognitive impairments.
4. **Environmental factors**: Exposure to lead, poor nutrition, and inadequate health care can adversely affect a child's development. Socioeconomic factors, including poverty and limited access to educational resources, also play a significant role.
5. **Neurobiological factors**: Disorders of the nervous system, such as epilepsy or neurodegenerative diseases, can influence cognitive, motor, and social development.
6. **Trauma and stress**: Early childhood trauma, chronic stress, or adverse childhood experiences (ACEs) can have lasting effects on emotional, social, and even physical development.
7. **Learning disabilities**: Conditions like dyslexia or attention-deficit/hyperactivity disorder (ADHD) have specific neurological bases that affect the processing of information and can impact academic and social skills development.
8. **Autism spectrum disorder (ASD)**: This neurodevelopmental disorder is characterized by challenges in social interaction, communication, and repetitive behaviors, with the cause being a complex interplay of genetic and environmental factors.

By understanding these etiologies, educators in special education can develop more effective individualized educational plans (IEPs), implement appropriate interventions, and create supportive learning environments that cater to the unique needs of each student.

Classroom Scenario – Integrating Etiology in a Special Education Classroom

Setting: Sunflower Middle School, a diverse classroom with students of varying disabilities

Characters:

- Ms. Carter, a special education teacher with expertise in developmental psychology
- Jayden, a student with autism spectrum disorder (ASD)
- Sophia, a student with cerebral palsy (CP)
- Liam, a student with Down syndrome (DS)

Ms. Carter is a special education teacher who begins her day at Sunflower Middle School by reviewing her students' Individualized Education Programs (IEPs) and recent evaluations. Understanding the etiology, or the cause and development of their conditions, is crucial in tailoring her instructional methods.

In her interaction with Jayden, who has autism spectrum disorder (ASD), Ms. Carter employs strategies that address his needs for routine and structure, which are informed by understanding that ASD is a neurodevelopmental condition that affects social interaction and behavior. She uses visual schedules to ease transitions between activities and incorporates his interests to engage him in learning.

Sophia, who has cerebral palsy (CP), requires physical accommodations due to her motor disabilities. Ms. Carter collaborates with occupational therapists to understand the specific etiology of Sophia's CP, which is due to a brain injury during birth. This knowledge allows for the design of a classroom layout that is wheelchair-accessible and the selection of adaptive tools to assist Sophia in writing and using a computer.

For Liam, who has Down syndrome (DS), Ms. Carter integrates activities that stimulate cognitive development and social skills. Understanding that DS is a genetic disorder that often results in intellectual disability and developmental delays, she focuses on repetitive learning and memory games to enhance his retention and employs peer tutoring to foster social integration.

Throughout the day, Ms. Carter employs differentiated instruction, pairing etiological insights with evidence-based teaching practices. She knows that the etiology of her students' disabilities provides a framework for understanding their unique challenges and potential. By the end of the day, each student has engaged in activities designed to support their specific developmental needs, and Ms. Carter reflects on the progress made, ready to adjust her strategies as her students continue to grow and develop.

Conclusion:

Ms. Carter's use of etiological understanding is central to providing effective support. It informs her approach to each child's learning and reflects the dynamic interplay between a child's condition and their educational experience. By considering the origins and characteristics of each disability, Ms. Carter can offer a responsive and nurturing educational environment tailored to her students' diverse needs.

Developmental milestones

Typical developmental milestones serve as benchmarks of average abilities and skills that children tend to reach in certain age ranges, and they can differ notably for individuals with exceptionalities.

Linguistic:

Linguistic or language-based exceptionalities involve difficulties processing linguistic information, which may manifest as challenges in understanding or producing spoken or written language. This encompasses a range of disorders such as dyslexia, which affects reading abilities; dysgraphia, which impacts writing skills; and specific language impairment, which can hinder the acquisition and use of spoken language. These exceptionalities may result from genetic, neurobiological, or environmental factors, and they require specialized instructional strategies to support effective communication and learning.

Examples of language-based exceptionalities include deficits in phonemic and phonological awareness, phonics, fluency, vocabulary, comprehension, and writing.

Quick Tip

Special educators use the term "exceptionality" to refer to students with different learning needs from the general population due to various conditions that may affect their academic performance. The term shifts the emphasis from a deficit model, which focuses on what students can't do, to a strength-based model, which recognizes what students can do and how their unique characteristics can be accommodated or enhanced within an educational setting. Exceptionality includes both students who have disabilities and those who are gifted and talented, acknowledging that any divergence from the norm—whether it involves challenges or advanced abilities—may require specialized educational approaches.

- Typical: Children usually begin cooing and babbling in infancy, say their first words around their first birthday, and combine words into sentences as toddlers.
- Exceptionalities: Individuals with linguistic exceptionalities, such as developmental language disorders or autism spectrum disorders, may experience delayed speech onset, have a limited vocabulary, struggle with grammar, or use alternative communication methods.

Physical:

Physical exceptionalities involve conditions that affect an individual's physical capabilities and may include orthopedic impairments, such as cerebral palsy or spina bifida, which can impact movement and dexterity. Additionally, they can encompass chronic health issues like asthma, diabetes, or epilepsy that can affect a student's stamina, strength, or vitality. These exceptionalities require accommodations to ensure accessibility and may necessitate adjustments in the educational environment to support the individual's physical needs and promote their full participation in learning activities.

Examples of physical exceptionalities include difficulty in fine and gross motor skills.

- Typical: Physical milestones include rolling over, sitting up, crawling, walking, and developing fine motor skills like grasping and drawing.
- Exceptionalities: Children with physical exceptionalities, such as cerebral palsy or muscular dystrophy, may reach these milestones later than typical or may require adaptive equipment and therapies to achieve different levels of mobility and dexterity.

Cognitive:

Cognitive exceptionalities involve difficulties in the mental processes related to learning, understanding, and applying knowledge. These can include impairments in processing speed, memory, attention, problem-solving, and executive functioning. Cognitive exceptionalities may manifest as specific learning disabilities such as dyscalculia, affecting mathematical abilities or nonverbal learning disabilities impacting spatial and social skills. They also encompass intellectual disabilities, where there is a significant limitation in both intellectual functioning and adaptive behavior, which covers many everyday social and practical skills. These challenges necessitate individualized educational strategies and supports to facilitate learning and development.

Quick Tip

Fine motor skills involve the coordination of small muscles, typically in the hands and fingers, with the eyes to execute precise movements, such as writing, buttoning a shirt, or manipulating small objects. Gross motor skills refer to using large muscle groups to perform bigger movements like walking, jumping, or throwing a ball, essential for mobility and overall physical coordination. Both sets of skills are crucial for daily functioning and are part of physical development.

- Typical: Cognitive milestones encompass problem-solving, memory, attention, and the understanding of concepts like cause-and-effect, time, and numbers.
- Exceptionalities: Individuals with cognitive exceptionalities, including intellectual disabilities or brain injuries, may develop these skills at a slower pace or may require specific educational strategies to learn effectively.

Social/emotional:

Social/emotional exceptionalities involve challenges in managing emotions, behaviors, and interactions with others. These can manifest as difficulty in forming and maintaining relationships, responding appropriately to social cues, and expressing or regulating emotions. Individuals with these exceptionalities may exhibit behaviors that interfere with learning and socialization, such as withdrawal, aggression, or disruption in the classroom. Support for these individuals often includes social skills training, counseling, and behavioral interventions tailored to help them navigate social interactions and emotional responses effectively.

- Typical: Social and emotional milestones involve smiling, recognizing familiar people, playing with others, showing empathy, and developing self-awareness and regulation.
- Exceptionalities: Those with social/emotional exceptionalities, such as those on the autism spectrum, may show different patterns of social interaction, struggle with empathy, or have challenges with emotional regulation.

For individuals with exceptionalities, milestones may not only be achieved at different ages but might also require interventions such as speech therapy, occupational therapy, or behavioral therapy to support their development in these areas.

Quick Tip

Emotional behavioral disturbance (EBD) is a condition characterized by persistent and significant emotional or behavioral responses that adversely affect a child's performance in educational settings. This can manifest as difficulties with interpersonal relationships, inappropriate behaviors or feelings under normal circumstances, pervasive unhappiness or depression, and a tendency to develop physical symptoms or fears associated with personal or school problems. Children with EBD may exhibit a range of behaviors from withdrawal to aggression, and their educational performance is often significantly hindered due to these challenges. It is important that teachers use behavioral supports and interventions that are tailored to the individual needs of each student.

Developmental Delay vs Developmental Disability

A developmental delay is something a student can grow out of. For example, with enough speech therapy and practice, a student can work through speech delays. However, a developmental disability is something a student will not grow out of. For example, if a student has cerebral palsy, he or she will not be able to eradicate that disability with therapy. The student can live a fulfilling life and achieve academically. However, the student will have cerebral palsy for life.

Examples of developmental delays:

- **Motor skills delay**: These delays are seen in children who reach milestones in gross motor skills (like crawling, walking, and jumping) or fine motor skills (like grasping small objects, drawing, and using utensils) later than their peers.
- **Speech and language delay**: This includes delays in the onset of babbling, the first words, and the development of vocabulary and sentence structure. Children may also show difficulties in understanding and processing language.
- **Cognitive delay**: These are delays in cognitive development, affecting a child's ability to learn new skills, solve problems, and adapt to new situations.
- **Social and emotional delay**: Children with these delays may struggle with understanding social cues, playing with other children, or forming attachments to caregivers and family members.
- **Vision and hearing delay**: Delays in vision and hearing can impact a child's ability to develop other skills. They might not respond to visual cues or may have delayed speech due to an inability to hear properly.
- **Self-help/adaptive delay**: Some children may take longer to develop daily self-care skills such as dressing, eating, and toilet training.

Examples of developmental disabilities:

- **ADHD** – People with ADHD may have trouble paying attention, controlling impulsive behaviors (may act without thinking about what the result will be), or be overly active. Although ADHD cannot be cured, it can be successfully managed, and some symptoms may improve as the child ages.
- **Autism spectrum disorder (ASD)** – ASD is a developmental disability that can cause significant social, communication, and behavioral challenges. The learning, thinking, and problem-solving abilities of people with ASD can range from gifted to severely challenged. It is a spectrum disorder, meaning there is a range of challenges for people with ASD. Some people with ASD need full-time care in their daily lives; others need therapy and do not need full-time assistance.
- **Cerebral palsy** — Cerebral palsy is a nondegenerative condition—meaning it does not get worse over time—that affects a person's motor skills and balance. Cerebral palsy is the most common motor disability in childhood. It is estimated that 1 in 345 children are born with cerebral palsy. The cause of cerebral palsy is a brain injury that occurs before, during, or immediately after birth.

- **Hearing loss** – Hearing loss can affect a child's ability to develop communication, language, and social skills. The earlier children with hearing loss start getting services, the more likely they are to reach their full potential.
- **Intellectual disability** – An intellectual disability limits a person's ability to learn at an expected level and function daily. Levels of intellectual disabilities vary in children. Children with an intellectual disability might have a hard time letting others know their wants and needs. They also may not be able to take proper care of themselves. Students with intellectual disabilities often need assistance when learning to speak, walk, dress, or eat.
- **Learning disability** – Learning disabilities are disorders that affect the ability to understand or use spoken or written language, complete mathematical calculations, coordinate movements, or direct attention. Types of learning disabilities include:
  - *Dyscalculia* affects a person's ability to understand numbers and learn math facts.
  - *Dysgraphia* affects a person's handwriting ability and fine motor skills.
  - *Dyslexia* affects reading and related language-based processing skills.
  - *Non-verbal disabilities* affect a person's skills to interpret nonverbal cues like facial expressions or body language.
- **Vision impairment** – Vision impairment is any kind of vision loss—total blindness or partial vision loss. Some people are completely blind, but many others have what's called legal blindness, and both are considered vision impairments.
- **Behavior disability** - An emotional disability characterized by the following:
  - An inability to build or maintain satisfactory interpersonal relationships with peers and/or teachers.
  - An inability to learn that cannot be adequately explained by intellectual, sensory, or health factors.
  - Consistent or chronic inappropriate type of behavior or feelings under normal conditions.
  - Displayed pervasive mood of unhappiness or depression.
  - A displayed tendency to develop physical symptoms, pains, or unreasonable fears associated with personal or school problems.

Test Tip

According to the CDC, recent estimates in the United States show that roughly one in six, or 17 percent, of children aged 3 through 17 years have one or more developmental disabilities.

Understanding the adaptive behavioral needs of individuals with exceptionalities

Special education teachers can understand the adaptive behavioral needs of individuals with exceptionalities through a multifaceted approach.

1. **Assessment and evaluation**: Conduct formal and informal assessments to identify specific strengths and challenges, including standardized tests, observations, and interviews with students, parents, and other educators.
2. **Collaboration with professionals**: Work with a team of professionals, such as psychologists, speech and language therapists, occupational therapists, and medical practitioners, who can provide insights into the individual needs of students.
3. **Continued education and training**: Stay informed of the latest research and strategies in special education through professional development opportunities, workshops, and specialized training.

4. **Individualized Education Plans (IEPs)**: Develop and implement IEPs that address the unique needs of each student, including specific behavioral goals and strategies tailored to the student's abilities and challenges.
5. **Observation and documentation**: Observe students regularly in various settings and document their behavior to understand triggers, effective strategies, and areas needing support.
6. **Parental and caregiver involvement**: Engage with parents and caregivers to gain a comprehensive view of the child's behavior across different contexts and to ensure consistency in approaches between home and school.
7. **Positive behavioral supports**: Implement positive behavior intervention supports (PBIS) that encourage appropriate behavior through reinforcement rather than punishment.
8. **Cultural competence**: Be aware of and sensitive to the cultural and familial backgrounds of students, which can influence behavior and the interpretation of behavior.
9. **Flexibility and responsiveness**: Be willing to adapt strategies and approaches as students grow and their needs change, as well as being responsive to the effectiveness of interventions.
10. **Empathy and patience**: Cultivate an attitude of empathy, patience, and respect for each student's experience, recognizing that adaptive behaviors are often developed as coping mechanisms for underlying challenges.

By integrating these strategies, special education teachers can create a supportive and effective learning environment that addresses the adaptive behavioral needs of students with exceptionalities, promoting their growth and success in school.

Classroom Scenario - Nurturing Individual Potential: A Day in the Adaptive Special Education Classroom

Setting: The adaptive special education classroom at Harmony Elementary School

Characters:

- Ms. Thompson, a dedicated special education teacher
- Leo, a student with an intellectual disability
- Amina, a student with autism spectrum disorder (ASD)
- Ethan, a student with attention deficit hyperactivity disorder (ADHD)
- Ms. Gonzalez, an occupational therapist (OT)
- Mr. Jacobs, a speech-language pathologist (SLP)

Scenario:

Ms. Thompson prepares for a bustling day in her adaptive special education classroom at Harmony Elementary School. With a thorough understanding of the adaptive behavioral needs of her students, she has a full schedule planned, grounded in a multifaceted approach to education.

The morning begins with an assessment and evaluation session for Leo, who has an intellectual disability. The assessment focuses on his communication skills. Ms. Thompson, alongside Mr. Jacobs, the speech-language pathologist, employs interactive tools to measure Leo's progress. They document his responses meticulously, noting areas where support is needed.

In the spirit of collaboration, Ms. Thompson then meets with Ms. Gonzalez, an occupational therapist, to discuss Amina, a student with ASD, and her motor skill development. Together, they integrate sensory activities into Amina's Individualized Education Plan (IEP), ensuring that classroom activities align with her therapy goals.

During a reading activity, Ms. Thompson observes Ethan, who has ADHD, becoming increasingly restless. Drawing upon her continued education and training in positive behavioral and intervention supports (PBIS), she gently redirects his energy through a hands-on learning station designed to sustain his attention. Observation and documentation are key; she notes his responses to different stimuli for future reference.

Lunchtime offers a valuable opportunity for parental and caregiver involvement. Ms. Thompson has organized a 'Family Lunch' event, allowing parents to engage with the learning environment. This session provides insight into the cultural backgrounds of her students, enhancing her cultural competence and ensuring that she respects and integrates their diverse heritage into her teaching.

Throughout the afternoon, unexpected situations arise. Amina experiences sensory overload, and Ms. Thompson quickly adapts the lesson to provide a calming environment, demonstrating the importance of being attuned to students' needs.

As the school day nears its end, Ms. Thompson's empathy and patience shine through. She speaks with each student, acknowledging their efforts and encouraging their progress. She understands that success in her classroom is not measured solely by academic achievement but by the personal growth and well-being of her students.

Conclusion

This scenario exemplifies how a special education teacher can create a supportive and dynamic learning environment by employing a comprehensive approach that includes assessment, collaboration, continuous professional development, and a deep commitment to understanding and supporting the unique needs of each student.

Individual Learning Preferences

The importance of individual learning preferences in special education is paramount as they directly influence how students engage with material, process information, and demonstrate understanding. Recognizing and accommodating these preferences ensures that instruction resonates with each learner's strengths, enhancing motivation, promoting self-efficacy, and improving academic outcomes.

Tailoring educational experiences to meet these individual preferences allows educators to provide the differentiated support that students with exceptionalities require, creating pathways to more meaningful and accessible learning opportunities. It is this attention to individual learning styles and preferences that is a cornerstone of effective special education, as it affirms the belief that all students can learn and achieve when provided with the appropriate accommodations and instructional approaches.

Special education teachers must consider environmental and biological factors impacting an individual's academic performance.

Environmental Factors

Environmental factors play a significant role in the development and learning of all individuals, including those with disabilities. These factors can influence development in several ways:

1. **Family dynamics**: The child's immediate home environment, including relationships with parents and siblings, parental involvement in education, and supportive communication, can significantly affect their emotional and educational development.
2. **Socioeconomic status**: Access to resources such as quality education, nutritious food, health care, and stable housing, often tied to socioeconomic status, can impact cognitive development and academic achievement.
3. **Cultural and linguistic context**: The cultural and linguistic background of a child can shape their learning experiences and interactions with the educational system. Bilingualism, for example, can affect language development, and cultural values can influence behavior and socialization.

4. **Educational environment**: The quality of the schools and classrooms, including the availability of specialized support services, class size, educational materials, and teacher expertise, can make a substantial difference in the educational outcomes of students with disabilities.
5. **Social interactions**: Peer relationships and social networks can influence social development and the acquisition of social skills. Positive interactions can improve self-esteem and motivation, while negative experiences like bullying can have adverse effects.
6. **Technology and media**: Access to and use of technology and media can offer enhanced learning opportunities, assistive tools, and information. However, they can also present challenges, such as distractions or exposure to inappropriate content.
7. **Community services**: The availability and quality of community services, including recreational programs, therapy, and support groups, can provide additional learning opportunities and support outside of the traditional educational setting.
8. **Policy and legislation**: Laws and policies related to education, disability rights, and funding for support services can affect how well a society supports the development and learning of individuals with disabilities.
9. **Physical environment**: Features such as safety, cleanliness, exposure to toxins, and the design of learning and living spaces can affect health and cognitive functioning.
10. **Life experiences**: Unique individual experiences, including travel, participation in extracurricular activities, and exposure to various careers or hobbies, can broaden learning and development.

These environmental factors interact with individual abilities and disabilities, often creating a complex interplay that can either facilitate or hinder development and learning. For special educators, understanding these environmental influences is critical in providing comprehensive support that goes beyond addressing the disability itself to foster optimal development and learning outcomes for their students.

There are many environmental and social influences on student development and achievement. The most widely known theorist in this area is Abraham Maslow.

Abraham Maslow

Maslow is widely known for the Hierarchy of Needs (as shown in the diagram). Maslow asserted that people are motivated by five basic factors: physiological, safety, love, esteem, and self-actualization.

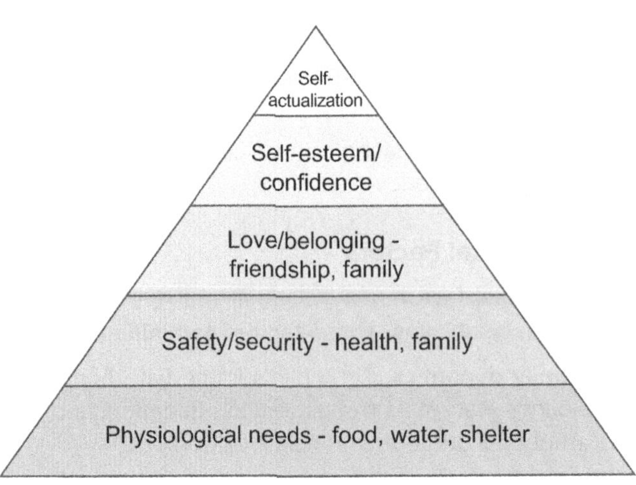

According to Maslow, when a lower need is met, the next need on the hierarchy becomes the focus of attention. If students lack a lower need, they cannot be motivated by one of the other needs. For example, if a student does not have basic needs like food or shelter, the student will not be motivated by esteem. Food and water are fundamental to all the other needs.

- **Maslow in the classroom**
  - Meeting students' needs before moving on to high-level assignments/activities
  - Considering students' situations at home before assigning work

Classroom Scenario – Catering to the Whole Child: Maslow's Hierarchy in the Special Education Classroom

Setting: Room 102, a special education classroom at Oakwood Elementary School

Characters:

- Mr. Elliot, a compassionate special education teacher
- Grace, a student with a speech and language impairment
- Marcus, a student with an emotional behavior disturbance (EBD)
- Bella, a student with autism spectrum disorder (ASD)

Mr. Elliot starts his day by reviewing his lesson plans. He firmly believes in addressing the holistic needs of his students, guided by Maslow's Hierarchy of Needs, to create an optimal learning environment.

The day begins with Mr. Elliot ensuring that the most fundamental level of Maslow's pyramid—physiological needs—are met. The classroom is well-lit and ventilated with a comfortable temperature. He has arranged for a nutritious snack for his students, understanding that hunger can greatly affect concentration and learning.

Next, Mr. Elliot turns his attention to the safety needs of his students. He has created a predictable routine that helps Marcus, who suffers from EBD, feel secure and oriented in the classroom. Personalized calm-down kits are readily available, providing a sense of comfort and safety.

As students begin to work on a group project, Mr. Elliot fosters a sense of belonging and love. For Grace, who struggles with speech, he encourages peer support, pairing her with empathetic classmates who facilitate inclusive participation, thereby nurturing her social skills and sense of belonging.

Midday approaches, and Mr. Elliot observes his students to that ensure their esteem needs are being addressed. He takes time to praise Bella, who has ASD, for her unique approach to a math problem, thereby bolstering her self-esteem and confidence. Mr. Elliot displays students' work on the "Wall of Achievement," where everyone's efforts are recognized.

In the afternoon, Mr. Elliot dedicates time to self-actualization—the peak of Maslow's pyramid. He provides a variety of materials and activities that allow students to explore and express their talents and interests. Art supplies, building blocks, and interactive computer programs are available for students to engage with, facilitating a journey of personal growth and self-fulfillment.

Conclusion:

This scenario illustrates how the principles of Maslow's Hierarchy of Needs can be integrated into a special education setting to support the comprehensive development of students with disabilities, ultimately creating a stable and conducive environment for learning and personal development.

Quick Tip

Core qualities of life include emotional, physical, and material well-being, social inclusion, and human rights.

Biological Factors

Biological factors encompass genetics, neurochemistry, and brain structure and function. For instance, hormonal imbalances can affect mood and behavior, genetic conditions such as Down syndrome can impact cognitive development, and irregularities in brain structure can influence learning processes and behavior regulation. Such factors may determine a student's innate capabilities and challenges, affecting their behavior in a learning environment and their capacity to perform academically.

Biological factors include:

1. **Genetic disorders**: Conditions such as Down syndrome, Fragile X syndrome, and Turner syndrome are caused by chromosomal abnormalities and can result in cognitive delays, learning disabilities, and other developmental issues.
2. **Neurodevelopmental disorders**: Autism spectrum disorder (ASD) and attention-deficit/hyperactivity disorder (ADHD) are believed to have strong biological bases, impacting attention, behavior, communication, and social interaction.
3. **Brain injuries**: Traumatic brain injury (TBI), whether congenital or acquired, can cause cognitive impairments, physical disabilities, and changes in behavior, affecting a student's ability to learn and interact.
4. **Sensory processing disorders**: Issues with processing sensory input, which can be part of disorders like ASD or standalone, affect how students interact with their environment and can lead to difficulties in concentration and behavior.
5. **Neurochemical imbalances**: Conditions like depression, anxiety, and bipolar disorder involve imbalances in brain chemicals and can significantly affect mood, energy levels, concentration, and motivation.
6. **Prenatal exposure to harmful substances**: Exposure to drugs, alcohol, or certain infections in utero can lead to fetal alcohol spectrum disorders or other developmental disabilities that impact cognitive and behavioral functioning.
7. **Hormonal imbalances**: Disorders like hypothyroidism or adrenal hyperplasia, which affect the body's hormone levels, can influence energy, growth, metabolism, and mood, all of which can affect learning and behavior in school.
8. **Metabolic disorders**: Conditions such as phenylketonuria (PKU) or diabetes require careful management to prevent impacts on cognitive functions and physical well-being, which in turn can affect educational performance.
9. **Epilepsy**: Seizure disorders can disrupt regular brain activity, leading to potential impacts on consciousness, sensory perception, or motor skills, which can intermittently affect learning and attention.
10. **Hereditary factors**: A family history of learning disabilities or other educational challenges may suggest a genetic predisposition that could manifest in a child's learning and behavioral development.

Co-occurring or Comorbid Conditions

Co-occurring or comorbid conditions refer to two or more disorders or disabilities in the same individual. These can include a combination of learning disabilities, developmental disorders, emotional or behavioral disorders, and physical disabilities.

For example, a student may have both attention-deficit/hyperactivity disorder (ADHD) and dyslexia, or autism spectrum disorder (ASD) with accompanying anxiety or depression. The presence of comorbid conditions can complicate diagnosis and intervention, as the symptoms of one disorder may mask or exacerbate the symptoms of another, making it challenging to address each condition effectively. Therefore, special education professionals must carefully assess students and plan individualized educational programs, considering all aspects of a child's developmental profile to meet their unique learning needs.

Self-Regulation

Self-regulation refers to an individual's ability to manage their emotions, behavior, and body movements in response to a situation. Students with challenges in self-regulation may struggle with coping with stress, maintaining focus in the classroom, acting in socially appropriate ways, or controlling their impulses. These difficulties can lead to disruptive behavior and hinder academic achievement. Conversely, students who develop strong self-regulation skills are often better able to adapt to the demands of the classroom, engage in learning, and achieve academic success.

Understanding these factors is critical for educators in designing effective strategies and supports. Interventions might include behavioral plans for students with self-regulation challenges, specialized instruction for those with additional disabilities, and collaboration with medical professionals to address biological factors. By considering the multifaceted nature of students' experiences, educators can better support their behavioral and academic growth.

The following table provides several ways special education teachers can use self-regulation strategies with students with exceptionalities.

Strategy	Explanation
Structured Routines	Establish predictable routines and schedules to provide stability and reduce anxiety.
Visual Schedules	Use visual timetables or charts to help students understand and anticipate upcoming transitions or activities. This is particularly helpful for students with ASD.
Modeling Behavior	Demonstrate appropriate behavior, emotional responses, and problem-solving in real-time for students to emulate. This is particularly helpful for students with EBD.
Social Stories	Create narratives that describe social situations and appropriate responses to help students navigate interpersonal interactions. This is particularly helpful for students with ASD.
Calm-Down Kits	Provide tools such as stress balls, fidget devices, or noise-canceling headphones that students can use when feeling overwhelmed. This is particularly helpful for students with EBD.
Mindfulness and Relaxation Techniques	Teach deep breathing, guided imagery, or meditation to help students manage stress and focus.
Positive Reinforcement	Use a reward system to encourage and reinforce self-regulatory behaviors.
Choice-Making Opportunities	Allow students to make choices about their learning activities to promote autonomy and engagement.
Breaks and Sensory Activities	Integrate movement breaks, sensory play, or quiet times into the day to help students regulate their sensory needs and energy levels.

Strategy	Explanation
Self-Monitoring	Teach students to recognize their emotions and behaviors using tools like mood charts or behavior journals and to use strategies proactively.
Executive Functioning Support	Provide support with organization, time management, and planning to reduce frustration and promote independence.
Cognitive Behavioral Approaches	Apply cognitive-behavioral strategies to help students identify and challenge negative thoughts and to develop more adaptive thinking patterns.
Collaboration with Specialists	Work with occupational therapists, speech-language pathologists, or psychologists for specialized strategies tailored to individual needs.
Peer Support and Buddy Systems	Pair students with peers who can model appropriate behavior and offer support.
Safe Spaces	Designate a specific area in the classroom where a student can go to regain composure and practice self-regulation strategies.

The ecological perspective in special education

The ecological perspective in special education is a framework that considers the complex interplay between a child with exceptionalities and their environment. It posits that a child's development and learning are influenced not only by their individual characteristics but also by the systems and contexts they are part of, such as family, school, community, and society.

This perspective emphasizes the importance of understanding and addressing the multiple environmental factors that affect a child's educational experiences and outcomes. It suggests that interventions should not solely focus on the child but also on modifying the environment to better support the child's needs. For example, changes might be made in teaching strategies, classroom settings, and curriculum design to accommodate and facilitate the learning of students with special needs.

This approach advocates for a holistic understanding of students within their ecosystems, encouraging collaboration among educators, families, and other professionals to create an inclusive and supportive learning environment.

Test Tip

When teachers engage in differentiated instruction, adjust the learning setting, or put into practice inclusion strategies, they are applying an ecological perspective. This approach considers the entire learning environment and how it can be adapted to meet the diverse needs of students. For instance, a teacher might alter aspects of a cooperative learning activity to better serve a student with emotional behavioral disturbances, ensuring that the environment is conducive to the learning and participation of all students.

Auditory and Information Processing

Exceptionalities can significantly affect auditory and information-processing skills in various ways, depending on the nature and severity of students' conditions. Here's how some exceptionalities might impact these areas:

1. **Auditory Processing Disorder (APD)**: Students with APD have difficulty processing auditory information. They may struggle to differentiate similar sounds, understand speech in noisy environments, or remember verbal instructions.
2. **Attention-Deficit/Hyperactivity Disorder (ADHD)**: Students with ADHD often have challenges with selective attention and may be easily distracted by background noise, which can interfere with their ability to process auditory information effectively.
3. **Autism Spectrum Disorder (ASD)**: Individuals with ASD may experience hypersensitivity to sounds, which can be distracting or even painful, leading to difficulties in processing auditory information. They may also have a literal understanding of language, making inference and abstract language comprehension challenging.
4. **Specific Learning Disabilities (SLD)**: Specific learning disabilities, such as dyslexia, can affect the processing of written and sometimes spoken information, making it difficult for students to decode text, spell, or comprehend complex sentences.

Quick Tip

A common strategy to support students with autism spectrum disorder (ASD) involves the use of visual aids. These graphic representations can help simplify and clarify processes that might otherwise be too complex or stressful for them to understand and engage with effectively.

5. **Intellectual Disabilities**: Students with intellectual disabilities experience significant limitations in both intellectual functioning and adaptive behavior, which covers a range of functional skills.
6. **Language Disorders**: Children with language disorders may have difficulty understanding language (receptive language) or using language (expressive language), which affects their ability to process and convey information.
7. **Sensory Impairments**: Hearing loss or deafness affects auditory information processing. Even mild hearing impairment can impact students' abilities to follow verbal instructions or engage in conversations.
8. **Neurological Disorders**: Conditions such as epilepsy or cerebral palsy can affect the brain's ability to process auditory information and other types of sensory input accurately and efficiently.
9. **Traumatic Brain Injury (TBI)**: A TBI can result in difficulties with attention, memory, and information processing speed, as well as auditory comprehension challenges.
10. **Emotional Disorders**: Anxiety, depression, and other emotional disorders can interfere with cognitive processes, including attention and memory, which are essential for processing auditory and other types of information.

Special educators, often in collaboration with other specialists, develop strategies to support students with these challenges, such as using visual supports to complement auditory information, providing repeated and clear instructions, using assistive technology (like FM systems), and teaching compensatory strategies to help students process information more effectively.

Quick Tip

Frequency modulation systems (FM systems) are assistive listening devices that enhance the auditory reception of sounds for individuals with hearing impairments, particularly in educational settings.

An FM system typically consists of a transmitter microphone used by the speaker (often the teacher) and a receiver worn by the student. The transmitter captures the speaker's voice and sends it directly to the receiver, which can be tuned to a specific frequency. The receiver transmits the sound to the student's hearing aids, cochlear implants, or headphones. This direct transmission reduces the effects of distance, reverberation, and ambient noise, which can be particularly disruptive in a classroom environment.

These systems are beneficial not only for students with hearing loss but also for those with auditory processing disorders, attention deficits, or language difficulties.

Interactions with Families and Communities

Sensory impairments and physical and health exceptionalities can significantly influence an individual's interactions with their families and communities in several ways:

1. **Communication barriers**: Sensory impairments, such as hearing loss or vision impairment, can make communication challenging, potentially leading to misunderstandings or feelings of isolation if appropriate accommodations (like sign language or braille) are unavailable.
2. **Social participation**: Physical disabilities may limit an individual's ability to engage in community activities or events, especially if they are held in locations that are not accessible, thus reducing opportunities for socialization.
3. **Dependence on caregivers**: Individuals with significant disabilities may require assistance with daily living activities, which can affect family dynamics and create a dependency relationship that may impact the independence of the individual.
4. **Health care needs**: Chronic health conditions may necessitate frequent medical appointments or treatments, which can be time-consuming and stressful for families and may also limit participation in community activities.
5. **Educational integration**: Disabilities can affect educational experiences and how individuals feel integrated within school communities, impacting their social networks and sense of belonging.
6. **Emotional impact**: The presence of a disability has emotional repercussions not only for the individual but also for family members, who may experience a range of feelings from concern to compassion, potentially affecting family interactions and roles.
7. **Financial strain**: The cost of managing a disability, including medical care, therapy, assistive devices, and home modifications, can create financial stress for families.
8. **Advocacy and awareness**: Families may find themselves in the role of advocates for their loved ones, working to raise awareness and promote inclusivity within the community, which can be both empowering and demanding.
9. **Access to support services**: The availability and quality of support services such as respite care, support groups, and educational resources can affect how much families and individuals with disabilities can engage with their communities.
10. **Cultural and societal attitudes**: Cultural beliefs and societal attitudes toward disability can affect how individuals and their families are treated and perceived in the community, influencing interactions and the level of support or discrimination they may encounter.

Families and communities are crucial in supporting individuals with sensory impairments and physical and health exceptionalities. The goal is to create inclusive environments that cater to diverse needs, promoting positive interactions and full participation in family and community life.

Adapting the Learning Environment for Students with Exceptionalities

Special education teachers can adapt the learning environment to provide optimal learning opportunities for individuals with exceptionalities by implementing various strategies. For example, teachers can integrate specialized health care supports and consider a spectrum of placement options.

Health care supports may include on-site nursing care for students with medical needs, occupational and physical therapy to assist with mobility and daily living skills, and the administration of medications. Accommodations might also involve modifying classroom furniture, ensuring that seizure safety protocols are in place, and coordinating with health professionals for individualized health plans.

Regarding placement options, teachers can collaborate with multidisciplinary teams to determine the least restrictive environment (LRE) for each student, ranging from full inclusion in a general education classroom with necessary supports to more specialized programs such as self-contained classrooms or specialized schools.

Transition programs and vocational training might also be offered as part of the continuum of services to prepare students for life beyond school. By carefully considering and addressing both the health-related and educational needs of students, teachers can create a comprehensive, supportive educational experience that fosters both academic and personal growth.

Quick Tip

To effectively meet each student's needs, special education teachers must maintain consistent and clear communication with a multidisciplinary team. This team should include school nurses, occupational therapists, physical therapists, and other pertinent health care professionals. Such collaboration ensures a comprehensive understanding and management of the health-related needs of students with exceptionalities. With appropriate and timely support integrated into the educational framework, this cooperative approach facilitates incorporating health care plans into the daily classroom environment. It contributes to creating and maintaining a learning space that is not only safe but also nurturing for every student.

Least Restrictive Environment

The concept of the least restrictive environment (LRE) in special education is grounded in the legal mandate from the Individuals with Disabilities Education Act (IDEA). It stipulates that students with disabilities should be educated with their non-disabled peers to the maximum extent appropriate. The principle behind LRE is that students with special needs should have access to the same educational opportunities as other students and should not be segregated unless their disability is such that they cannot achieve satisfactory education in a general education setting, even with the use of supplementary aids and services.

Examples of LRE include:

1. Full inclusion: A student with disabilities participates in the same programs and classes as their peers without disabilities, receiving the necessary support within that setting, such as an aide or specialized instructional strategies.
2. Resource room: A student spends part of the day in a general education class and part of the day receiving more intensive instruction in a small group setting outside the general classroom, such as a resource room.

3. Special classes: For students whose needs cannot be met in the general education classroom, even with supports, special classes with a lower student-to-teacher ratio may be provided for a portion or entire day.
4. Special schools: Some students may attend specialized schools that are equipped to handle more significant needs that cannot be appropriately met in a traditional school setting.

The LRE is individualized and based on the student's unique needs, ensuring that they receive the most effective instruction in the most integrated setting possible. The goal is to prevent isolation and provide a spectrum of placements to accommodate the diverse needs of students with disabilities.

Classroom Scenario - Bridging Special and General Education: Fostering an Inclusive Learning Environment

Setting: Junction Valley Middle School, a collaborative educational setting with both general and special education classrooms

Characters:

- Ms. Harding, a special education teacher with a passion for inclusion
- Mr. Benson, a general education teacher open to collaborative teaching
- Sarah, a student with mild autism
- Alex, a student with learning disabilities
- General education students

Scenario:

Ms. Harding and Mr. Benson are preparing for a joint lesson on environmental science. Their goal is to ensure that Sarah and Alex, who are usually taught in a special education setting, can participate fully in the general education classroom. They are committed to the principle of the least restrictive environment (LRE), aiming to provide all students with the opportunity to learn alongside their peers to the greatest extent appropriate.

The day starts with Ms. Harding briefing Mr. Benson on the specific accommodations that Sarah and Alex will need. For Sarah, it involves providing written instructions and visual aids to complement verbal explanations, and for Alex, it means offering additional time to process information and respond to questions.

As students file into Mr. Benson's classroom, Ms. Harding facilitates the transition. She has worked with Sarah and Alex beforehand, preparing them for the change in environment and what to expect. Mr. Benson greets them warmly, making them feel welcome.

During the lesson, Mr. Benson leads the discussion while Ms. Harding moves around the room, providing support as needed. They utilize cooperative learning groups, ensuring that Sarah and Alex are integral members of their teams. Ms. Harding subtly assists other students in the group to use clear communication, fostering a supportive peer network.

To assess learning, the teachers have designed a project allowing multiple means of expression. Sarah, who is artistically inclined, is encouraged to create a visual representation of the lesson, while Alex, who has strong verbal skills, is supported in presenting his understanding through an oral explanation.

Throughout the lesson, Ms. Harding and Mr. Benson maintain a flexible and responsive approach. They communicate non-verbally, are ready to adapt the lesson pace, and step in with additional scaffolding if they observe students struggling.

Conclusion:

This scenario demonstrates the importance of collaboration between special and general education teachers to ensure that students with disabilities can access inclusive educational experiences. By working together, they ensure that the unique needs of each student are met while fostering the least restrictive environment for special education students.

Test Tip

When reviewing answer options, prioritize those referencing the least restrictive environment (LRE). For instance, if a teacher is making accommodations for special education students in a manner that allows them to remain integrated with their non-disabled peers, this exemplifies adherence to LRE principles. Such answer choices that align with this inclusive approach are often the correct ones.

Theoretical approaches to student learning and motivation

Behaviorist theory influences how teachers create motivational learning environments, engage students during instruction, and manage classroom behaviors. This is especially important in special education. In this section, we will explore terms and concepts of motivational theories you may see on the exam. On the exam, you will relate a learning or scenario to a concept or theory or, conversely, apply a theory to a classroom management, learning, or instructional situation.

Motivation theory

The best teachers motivate students by designing and delivering engaging and relevant instruction. Increasing special education students' motivation, regardless of disability, is a common theme on the exam. These types of test questions will be presented as scenarios, and you will be expected to choose the most effective approach. The best teachers motivate all students—high-achieving, low-achieving, culturally diverse, and economically diverse students. Effective teachers use many motivational tools in their instruction and learning environment when needed.

Self-determination

Self-determination is the ability to make decisions for oneself and to control one's own future. Students with strong self-determination are motivated by opportunities to collaborate on instructional design, set goals for themselves, and navigate obstacles to succeed. The application of self-determination theory is best understood through intrinsic motivation.

Self-advocacy

Self-advocacy is speaking up for oneself and expressing needs and wants. This is very important in special education because as students get older, they will have to express their needs for accommodations so they can thrive. Teaching students to do this early will serve them later in life when they are on their own.

Test Tip

On the exam, prioritize answer choices that support and encourage students' self-advocacy–the ability to speak up for oneself and articulate one's needs and desires. It is vital that students with disabilities develop self-advocacy skills. This empowerment ensures they can actively seek out the instruction and accommodations necessary for their success and equitable access to education.

Intrinsic motivation

Intrinsic motivation is behavior driven by internal rewards rather than external rewards. According to self-determination theory, intrinsic motivation is driven by three things: autonomy, relatedness, and competence.

- **Autonomy**. This has to do with students' independence and self-governance. Allowing students to decide how and what they learn helps to increase autonomy and increase motivation. Students should be permitted to self-select books and work on things that interest them.
- **Relatedness.** Students must see the value in what they are learning in relation to their everyday lives. The best teachers make learning relatable and applicable to the real world.
- **Competence.** Students must feel they are equipped to meet expectations. It is important to challenge students while providing them with activities based on readiness levels and ability.

Extrinsic motivation

Extrinsic motivation refers to behavior that is driven by external rewards. Providing students with a party if they reach their reading goal or allowing students extra playtime because they cleaned up the classroom are examples of extrinsic motivation. Grades can also be considered extrinsic rewards. Extrinsic motivation is often unsustainable because once the reward is removed, the student is no longer motivated to achieve. However, in the special education classroom where the teacher is trying to change undesirable behaviors, extrinsic rewards are often used.

Contingency-Based Classroom Management

Contingency-based self-management creates an environment where students are responsible for managing their own behaviors; students are rewarded for appropriate behavior. Group contingency happens when the teacher reinforces the entire class or a smaller group of students for completing tasks, engaging in appropriate classroom behaviors, or other achieving other targeted behavior objectives. For example, when a group of students cleans up after a project, the teacher gives each student in the group a sticker. Group contingencies are most often used as a basic classroom management strategy. Studies have shown group contingencies often decrease inappropriate behavior and increase prosocial behavior in special education classrooms and can sometimes improve school-wide indicators of success.

Other Approaches to Student Learning and Motivation

Desensitization – A technique where a person is exposed to small doses of anxiety-inducing stimuli alongside a relaxation technique. This is used in reinforcement theory in which there is a weakening of a response, usually an emotional response, used to change a behavior. For example, for a student with social anxiety, the teacher may bring the student to a corner of the playground and help the student with relaxation techniques so the student becomes less anxious.

Extinction – Reinforcement provided for problem behavior (often unintentionally) is discontinued to decrease or eliminate occurrences of these types of negative (or problem) behaviors. For example, a young student engages in tantrums during lunch because she does not want to eat her food. If the teacher puts the student in timeout, the tantrums will continue because going to timeout eliminates lunchtime, which was the student's goal--not to eat lunch. Instead, the teacher ignores the tantrums and insists the student eat her food during lunch. Eventually, the tantrums will decrease because the student is not receiving the desired outcome.

Manipulating the Antecedent Stimulus – A type of intervention that changes the student's behavior by manipulating conditions that ***precede*** such behavior. For example, arranging the classroom layout so students are less likely to bump into each other, causing disruptions. This involves:

- Presenting the cues for the desired behavior in the child's environment
- Arranging the environment or setting up a biological condition so that engaging in the desirable behavior is more valuable to the child
- Decreasing the physical effort the child needs to engage in the desired behavior

Manipulating the Consequent Stimulus – A type of intervention that changes a student's behavior by manipulating conditions that ***follow*** such behavior. For example, when a student misbehaves, they receive a timeout or another consequence. This is often referred to as punishment.

Planned Ignoring – When a teacher identifies undesirable behaviors used for attention and then ignores those behaviors. This reduces undesirable behaviors.

Premack Principle – Also known as the first-then principle. A teacher using the Premack Principle says, "First clean up your centers, then we can go on the playground."

Satiation – Satiation is used to reduce undesirable behaviors. For example, a student repeatedly gets up and disrupts during class. To combat this behavior, the teacher will encourage the student to get up more often until the student gets tired of getting up. The teacher can set a timer for every two minutes, and when the time goes off, the student is instructed to stand up. At first, the student may enjoy the arrangement. However, over time, the student will grow tired of getting up every two minutes, eliminating the behavior altogether.

Human Development and Individual Learning Differences Practice Questions

1. Ms. Thompson is a special education teacher who closely observes her students throughout the day to ensure they reach their developmental milestones. She has four students, each demonstrating different behaviors corresponding to typical developmental milestones for their ages.

   - Student A recently started forming two- to three-word sentences, such as "I want juice" or "Go outside."
   - Student B has begun tying his shoelaces and riding a tricycle with better coordination.
   - Student C can perform basic addition and subtraction and is curious about time.
   - Student D is keen on making friends, understanding others' feelings, and developing her sense of empathy.

   Based on the information above, which student demonstrates typical cognitive developmental milestones?

   A. Student A

   B. Student B

   C. Student C

   D. Student D

2. Which of the following would be considered a language-based learning exceptionality?

   A. A student has difficulty with identifying letter-sound correspondence during a phonics lesson.

   B. A student has difficulty engaging with others in appropriate behavior on the playground.

   C. A student has difficulty controlling impulsive behavior during a reading activity.

   D. A student has difficulty with fine motor skills during a handwriting activity.

3. Julia is a third-grade special education student who struggles with maintaining relationships with her classmates and teacher. She often shows aggression on the playground and is sometimes withdrawn during cooperative learning. Which of the following exceptionalities is Julia most likely exhibiting?

   A. Cognitive disturbance

   B. Linguistic disturbance

   C. Emotional behavioral disturbance

   D. Physical disturbance

4. A sixth-grade special education teacher wants to be sure she is supporting her students with exceptionalities. Which of the following would be most effective in achieving this objective?

   A. Using a standards-based approach where all instruction is similar for every student to ensure equality

   B. Modifying the learning environment to meet the specific needs of each student based on their IEPs and learning preferences

   C. Instructing each student separately with different content and assessments so everyone can meet a different standard

   D. Using a self-contained model where students are separated from the general population so they can focus on the skills they need

5. Jose is a fifth-grade student with some language processing delays. He enjoys reading time and works diligently on his English language arts assignments. He does struggle with phonics. Which of the following would be the most appropriate accommodation for Jose?

   A. Place Jose in a self-contained special education classroom where he can receive intense interventions in English language arts.

   B. Place Jose in a part-time resource room where he can receive moderate English language arts interventions.

   C. Place Jose in the general education classroom and provide him with a speech and language pathology specialist.

   D. Place Jose in general education with his non-disabled peers while providing targeted interventions in phonics.

6. Ms. Jones, a special education teacher, begins a unit on using the library. She will go through the steps of entering the library, searching for books, checking out books, and walking back to class. Ms. Jones wants to modify the lesson for two students with autism spectrum disorder (ASD). Which of the following approaches would be most effective in accommodating these students?

   A. Allow the students with ASD to skip the lesson because they will become overwhelmed by the sensory aspects of the library.

   B. Turn off the main lights in the library so students with ASD feel more comfortable when entering the space.

   C. Allow the students with ASD to complete a different lesson in the classroom that goes through the steps of checking out a book.

   D. Provide the students with ASD a visual checklist with graphics of the process they can complete as they go through the steps of using the library.

7. A special education teacher is helping her students with self-regulation. The lesson's objective is the following.

   Students will manage their emotions, behavior, and body movements during story time.

   Which of the following would be most effective in helping students achieve this objective?

   A. Practice procedures and routines.

   B. Grade students based on their behavior.

   C. Pair students with others to model behavior.

   D. Display the steps for the assignment.

8. Which of the following may indicate that a student suffers from an auditory disorder?

   A. The student is unable to remember the steps during a classroom procedure.

   B. The student is unable to follow repeated verbal commands by the teacher.

   C. The student is unable to follow written instructions for a classroom procedure.

   D. The student is unable to follow mathematical processes for simple equations.

9. Which of the following may indicate the student has an intellectual disability?

   A. The student cannot perform complex mathematical processes.

   B. The student experiences extreme sensitivity to light and sound.

   C. The student cannot complete functional tasks.

   D. The student cannot read fluently through grade-level text.

10. Which of the following scenarios indicates a student exhibits a co-occurring or comorbid condition?
    - ☐ A. A student with attention deficit hyperactivity disorder (ADHD) struggles with reading instruction, specifically with phonics.
    - ☐ B. A student who has autism spectrum disorder (ASD) experiences extreme sensitivity to light and sound.
    - ☐ C. A student with auditory processing disorder (APD) struggles to hear a guest speaker during class.
    - ☐ D. A student with an intellectual disability struggles with functional tasks and suffers from depression and anxiety.
    - ☐ E. A student with traumatic brain injury (TBI) struggles with language processing and experiences seizures.

Human Development and Individual Learning Differences Answer Explanations

Number	Answer	Explanation
1.	C	Bella (choice C) is correctly demonstrating cognitive milestones for a 7-year-old. Cognitive development at this age includes understanding more complex concepts such as basic mathematics and the concept of time. This aligns with typical cognitive development stages for early school-age children. The behaviors demonstrated by Jamie (choice A), Aiden (choice B), and Sophia (choice D) correspond with linguistic, physical, and social/emotional developmental milestones, respectively, but not directly to cognitive milestones in the context provided. Jamie is showing linguistic progress, Aiden is exhibiting physical development, and Sophia is displaying social/emotional development, which is distinct from cognitive development milestones.
2.	A	Linguistic or language-based exceptionalities involve difficulties processing linguistic information, which may manifest as challenges in understanding or producing spoken or written language. Difficulty in phonics is considered a linguistic or language-based exceptionality. Choice B and C are social/emotional exceptionalities. Choice D is a physical exceptionality.
3.	C	A child with emotional behavioral disturbance (EBD) will often have difficulty developing and maintaining relationships. Children with EBD may exhibit a range of behaviors from withdrawal to aggression, and their educational performance is often significantly hindered due to these challenges.
4.	B	The ecological perspective in special education is a framework that considers the complex interplay between a child with exceptionalities and their environment. When teachers differentiate instruction, modify the learning environment, or implement inclusion strategies, they use an ecological perspective. None of the other approaches listed are effective in special education. Choice A is ineffective because expecting all students to learn with one universal approach will not meet the needs of specific students. Choice C is ineffective because educating each student separately is not possible and is not inclusive. Choice D is the opposite of inclusion and segregates special education students from their non-disabled peers, which is the opposite of the least restrictive environment (LRE).

Number	Answer	Explanation
5.	D	This student is struggling with one skill and should receive interventions in that area. However, the least restrictive environment for this student would be the general education classroom, where he can participate with his non-disabled peers and still receive support in phonics. He does not have a severe disability; therefore, choices A and B are not appropriate. He also does not have a speech impairment, making choice C incorrect as well.
6.	D	A typical accommodation for students with ASD is to provide graphic representations for processes that may overwhelm them. Choices A and C exclude the students with ASD from the activity, which is not LRE. Choice B is not effective because the scenario did not emphasize that these students have sensitivity to light. Choice D may negatively impact the other students in the class who do not have ASD.
7.	A	Establishing predictable routines and procedures provides stability and reduces anxiety, which allows students to regulate their behavior.
8.	B	Students with auditory processing disorder (APD) may struggle to differentiate similar sounds, understand speech in noisy environments, or remember verbal instructions. In this case, the student did not process repeated verbal commands, which indicates the student may have an auditory processing disorder.
9.	C	An intellectual disability is characterized by significant limitations in both intellectual functioning and in adaptive behavior, which covers a range of everyday social and practical skills. Functional skills include hygiene, dressing, eating, and managing money.
10.	A, D & E	Co-occurring or comorbid conditions refer to two or more disorders or disabilities in the same individual. These can include a combination of learning disabilities, developmental disorders, emotional or behavioral disorders, and physical disabilities. In choice A, the student has ADHD and language processing disorder. The student in choice D has an intellectual disability and anxiety and depression. The student in choice E has TBI, language processing, and epilepsy. In choices B and C there is only one condition mentioned for each student.

This page intentionally left blank.

Effective Planning and Instruction and Productive Learning Environments

For this component of the examination, a thorough understanding of the following key areas is required:

A. Planning and Instruction

B. Productive Learning Environments

Within these overarching themes, candidates must demonstrate knowledge of employing effective teaching strategies in the special education classroom. This encompasses providing constructive feedback, imparting social behavior skills, and bolstering social-emotional competencies. Mastery of these practices is essential for fostering an environment that encourages active participation from students, enhances their motivation, provides ample response opportunities, and strengthens their ability to self-regulate their learning.

Additionally, examinees should be proficient in delivering explicit and systematic instruction when teaching content and strategies to advance students' cognitive and metacognitive abilities.

Success in this part of the exam also hinges on an understanding of the adaptive behavioral requirements of individuals with exceptionalities. It is crucial for candidates to recognize the influence of environmental and biological factors on students with exceptional needs.

Planning and Instruction

In special education, planning and instruction are meticulously tailored to accommodate the diverse learning needs and goals of each student, as outlined in their Individualized Education Programs (IEPs). This process involves designing differentiated learning activities, employing specialized instructional strategies, and providing necessary accommodations and modifications. The aim is to ensure equitable access to the curriculum, foster skill acquisition, and promote academic and social success, in alignment with mandated educational standards and students' personalized educational objectives.

Standards Alignment

The foundational aspect of crafting a successful lesson plan is aligning the plan with state-adopted educational standards. These benchmarks delineate the academic achievements that students are expected to reach. Annual state assessments in critical areas such as reading, writing, and mathematics evaluate student proficiency in these standards. Consequently, integrating these standards into the heart of instructional planning and curriculum design is the most efficacious approach to educational planning.

Vertical Alignment

Vertical alignment occurs when lessons and activities in the classroom support one grade level to the next or one skill to the next. State standards are vertically aligned—every skill in each standard supports one grade level to the next. For example, the skills outlined in the standards for seventh-grade math are designed to help students prepare for what they will need in eighth-grade math, ninth-grade math, and so on. While the standards are designed to be vertically aligned, it is the responsibility of the educator to ensure students are receiving lessons that are vertically aligned. Educators can vertically align their lessons by:

- Collaborating with other teachers in different grade levels
- Paying close attention to the standards that come before and after the year being taught
- Attending professional development that focuses on standards alignment

Horizontal Alignment

Horizontal alignment occurs when lessons are aligned to other academic disciplines and content areas. For example, ninth-grade social studies teachers plan with the ninth-grade English teachers to design a common lesson focusing on the Civil Rights Movement. This lesson will fulfill social studies standards in US history and English language arts standards in reading and writing. This relationship between the two content areas to focus on common content, goals, and standards is horizontal alignment. Effective educators can be sure lessons are horizontally aligned by:

- Collaborating with other teachers in different content areas
- Researching other content areas that relate to the content being taught
- Looking for connections where the curriculum can support other content areas

Measurable Objectives

Learning objectives are the behaviors or skills students are expected to acquire in a lesson. These objectives should be measurable, meaning teachers should be able to determine if the objective is met by a formative or summative assessment. We will discuss this more in-depth in the following sections. Measurable objectives allow teachers to determine if students understood the lesson and met the standards.

Flexibility

Another important element of an effective lesson plan is flexibility. Lessons do not always go according to plan. For example, it may take longer than expected for students to understand a concept or complete an activity. Therefore, lesson plans should be flexible, and teachers should modify the lessons according to students' needs.

Lesson Plans

Lesson plans help to guide and focus instruction. Special education teachers must use lesson plans to organize time, resources, and instruction to maximize student learning. When lesson planning for special education students, using backward design is most effective. In backward design, the teacher starts with the standard or goal the teacher wants students to achieve and then plans the lessons according to that standard or goal.

Backward Design

In backward design, alignment is critical. Start with the standards, plan the assessments, monitor students' progress at key intervals, and adjust short-term objectives accordingly.

Steps to Backwards Design

1. Identify the state-adopted standards for the concepts you are teaching. Be sure you are following the scope and sequence outlined by the state standards. The goal is student mastery of the standard(s).
2. Choose what assessments you will use to determine if the students mastered the standard(s).
3. Plan the lesson and activities.
4. Monitor progress as students move through the unit, lesson, or activity.

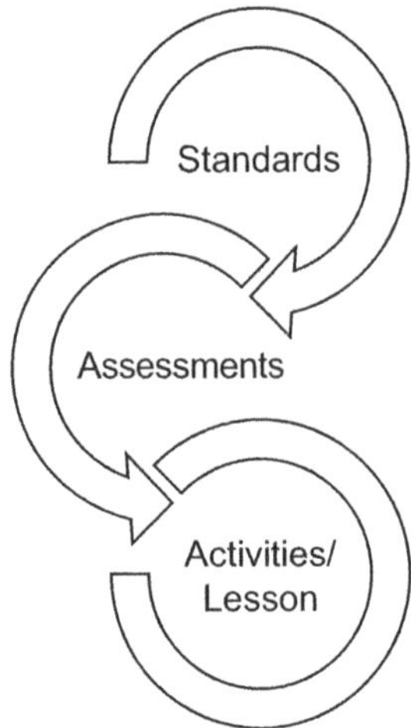

- Start with the state adopted standards. That is the end goal–to have the students master the standard(s).
- Determine how you will know the students mastered the standard and what assessments you will use to measure success.
- Decide what lessons and activities you will have students engage in to work toward standards mastery.

Using Data

Special education teachers can use information from multiple assessments to inform their instructional decisions and provide constructive feedback through the following strategies:

Test Tip

As a special education teacher, adopting a data-driven approach is crucial. It guarantees that instructional choices are grounded in tangible, objective evidence of a student's performance and specific needs, avoiding reliance on subjective opinion or conjecture. Data offers a quantifiable and transparent account of a student's developmental trajectory, highlighting progress and difficulties. This facilitates the accurate customization of educational plans, including Individualized Education Plans (IEPs), to suit each student's unique circumstances. When encountering an exam response that refers to data-driven decision-making, consider carefully, as it is likely indicative of a correct choice.

1. **Data-Driven Instruction**: By analyzing errors and response patterns across various assessments, teachers can identify specific areas where a learner struggles. This allows for targeted instruction that focuses on those identified skills or knowledge gaps.
2. **Individualized Education Programs (IEPs)**: Assessment data can be used to adjust Individualized Education Programs (IEPs) or 504 plans to better align with the student's needs, ensuring that goals are measurable, and instruction is tailored to the learner's abilities.
3. **Differentiation of instruction**: Teachers can differentiate content, process, product, and learning environment based on the learner's needs. For instance, if assessments indicate difficulty understanding a concept through reading, the teacher may provide audio materials or hands-on activities to aid comprehension.
4. **Scaffolding**: If assessments reveal that students are making errors due to gaps in foundational knowledge, teachers can scaffold instruction by breaking down tasks into smaller, more manageable steps, thereby building the students' skills incrementally.
5. **Constructive feedback**: Specific error patterns from assessments can guide teachers in providing detailed and constructive feedback. Instead of simply indicating that an answer is incorrect, feedback can focus on the nature of the mistake and suggest strategies for improvement.
6. **Progress monitoring**: When teachers continuously look at data, both qualitative and quantitative, to measure academic improvement, they are progress monitoring. Teachers can use this data to adjust the pace of instruction, provide additional support where needed, and celebrate improvements, no matter how small.
7. **Collaboration with other professionals**: Teachers can share assessment data with other professionals (such as speech-language pathologists or occupational therapists) to develop a comprehensive understanding of the student's needs and to coordinate support strategies.
8. **Reflective teaching practices**: Teachers can reflect on the effectiveness of their instruction based on student performance on assessments. If multiple students make similar errors, it may indicate a need to revisit the teaching approach for that concept or skill.
9. **Formative assessment application**: Teachers can use formative assessments not just to gauge understanding but to inform immediate instructional adjustments. This can be as simple as reteaching a concept when students demonstrate misunderstanding or as complex as restructuring a unit plan based on assessment trends.
10. **Error analysis**: Conducting an error analysis can provide insights into students' thought processes, revealing misconceptions or partial understandings that can be directly addressed in subsequent instruction.

By thoughtfully analyzing assessment data and responding with appropriate interventions, special education teachers can create a responsive learning environment that supports the growth and development of each student. This reflective and informed approach to teaching ensures that feedback is not only corrective but also empowering, guiding students toward greater autonomy and success in their learning journeys.

Measurable Goals

Goals are different from objectives in that goals are usually bigger milestones, and they often govern longer periods of time. For example, an objective is something a student can achieve in one class period, while a goal is something the student may achieve over a semester or school year.

The best way to ensure the goals you and your students set are measurable is to use the SMART goal method.

- **Specific.** The goal must contain a statement that details specifically what the student will accomplish.
- **Measurable.** There must be a way to measure progress toward the goal—using assessment data.
- **Achievable.** The goal must be within the scope of abilities of the student.
- **Relevant.** The goal must be relevant to what the student is doing in school/life.
- **Timely.** The goal must be completed within a targeted time frame.

S Specific
M Measurable
A Attainable
R Relevant
T Timely

Examples of SMART goals:

- By the end of the quarter, Patricia will increase written language skills by using proper spelling and punctuation in 4 out of 5 trials with 80 percent accuracy as measured by formative assessments.
- By the end of the semester, Jocelyn will increase her fluency from 93 words per minute to 125 words per minute as measured by informal fluency reads.

Ways to Track and Measure Students' Goals

Data folders – Students use data folders to track their progress by recording their achievements. Teachers and students reference data folders throughout the year to progress monitor, set new goals, and conduct student-led conferences. This is an example of teachers and students using data together to make decisions.

Portfolios – A student portfolio is a compilation of academic work and other forms of educational evidence assembled for the purpose of:

- Evaluating coursework quality, learning progress, and academic achievement
- Determining whether students have met learning standards or other academic requirements for courses, grade-level promotion, and graduation

Quick Tip

Goals are a crucial element of an Individual Education Plan (IEP) for students in special education. For an IEP to comply with legal requirements, it must specify measurable goals. Further details on this subject are provided in subsequent sections of this study guide. It is important to note that the fundamental purpose of an IEP is to facilitate a student's achievement in academic, social, and behavioral areas. Therefore, when answering exam questions, consider choices that concentrate on scenarios involving goals. Likewise, in your teaching practice, prioritizing goal setting and attainment is equally important.

- Helping students reflect on their academic goals and progress as learners
- Creating a lasting archive of academic work products, accomplishments, and other documentation

Compiling, reviewing, and evaluating student work can provide an authentic picture of what students have learned and can do.

Constructivism

Constructivism in education is a learning theory that posits learners construct their own understanding and knowledge of the world, through experiencing things and reflecting on those experiences. It emphasizes active engagement, inquiry, problem-solving, and the importance of social interaction in learning. According to constructivist theory, learning is a process of adjusting mental models to accommodate new experiences. Constructivists argue that learning is more effective when a learner is actively engaged in constructing their own knowledge rather than passively receiving information.

In the context of special education, constructivism holds significant implications for instructional design and teaching strategies. It supports the idea that learning should be tailored to the individual's needs, backgrounds, and experiences, a principle that aligns closely with the personalized approaches often required in special education. Here are several ways in which constructivism relates to special education:

1. **Individualized learning**: Constructivism advocates for learning experiences that are tailored to the individual's current understanding and abilities. This approach is particularly beneficial in special education, where educators design Individualized Education Programs (IEPs) that cater to the unique needs of each student with disabilities.
2. **Active engagement**: Constructivist approaches encourage learners to engage actively with materials, ideas, and peers. This active engagement is crucial in special education, as it helps to ensure that learning is meaningful and accessible to students with diverse learning needs, including those with physical, cognitive, or emotional challenges.
3. **Use of concrete materials and experiences**: Constructivism emphasizes the importance of concrete, hands-on experiences in learning. In special education, using manipulatives, visual aids, and experiential learning activities can be particularly effective for students who may struggle with traditional, abstract forms of instruction.
4. **Social interaction**: The constructivist theory underscores the value of social interaction in learning. Collaborative learning environments, peer tutoring, and cooperative learning strategies can be especially beneficial for students in special education, offering opportunities for social development and the acquisition of social skills, in addition to academic learning.
5. **Problem-solving and critical thinking**: Constructivism encourages learners to explore, question, and solve problems, developing critical thinking and self-regulation skills. For students with special educational needs, engaging in problem-solving activities can be empowering, fostering independence and self-efficacy.
6. **Adaptive learning environments**: Constructivism calls for learning environments that adapt to the learner's needs, allowing for modifying tasks and expectations to support learning. This principle is at the heart of special education, where accommodations and modifications are made to ensure that all students have access to meaningful educational opportunities.

In summary, constructivism's focus on active, personalized learning and its emphasis on the role of experiences in shaping understanding make it a valuable framework for informing practices in special education. By adopting constructivist principles, educators can create more inclusive, responsive, and effective learning environments for all students, including those with special needs.

Effective strategies for promoting active student engagement

Promoting active student engagement and supporting various aspects of student development, particularly during transitions and emergency drills, require thoughtful and deliberate strategies. Here are some approaches tailored to these specific situations:

Strategy	Transitions	Safety Drills
Establish and practice routines and procedures.	Provide a structured and predictable environment, which will reduce anxiety and confusion. Knowing what to expect during transitions can be especially comforting for students with autism, anxiety disorders, or cognitive impairments.	Use well-rehearsed routines to ensure that safety drills are carried out efficiently and effectively. Students who are familiar with the drill process are more likely to respond quickly and correctly, which is essential in an actual emergency. This also reduces stress and anxiety when an emergency occurs.
Provide constructive feedback.	Offer specific, positive feedback for successfully navigating transitions, and gently guide students through steps where they encounter difficulty, using it as an instructional moment.	After drills, discuss what went well and where there is room for improvement in a calm and constructive manner, ensuring students understand the importance of their actions.
Teach social behaviors.	Model and rehearse transition-related social behaviors, such as raising a hand before speaking or waiting in line. Social stories and role-playing can be effective in teaching these behaviors.	Clearly outline expectations for behavior during drills, such as staying quiet and following instructions, and practice these behaviors through regular drills and debriefs.
Support social-emotional skills.	Encourage self-awareness and self-management by discussing feelings that might arise during transitions, like anxiety or excitement, and teach coping strategies, such as deep breathing or counting to ten.	Recognize that drills may be stressful for students, especially those with exceptionalities. Provide reassurance and discuss emotions while teaching and reinforcing calming techniques.
Increase opportunities to respond.	Provide students with choices during transitions, such as the order of tasks or the materials they use, to give them a sense of control and agency.	Involve students in the safety planning process, like checking that the path is clear or helping to lead the class to the designated safe area, to encourage engagement and responsibility.
Enhance self-regulation of learning.	Teach students to set personal goals for transitions, monitor their own progress, and reflect on their performance to build self-regulation skills.	Incorporate self-reflection into the debrief process by asking students to think about how they felt and behaved during the drill and what they might do to improve next time.

Explicit and systematic instruction to develop cognitive and metacognitive skills

Special education teachers can employ explicit and systematic instruction to effectively teach content and strategies that develop learners' cognitive and metacognitive skills. This approach especially benefits students with learning difficulties by providing clear, structured, and incremental learning experiences. The following are specific strategies for addressing deficits in perception, comprehension, memory, retrieval, and effective grouping:

Strengthening and compensating for deficits in perception

In special education, a deficit in perception refers to difficulties in the ability to interpret and make sense of sensory information. Perception involves taking in information through the senses — sight, hearing, touch, taste, and smell — and then processing, organizing, and interpreting this information to understand the environment and interact with it effectively. A deficit in this area can manifest in various ways, depending on which sense is affected and the severity of the impairment. Key aspects include:

Visual perception: Difficulties in interpreting and understanding visual information. This might include challenges in distinguishing shapes, recognizing patterns, understanding spatial relationships, or difficulties with visual-motor coordination.

Auditory perception: Challenges in processing and making sense of auditory information. This can involve problems in distinguishing between sounds, understanding spoken language, or difficulty filtering out background noise.

Tactile perception: Issues with processing and interpreting touch sensations. This could manifest as hypersensitivity or hyposensitivity to touch, affecting fine motor skills or causing discomfort with certain textures.

Proprioceptive and vestibular perception: Difficulties in understanding the position and movement of the body, which can affect balance, coordination, and the ability to navigate through space.

To help strengthen skills in these areas and compensate for deficits, special educators can use the following approaches.

- Use multi-sensory teaching methods, such as visual aids, tactile materials, and auditory input, to enhance perception.
- Break down complex information into smaller, manageable units.
- Provide explicit instruction in recognizing patterns, sequences, and critical features of concepts.

Strengthening and compensating for deficits in comprehension:

Deficits in comprehension in the context of special education refer to difficulties in understanding and processing information. These challenges can affect various aspects of learning and communication. Students with comprehension deficits might struggle to grasp the meaning of spoken or written language, instructions, social cues, or concepts. Key characteristics and implications of comprehension deficits include:

Language comprehension: Difficulty in understanding spoken words and sentences. This might manifest as challenges in following verbal instructions, engaging in conversations, or comprehending stories and lectures.

Reading comprehension: Challenges in understanding and interpreting written text. Students may struggle to identify the main idea, make inferences, understand the sequence of events, or draw conclusions from what they read.

- **Literal comprehension** – The student can answer questions that can be found in the text.
- **Inferential comprehension** – The student can answer questions that are indirectly referenced in the text but not explicitly stated.
- **Evaluative comprehension** – The student can move beyond the text and form an opinion about the text based on what is read.

Effective Planning and Instruction and Productive Learning Environments

Social comprehension: Difficulties in interpreting social cues, such as body language, tone of voice, or facial expressions, which can affect social interactions and relationships.

Conceptual comprehension: Trouble grasping abstract concepts, such as time, quantity, or theoretical ideas, which can impact learning in subjects like math and science.

Instructional comprehension: Difficulties in understanding and following multi-step instructions, which can affect a student's ability to complete tasks or participate in classroom activities.

To help strengthen skills in these areas and compensate for deficits, special educators can use the following approaches.

- Employ instructional methods like guided reading and questioning techniques to improve comprehension.
- Use graphic organizers to help students organize and relate information.
- Teach summarizing and paraphrasing skills to aid in understanding and processing information.
- Model think-aloud strategies during reading to show students how to use their brains.

Teachers must use instructional approaches, activities, and interventions that are developmentally appropriate and help to accommodate all learners. Teachers must also consider students' physical, intellectual, and behavioral capabilities. For example, a student may require a wheelchair and not have control or use of her hands; however, she may also have high-level cognitive skills and require challenging content and material. The teacher must meet the specific needs of every student.

There are several instructional approaches teachers can use in the special education and general education classroom.

- **Metacognitive** – teaching students to think about their thinking and plan, monitor, evaluate, and make changes to their own learning behaviors.
- **Diagnostic prescriptive –** Identifying the most effective instructional strategies for children who differ on any number of variables believed to be related to academic learning. This requires teachers to analyze formative and summative data and apply methods and interventions to meet the needs of a particular student.
- **Direct instruction** – a teacher-directed method that involves the teacher standing in front of the room, giving directions, or modeling a lesson. This is usually done as a whole-group lesson.
- **Cooperative learning** – students work together in small groups to complete tasks, analyze text, work in labs, etc. The students oversee their learning in this method, and the teacher is a facilitator.
- **Multiple-modality** – involves providing diverse presentations and experiences of the content so that students use different senses and skills during a single lesson. Often multiple modalities address different learning preferences.

Student-Centered Environment

In a student-centered environment, teachers pay attention to learning preferences, readiness levels, and developmentally appropriate practices. Below are considerations when designing a student-centered or learner-centered classroom environment.

- **Visual learners.** These students thrive when images and graphics accompany the learning to organize information.
- **Auditory learners.** These students grasp concepts best through listening and speaking situations (think lectures and podcasts).
- **Kinesthetic learners.** These students prefer hands-on learning experiences and moving their bodies.
- **Read and write learners**. These students prefer reading and writing activities to make sense of abstract concepts.

Test Tip

In the context of this examination, the term *differentiation* is key. You are also encouraged to be vigilant for terms and phrases associated with differentiation, such as *interventions, adapting instruction to meet diverse student needs*, and *accommodations*. These concepts often point to the correct answers when selecting among instructional practice options, as they are central to effective teaching strategies.

Strengthening and compensating for memory deficits:

Deficits in memory in special education refer to challenges with the ability to encode, store, and retrieve information. Memory is a crucial cognitive function that affects learning and daily functioning. Students with memory deficits may struggle in various educational settings and activities. These challenges can manifest in different forms:

- **Short-term memory**: Difficulty in holding information for a brief period. Students may struggle to remember instructions just given or cannot recall information from the beginning of a lesson by its end.
- **Working memory**: Challenges with manipulating information in the mind. This affects the ability to solve problems in one's head, do mental arithmetic, or follow multi-step instructions.
- **Long-term memory**: Difficulty in storing and retrieving information over longer periods. This might involve struggles in recalling facts, events, or procedures learned in the past.
- **Episodic memory**: Challenges with remembering specific events or experiences, such as what they did over the weekend or specifics of a field trip.
- **Procedural memory**: Difficulties in remembering how to perform tasks or activities that require steps, like tying shoes or playing a musical instrument.

Memory deficits in students can stem from various causes, including learning disabilities, neurological disorders, attention deficit hyperactivity disorder (ADHD), and emotional disturbances. To support these students, special education teachers can employ several strategies:

- **Repetition and reinforcement**: Repeating information and reviewing content can help reinforce memory.
- **Use of mnemonics**: Teaching mnemonic devices to aid in memorization of facts or sequences.
- **Chunking information**: Breaking down information into smaller, manageable "chunks" can make it easier to process and remember.
- **Visual aids**: Using charts, diagrams, and other visual tools to support memory.
- **Real-life connections**: Relating information to real-life situations or personal experiences to make it more memorable.
- **Organizational tools**: Encouraging the use of agendas, planners, and checklists to help remember tasks and assignments.
- **Teaching memory strategies**: Using categorization, association, and visualization techniques.
- **Consistent routines**: Establishing a predictable routine in the classroom can aid memory by creating a stable learning environment.

Strengthening and compensating for retrieval deficits

Deficits in retrieval within the context of special education refer to difficulties in accessing and pulling out information from memory when needed. Retrieval is a critical part of the learning process, as it allows students to recall previously learned information to apply to new situations or to demonstrate understanding. Here are several aspects of retrieval deficits:

- **Recall issues**: Difficulty in recalling information without cues or prompts, which can affect performance in testing situations or during class discussions.
- **Retrieval failure**: Inability to access specific information even though it has been studied, often described as the 'it's on the tip of my tongue' phenomenon.
- **Slower retrieval speed**: Some students may be able to eventually retrieve the information, but it takes them longer than their peers, which can affect their pace of learning and performance under time constraints.
- **Inconsistent retrieval**: The ability to retrieve information may be erratic, with students being able to remember the information at one time but not another.

To support students with retrieval deficits, educators can implement several strategies:

- **Cueing and prompting**: Providing cues or hints to help students recall information, such as the first letter of a word or a contextual hint.
- **Multiple retrieval opportunities**: Offering regular opportunities to retrieve information through quizzes, discussions, and review sessions to strengthen memory pathways.
- **Mnemonic devices**: Using memory aids that can help students recall information by associating it with something more memorable.
- **Structured retrieval practice**: Incorporating activities that require retrieval in a structured manner, such as fill-in-the-blank exercises or matching tasks, which can be less demanding than open-ended questions.
- **Spacing retrieval practice**: Spreading out retrieval practice over time (spaced practice) rather than cramming, which has been shown to improve long-term retention.
- **Errorless learning**: Starting with tasks that are easy enough to ensure success and gradually increasing difficulty to avoid the reinforcement of incorrect responses.

Quick Tip

Students with learning disabilities often require intensive support. This is sometimes referred to as a remedial approach. Remedial instruction is one-on-one or small-group instruction that focuses on the needs of the individual student.

Grouping Strategies for Mastery of Concepts:

Grouping strategies in special education serve as a dynamic tool to enhance learning by leveraging peer interactions and targeted instruction. Heterogeneous grouping allows students with diverse needs to collaborate, often leading to peer-mediated learning where students can model skills for each other, promoting social and cognitive development. Homogeneous grouping, on the other hand, enables educators to deliver specialized instruction tailored to a specific set of needs, allowing for intensive focus on skills or challenges. Both strategies can be interchanged or combined to provide a supportive learning environment, fostering inclusivity, and enabling special education students to reach their academic potential within the classroom.

Heterogeneous Grouping:

- Mix students of varying abilities to encourage peer learning and support.
- This approach is beneficial for collaborative projects, discussions, and problem-solving activities.

Homogeneous Grouping:

- Group students with similar skill levels or needs together to provide targeted instruction that addresses specific deficits.
- Use this strategy for direct instruction on foundational skills, remediation, or accelerated learning.

Caution

Homogeneous grouping can be an effective strategy for targeted educational interventions and should be employed as a short-term measure. Prolonged placement in homogeneous groups is not recommended as it may hinder a student's long-term academic growth. Studies indicate that exclusive reliance on this form of grouping for students facing academic challenges can be counterproductive. A more effective approach is to utilize heterogeneous grouping, which allows for a diverse range of abilities within each group, fostering a richer educational experience and promoting inclusive learning success.

Flexible Grouping:

- Change group compositions based on the specific learning activity, skill, or concept being taught.
- This allows for differentiation and the ability to address diverse needs within the classroom.

Peer Groups:

- Pair students to work on tasks together, allowing students to support and help one another.
- This method promotes social skills and can effectively reinforce concepts.

Caution

While collaborative work and peer assistance are effective methods to enhance learning, it's imperative that these strategies do not replace direct teacher involvement, especially when a student encounters academic hurdles. For instance, if a student is experiencing difficulties with reading comprehension at their grade level, it's essential that targeted interventions come directly from the teacher. Solely depending on classmates for assistance in cooperative learning scenarios may not sufficiently meet the specific educational requirements of a struggling student. It falls upon the teacher to provide the essential supports and resources necessary for each student's academic achievement.

Small Group Instruction:

- Provide instruction to small groups for more individualized attention.
- Use data from assessments to form groups based on specific instructional needs.

In all these methods, it is crucial for the teacher to provide clear, direct instruction with specific learning goals, provide regular feedback, and systematically monitor progress. This approach ensures that instruction is tailored to the unique needs of each student, facilitating effective learning and mastery of concepts.

Task Analysis

Task analysis is a type of systematic and explicit approach that breaks down instruction into manageable and achievable steps and is crucial for fostering student success. This method ensures instruction is consistent, personalized, and systematic, directly contributing to a student's learning achievements. Common techniques employed in task analysis include forward chaining, backward chaining, discrete trial instruction, and modeling. These methods are designed to gradually guide students through the learning process, enhancing their understanding and mastery of the material.

- **Forward chaining** is a teaching method where a complex skill or behavior is broken down into smaller, manageable steps. The learner is taught the first step first. Once the first step is mastered, the next step is introduced.
- **Backward chaining** is like forward chaining but in reverse. The learner begins with the last step of the task and works backward. The teacher completes all but the last task step, and the learner completes the final step. Over time, the learner is given more steps to complete until they can perform the entire task independently.
- **Discrete trial instruction (DTI)** is a structured method of teaching that breaks down skills into small, discrete components or trials. Each trial consists of a prompt or instruction, the student's response, and a consequence (usually a form of feedback). The trials are repeated until the skill is mastered.
- **Modeling** is when the teacher demonstrates a behavior or skill that the learner is expected to imitate. The teacher or a peer performs the task, providing a model for the learner. The learner observes and then attempts to replicate the behavior or skill.

Adapting the learning environment

Special education teachers can adapt the general curriculum to include specially designed instruction for individuals with exceptionalities through a process known as differentiation. This process involves modifying and tailoring instructional methods, materials, and assessments to meet the diverse needs of learners with disabilities. The goal is to provide equitable access to education and to ensure that students with exceptionalities can achieve academic success alongside their peers in the general education classroom.

Key strategies for adapting the general curriculum include:

1. **Individualized Education Programs (IEPs)**: This document outlines the student's specific learning needs, goals, and the services required to meet those goals. It's a collaborative effort involving teachers, parents, and other relevant stakeholders.
2. **Curriculum modification**: This is when teachers adjust the scope and sequence of the curriculum to align with the student's abilities and goals. This may involve simplifying content, reducing the number of concepts taught at one time, or providing alternative assignments that better suit the student's learning style.
3. **Differentiated instruction**: This is when teachers implement instructional strategies that cater to a range of learning styles and abilities. This might include using visual aids, hands-on activities, or technology-assisted instruction. The key is to present information in multiple ways to ensure it is accessible to all students.
4. **Accommodations vs. Modifications**: Accommodations are changes to the teaching or testing environment that remove barriers to learning and provide equal access to students. Modifications are changes to what the student is learning. Modifications might include altering the level of complexity of assignments or tests.
5. **Collaborative teaching**: This is when special education teachers work with general education teachers to plan and deliver instruction. This collaboration ensures that the curriculum is adapted in a way that is coherent and consistent across different learning environments.
6. **Ongoing assessment and feedback**: This is when teachers use formative assessments to monitor student progress and adjust instruction accordingly. This provides regular, constructive feedback to students to guide their learning and encourage growth.

7. **Professional development**: Teachers must stay informed about the latest research and best practices in special education. Participating in workshops, seminars, and other professional development opportunities will enhance instructional skills.
8. **Family and community involvement**: Parents and caregivers can provide valuable insights into the child's needs and strengths, and community resources can offer additional support and enrichment opportunities.

By implementing these strategies, special education teachers can effectively adapt the general curriculum to meet the unique needs of students with exceptionalities, fostering an inclusive and supportive learning environment that empowers all students to reach their full potential.

Quick Tip

Adhering to the Individualized Education Program (IEP) for each student is a fundamental duty of special education teachers. The IEP serves as a binding document that specifies necessary accommodations and assistive technologies for the student. It secures the educational rights of students with disabilities, affirming their entitlement to a free, appropriate public education (FAPE) that is customized to their unique needs. By following the IEP, educators maintain adherence to federal and state regulations, thereby safeguarding the legal rights of the students they serve.

Accommodations vs. Modifications

In special education, the terms "modifications" and "accommodations" refer to strategies and supports provided to students with disabilities to ensure equitable access to the curriculum and participation in the educational environment. While both are designed to assist students in overcoming or compensating for their disabilities, they differ fundamentally in their approach and impact on the student's educational experience.

Accommodations

Accommodations refer to changes in how instruction is delivered, materials are presented, or assessments are conducted. These adjustments allow students with disabilities to access the same curriculum as their non-disabled peers without altering the content or lowering the standards. Accommodations are designed to remove barriers to learning, ensuring that students can demonstrate their knowledge and skills in an equitable manner. Examples of accommodations include:

- Extended time on tests and assignments.
- Preferential seating to minimize distractions or enhance engagement.
- Large-print textbooks or audiobooks for students with visual impairments.
- Use of technology, such as speech-to-text software for students with writing difficulties.
- Alternate formats for assessments, such as oral presentations instead of written reports.

Modifications

Modifications, however, involve changes to the curriculum content, difficulty level, or performance expectations. These alterations are made to ensure that the educational content is accessible and appropriate for the student's cognitive abilities and learning needs. Modifications may simplify the material or adjust the quantity of work expected, thereby altering the standard or learning outcomes for the student. Examples of modifications include:

- Reduced homework or assignment expectations, such as fewer questions or problems to solve.
- Simplified reading materials that are at a lower reading level.

- Alternative projects or assessments that cater to the student's abilities and learning styles.
- Adjusted grading scales or performance criteria specific to the student's capabilities.

Key Differences

The primary difference between accommodations and modifications lies in their approach to the curriculum:

- **Accommodations** adjust the learning environment and instructional methods to provide equal access to the same curriculum for all students. They do not alter the curriculum content or the educational standards the student is expected to meet.
- **Modifications** entail changes to the curriculum content itself, adjusting the educational expectations and standards to align with the student's individual abilities and learning needs.

Choosing between accommodations and modifications depends on the student's Individualized Education Program (IEP), which outlines specific learning objectives and the supports necessary to achieve them. The decision is based on a careful assessment of the student's abilities, needs, and educational goals, with the aim of maximizing their learning potential while ensuring access to an appropriate and challenging education.

Teaching Approaches

Often in a special education classroom and general education classroom, teachers will have the opportunity to work with another professional or teacher in the same room. For example, a teacher and a paraprofessional may work together in a math class. Two teachers may work together in an elementary classroom. Having multiple instructors can be beneficial and create a supportive classroom environment. The following are some examples of coaching approaches.

- **Co-teaching** – the practice of pairing teachers together in a classroom to share the responsibilities of planning, instructing, and assessing students. Co-teaching is often implemented with general and special education teachers as part of an initiative to create a more inclusive classroom.
- **Station teaching** – the approach of having an instructor at each center or station. This promotes small group and individualized instruction for specific skills.
- **Alternative teaching** – a co-teaching model where one teacher works with a small group of students as the other teacher instructs the large group. This approach allows teachers to maximize time spent on differentiation and scaffolding techniques.
- **One teach, one assist** – the method where one teacher has the responsibility to deliver main instruction while the other teacher walks around the room and assists. The assist teacher may help students get supplies or help clarify if students have questions.
- **One teach, one observe** – this method is often used for data collection. The main teacher instructs the lesson, and the other observes students and collects formative data.
- **Parallel teaching** – this method involves two teachers. The teachers divide the class in half, and each teacher teaches the same thing to each respective half of the class.
- **Team teaching** – this involves two teachers in front of the class sharing the responsibility of whole-group instruction.

Instruction monitoring strategies for reading and writing

Special education teachers can use various monitoring strategies to enhance accuracy, fluency, vocabulary development, and comprehension in content-area reading and writing. These strategies are designed to provide structured and supportive learning experiences, helping students with disabilities to engage more effectively with content-area material. The following table outlines examples of teaching practices that can be applied to reading instruction.

Practice	Examples
Accuracy in Reading and Writing	**Error Analysis**: Track and analyze errors made by students in reading and writing to identify specific areas of difficulty. This can guide targeted instruction. **Guided Reading and Writing**: Provide scaffolded support during reading and writing tasks, gradually releasing responsibility to the student as their accuracy improves. **Peer-Assisted Learning**: Pair students for reading and writing activities, allowing them to learn from and correct each other under teacher supervision.
Fluency in Reading	**Repeated Reading**: Encourage students to read the same text multiple times to improve their speed, accuracy, and expression. **Progress Monitoring**: Regularly time and record students' reading to measure improvements in speed and fluency. **Model Fluent Reading**: Regularly read aloud to students, demonstrating fluent reading, including appropriate pacing and expression.
Vocabulary Development	**Pre-Teaching Key Vocabulary**: Introduce key vocabulary before reading new content. Use visual aids, context, and examples to explain words. **Word Walls**: Create a visual display of important vocabulary words in the classroom. Update the word wall as new terms are introduced. **Interactive Vocabulary Exercises**: Use games and technology-based tools to reinforce vocabulary learning in an engaging manner. **Teaching Context Clues:** Help students identify synonyms, antonyms, inferences, and examples to determine the meaning of words in context.
Comprehension in Content-Area Reading	**Graphic Organizers**: Use Venn diagrams, story maps, or concept maps to help students organize and retain information. **Questioning Techniques**: Employ guided questioning strategies during and after reading to check comprehension and encourage deeper thinking. **Summarization and Paraphrasing**: Teach students to summarize and paraphrase texts to ensure they understand the main ideas and details.
Writing in Content Areas	**Writing Templates and Frames**: Provide structured templates or sentence frames to help students organize their thoughts and content knowledge. **Process Writing**: Guide students through the steps of the writing process (prewriting, drafting, revising, editing, and publishing), offering support and feedback at each stage. **Self-Assessment and Reflection**: Encourage students to assess their own writing, identifying strengths and areas for improvement.
Technology Integration	**Assistive Technology**: Use technology tools designed to support reading and writing, such as text-to-speech software, word prediction programs, and audiobooks. **Digital Learning Tools**: Incorporate interactive digital tools like educational apps and online platforms that offer practice and reinforcement in reading and writing skills.

Practice	Examples
Regular Monitoring and Feedback	**Formative Assessments**: Conduct regular, informal assessments to monitor students' progress in reading and writing. This could include quick comprehension checks, writing samples, and oral reading records. **Feedback and Goal Setting**: Provide timely and specific feedback to students. Help them set achievable goals based on their performance data.
Collaboration and Professional Development	**Collaboration with Content-Area Teachers**: Work with teachers in specific content areas to align strategies and reinforce learning across subjects. **Continuous Professional Learning**: Stay informed about the latest research and best practices in teaching reading and writing to students with disabilities.

By systematically applying these strategies, special education teachers can effectively support their students in developing critical literacy skills in content-area reading and writing. These approaches not only address the immediate learning needs of students with disabilities but also foster long-term academic growth and a deeper engagement with content-area material.

Another way teachers can help students thrive in the classroom is to plan for activities that promote learning for all different students with different needs and preferences. The following is a table with several types of approaches teachers can use.

Activity	Definition	Example
Jigsaw	A cooperative learning activity in which each student or groups of students read and analyze a small piece of information that is part of a much larger piece. They then share what they learned with the class.	The teacher arranges students in groups. Each group reads and analyzes a piece of text. Group members then join with members of other groups, and each student shares and discusses his or her section of the text. As the group shares, the entire text is covered. It is referred to as Jigsaw because students complete the puzzle when they share their individual pieces.
Chunking	A reading activity that involves breaking down a difficult text into manageable pieces.	In a science class, students break down a lengthy and complex chapter on genetics by focusing on pieces of the text. The teacher has planned for students to read and analyze the text one paragraph at a time.
Think-Pair-Share	A cooperative learning activity in which students work together to solve a problem or answer a question.	Think – The teacher asks a specific question about the text. Students "think" about what they know or have learned about the topic. Pair – Students pair up to read and discuss. Share - Students share what they've learned in their pairs. Teachers can then expand the "share" into a whole-class discussion.

Activity	Definition	Example
Reading Response Journals	A writing activity where students use journals to react to what they read by expressing how they feel and asking questions about the text.	After reading a chapter of a book in class, the teacher asks students to use their reading response journals to respond to the story emotionally, make associations between ideas in the text and their own ideas, and record questions they may have about the story.
Evidence-Based Discussion	The teacher sets the expectation that students use evidence in the text to support claims they make during the discussion.	The class is discussing World War II. Students are asking and answering questions. When making claims, students identify support for those claims in the text.
Literature Circles	A small-group, cooperative learning activity where students engage and discuss a piece of literature/text.	In their cooperative groups, students read and analyze text together. Each student contributes to the learning. There is an administrator who decides when to read and when to stop and discuss. There is a note taker who writes down important information. There are two readers who take turns reading the text based on the administrator's suggestions.

Instruction monitoring strategies for math

Special education teachers can implement various monitoring strategies to enhance accuracy and proficiency in mathematics for individuals with learning needs. These strategies focus on individualized instruction, continuous assessment, and adaptive teaching methods to meet the unique requirements of each student. The following table outlines examples of teaching practices that can be applied to math instruction.

Practice	Examples
Baseline Assessment and Goal Setting	Begin with a thorough assessment to establish each student's current level of proficiency in mathematics. Set specific, measurable, achievable, relevant, and time-bound (SMART) goals for improvement in calculations and applications.
Differentiated Instruction	Tailor instruction to meet the diverse learning styles and abilities of students. This might involve using visual aids, manipulatives, or technology-assisted instruction. Break down mathematical concepts into smaller, more manageable steps to ensure understanding.
Use of Manipulatives and Visual Aids	Incorporate hands-on learning tools like counters, number lines, and geometric shapes to make abstract concepts more concrete. Use visual representations, such as graphs and charts, to aid comprehension.

Practice	Examples
Frequent Practice with Immediate Feedback	Provide regular practice opportunities in both calculations and real-world applications. Offer immediate, constructive feedback to correct misconceptions and reinforce correct procedures.
Progress Monitoring	Use ongoing formative assessments to track student progress toward their mathematical goals. Adjust instruction based on assessment data to address areas of need and reinforce strengths.
Technology Integration	Use educational software and apps that provide interactive math practice and track student progress. Implement assistive technology tools for students with specific learning disabilities in math (e.g., calculators, speech-to-text programs for word problems).
Metacognitive Strategies	Teach students to think about their thinking (metacognition) to develop self-monitoring and problem-solving skills. Encourage self-questioning techniques and reflective practices to enhance understanding and application of mathematical concepts.
Real-World Application	Connect mathematical concepts to real-life situations to enhance relevance and engagement. Involve students in problem-solving activities that require the application of math skills in practical contexts.

By implementing these strategies, special education teachers can effectively support students with diverse learning needs in developing accuracy and proficiency in mathematics. This approach not only addresses immediate learning challenges but also fosters long-term mathematical understanding and competence.

Universal Design for Learning (UDL)

The Universal Design for Learning (UDL) is an educational framework that aims to improve and optimize teaching and learning for all people based on scientific insights into how humans learn. Developed by researchers at the Center for Applied Special Technology (CAST), UDL guides the creation of inclusive and accessible learning experiences that accommodate individual learning differences.

UDL is rooted in three primary principles (what, how, and why):

1. **Multiple Means of Representation (the "what" of learning):** This principle emphasizes presenting information and content in various ways to address the diverse needs of learners. It recognizes that learners differ in how they perceive and comprehend information; thus, teachers should offer different ways of presenting content. This can include visual aids, auditory materials, hands-on activities, and interactive digital tools.
2. **Multiple Means of Action and Expression (the "how" of learning):** This principle allows learners various ways to express their knowledge. Recognizing that individuals have diverse strengths and preferences in how they express their knowledge and ideas, UDL encourages the provision of multiple options for students to demonstrate their learning, such as through writing, oral presentations, visual arts, or technology.

3. **Multiple Means of Engagement (the "why" of learning):** This principle addresses the importance of motivating students. It acknowledges that learners have varied interests and ways of engaging with content. UDL encourages educators to offer choices that foster motivation and engagement, such as providing real-world applications, offering choices in how to approach learning tasks, and creating collaborative or independent learning opportunities.

Implementing UDL in educational settings involves a proactive curriculum design that anticipates potential barriers to learning and incorporates a variety of teaching methods, materials, and assessments to meet the diverse needs of all students. It is about designing learning experiences that are accessible and effective for everyone, regardless of ability, disability, age, gender, or cultural and linguistic background.

This approach promotes inclusivity, equity, and accessibility in education, ensuring that all learners have equal opportunities to succeed.

Direct instruction

Direct instruction is a teacher-led approach that is structured, sequenced, and systematic. It is designed to teach specific skills and knowledge through direct and explicit teaching techniques, such as lectures or demonstrations of the material, rather than exploratory models such as inquiry-based learning.

Here are some key characteristics of direct instruction:

1. **Explicit teaching**: Teachers clearly explain what should be learned and how to perform tasks. They often use clear, concise language and demonstrate the skills or concepts students are expected to learn.
2. **Structured framework**: Lessons are carefully planned and follow a prescribed format. This includes an introduction to the lesson, a presentation of new content, guided practice with feedback, independent practice, and a summary or review.
3. **Skill sequencing**: Skills and concepts are broken down into small, manageable parts and taught in a logical, hierarchical sequence that builds from simple to complex.
4. **Paced instruction**: Teachers maintain an instructional pace to keep students engaged and to cover more material in less time. They monitor the pace and may adjust it based on student understanding.
5. **Frequent assessment**: Teachers assess students' understanding through questions and practice opportunities. Immediate feedback is provided to correct errors and reinforce learning.
6. **Maximized engagement**: The teacher aims to keep all students actively engaged throughout the lesson, often by asking questions and calling on students to answer, ensuring they are attentive and involved.
7. **Mastery learning**: The goal is for all students to achieve a high level of mastery before moving on to the next concept or skill. Additional support is provided to students who need it.

Direct instruction is particularly effective for teaching basic skills, such as reading and math, to diverse groups of students, including those with learning disabilities. It emphasizes clarity and precision in teaching and learning, and it's supported by a substantial body of research indicating its effectiveness in improving academic outcomes, especially for students at risk of educational failure.

The following table outlines examples of direct instruction.

Direct Instructional Strategies	Purpose	Example
Explicit teaching	Breaking down a topic into smaller parts and teaching them individually. The purpose is to simplify and clarify.	Teaching students to recognize and use suffixes like *-s, -es, -ed, -ing* by reciting and writing a list of words and categorizing them.
Drill and practice	Repetition of a specific set of facts. The intention is memorization.	Call and response practice of spelling words, phonemes, word patterns, math facts, or steps in a process.
Lecture	Speaking to students on a topic, typically using PowerPoint presentations, dry erase or chalkboard, or other visuals as props.	Introducing a social studies topic such as events leading to the Civil Rights Movement.
Demonstrations	Showing students a process, concept, or idea.	Demonstrating a science experiment. Modeling learning behaviors such as revising a piece of writing using a document camera.
Guides for reading, listening, viewing	Teacher-written guides used by students who are reading, listening, or viewing new material. The guides typically include previewing vocabulary, summarizing main ideas, and questioning to check for comprehension.	A guide for viewing a video being shown on photosynthesis. A "cause and effect in narrative writing" guide used by students as they listen to an episode of a mystery podcast.

Indirect instruction

Indirect instruction is a student-led educational approach grounded in the belief that learning is most effective when students are actively engaged in discovering information, solving problems, and developing new understandings through a process of inquiry and exploration. Indirect instruction contrasts with direct instruction, where the teacher primarily lectures and presents information, expecting students to absorb knowledge passively.

Key features of indirect instruction include:

1. **Student-centered learning**: The focus is on students' active participation and their ability to construct knowledge through personal experience. Teachers act as facilitators rather than the sole source of information, guiding students to discover answers and understand concepts independently or collaboratively.
2. **Inquiry and exploration**: Students are encouraged to ask questions, investigate, and explore concepts deeply. This approach fosters critical thinking and problem-solving skills, as learners are not simply given answers but must work through the process of finding solutions.

3. **Discussion and collaboration**: Indirect instruction often involves group work, discussions, and collaborative projects. These activities promote social learning and allow students to articulate their thoughts, defend their opinions, and learn from the perspectives of others.
4. **Use of scaffolding**: Teachers provide support or "scaffolds" to help students reach higher levels of understanding. These supports are gradually removed as students become more proficient, encouraging independence and self-directed learning.
5. **Integration of real-world problems**: This method often incorporates real-world problems and scenarios, making learning relevant and meaningful to students. It allows them to apply what they have learned in practical, tangible ways.

Indirect instruction can be particularly effective in fostering a deep understanding of content, critical thinking, and independent learning skills. It aligns well with constructivist theories of education, which argue that learners construct their own knowledge through experiences and reflection.

In the context of diverse classrooms, including special education settings, indirect instruction can offer flexible and differentiated learning opportunities. It allows students with various needs and abilities to engage with content at their own pace and in ways that are most meaningful to them. However, successful implementation of indirect instruction requires careful planning to ensure that all students are supported appropriately and that learning objectives are met.

The following table outlines examples of indirect instruction.

Indirect Instructional Strategies	Purpose	Examples
Problem-solving	Inclusive of many higher order thinking strategies including creative, critical, and analytical thinking. Allows students to apply learning by identifying problems and various solutions.	Math word problems. Finding the problem in a story and suggesting several possible solutions before reading to the end. Peer-resolution groups or playground representatives; students who are designated for helping their peers to resolve disagreements and disputes.
Inquiry	Students explore, ask, and seek answers to why and how things happen.	Using KWL charts and *Think, See, Wonder* routines. Asking and pursuing answers to phenomena of the natural world. Exploring numerical concepts or find the most efficient method for solving problems.
Cooperative learning groups	Students work on a project or task together.	Book clubs. Experimenting with building materials to make a sturdy bridge.

Indirect Instructional Strategies	Purpose	Examples
Discussions	Discussions are a way of co-constructing knowledge with students, checking for understanding, gauging student interest, and diving deeper into a topic. Useful across the curriculum.	Discussing why a math problem is wrong and how to fix it. Discussing cause-effect in a novel. Discussing engaging topics such as how to help stray animals.
Experiments	Developing, implementing, and understanding the process for proving claims and hypothesis. Students use problem-solving, inductive reasoning, and higher order thinking in the process of setting up and conducting experiments.	Building ramps that make cars go faster and farther. Consider what happens when combining different substances.
Simulations	A situation where an environment is designed for students to experience a scenario or setting. The idea is for them to interact and glean meaning from the experience.	Oregon Trail is a stimulus game entailing the hardships and realities of exploring the landscape and natural resources of the northwest in the early 20th century. Setting up an event, time, or place for students to have an experience. Pretending to be planets orbiting the sun.
Role play	Pretending to be characters in a story, time, place, or event to better appreciate specific feelings, perspective, and experience.	Acting out a scene from a novel. Role playing an event from US history. Children having a disagreement on the playground with positive and negative outcomes.

Instructional scaffolding

Instructional scaffolding is an educational technique that supports students' learning by providing temporary and adjustable assistance as they acquire new skills or knowledge. The concept is metaphorically derived from the scaffolds used in construction, which provide temporary support structures. In education, scaffolding involves a series of instructional techniques designed to move students progressively toward stronger understanding and, ultimately, greater independence in the learning process.

Key characteristics of instructional scaffolding include:

1. **Support during the learning process**: The teacher provides specific support tailored to the student's learning needs. This support can be through resources, guidance, encouragement, or direct instruction.
2. **Tailoring to individual needs**: The level and type of support provided are individualized based on each student's current level of knowledge and skill. It is not a one-size-fits-all approach but rather adjusts to meet the varying needs of learners.

3. **Gradual removal of support**: As students become more competent and confident, the scaffolding is gradually removed. This process is often called "fading" and is crucial to encourage independence and prevent over-reliance on support.
4. **Focus on the Zone of Proximal Development (ZPD)**: Scaffolding is particularly effective in the ZPD, a term coined by psychologist Lev Vygotsky. The ZPD is the difference between what a learner can do without help and what they can achieve with guidance and encouragement from a skilled partner.

Examples of instructional scaffolding include:

- **Modeling**: Demonstrating a task or concept to students before they attempt it.
- **Guided Practice**: Working with students as they try new tasks, providing guidance as needed.
- **Prompting**: Using hints or cues to lead students toward the correct response or action.
- **Questioning**: Asking questions that encourage students to think critically and explore concepts more deeply.
- **Feedback**: Providing constructive feedback to help students understand their progress and areas for improvement.
- **Graphic Organizers**: Using visual aids like charts, diagrams, or maps to help students organize and understand information.
- **Think-Alouds**: Verbalizing thoughts during problem-solving or reading processes to model metacognitive strategies.

Effective scaffolding ensures that students are constantly challenged yet not overly frustrated. It is a dynamic process, adjusting to the pace of the student's learning and gradually building their capacity to learn independently. Scaffolding is widely used in various educational settings, from early childhood education to adult learning, due to its adaptability and effectiveness in enhancing learning outcomes.

Classroom Scenario - Dynamic Teaching: Blending Direct and Indirect Instruction in a Science Lesson

Setting: Bright Horizons Middle School, Special Education Science Classroom

Characters:

- Mr. Allen, a versatile special education teacher
- Jasmine, a student with autism spectrum disorder (ASD)
- Omar, a student with dyslexia
- Carlos, a student with attention deficit hyperactivity disorder (ADHD)

Scenario:

In Mr. Allen's science classroom, students gather around their lab stations, eager to delve into today's lesson on the water cycle. Mr. Allen knows that his diverse learners will benefit from a combination of direct and indirect instructional strategies, along with appropriate scaffolding to ensure comprehension and engagement.

Direct Instruction: Mr. Allen begins with direct instruction, using a clear and concise lecture to introduce the water cycle. He employs a multisensory approach, showing a colorful diagram on the smart board and using a model to demonstrate evaporation, condensation, and precipitation.

Scaffolding for Jasmine: For Jasmine, who needs structure due to her ASD, he provides a graphic organizer. The organizer has labeled parts of the cycle and is paired with images to help her visually link each stage with its name and sequence.

Indirect Instruction: Switching to indirect instruction, Mr. Allen poses a question to the class: "Where do you think the water goes after it rains?" He encourages students to discuss in pairs, facilitating a peer-teaching moment. This allows students to explore ideas and make connections collaboratively.

Effective Planning and Instruction and Productive Learning Environments

Scaffolding for Omar: Omar, who has dyslexia, finds reading challenging. Mr. Allen gives him an audio recording of the text on the water cycle and a set of flashcards with key vocabulary and definitions. The flashcards have pictures representing each term, which Omar uses to match with statements his peers discuss.

Combining Strategies: Mr. Allen then directs the students to conduct a simple experiment to observe condensation. He guides them through the steps, modeling the first part and then letting the students continue, which blends direct instruction with hands-on learning.

Scaffolding for Carlos: Carlos, with ADHD, sometimes struggles to maintain focus during hands-on activities. Mr. Allen provides him with a checklist of steps for the experiment, which helps him stay on task. He also assigns Carlos the role of 'team leader' to channel his energy into a leadership position, guiding his group through the experimental process.

Conclusion:

As the lesson concludes, students share their observations. Mr. Allen reinforces their learning by connecting their findings back to the water cycle diagram, engaging the class in a reflective discussion. He assigns a homework task to draw or describe the water cycle in their own words, allowing for differentiation based on each student's strengths.

This scenario demonstrates how a special education teacher can effectively use a blend of direct and indirect instruction, augmented with thoughtful scaffolding, to engage students with diverse needs in a science lesson. By employing a range of strategies, Mr. Allen ensures that each student can access the content in a way that supports their individual learning style.

Individualized Family Service Plans (IFSPs) and Individualized Education Programs (IEPs)

An Individualized Family Service Plan (IFSP) and an Individualized Education Program (IEP) are both plans developed for children with special needs but serve different age groups and have distinct goals and structures.

IFSP:

- **Age Group**: The IFSP is for infants and toddlers up to age 3.
- **Family-Centered**: The IFSP focuses on the child and the family. It looks at the family's needs to support the child's development.
- **Developmental Focus**: The plan emphasizes early intervention services that are aimed at enhancing the development of infants and toddlers with disabilities.
- **Service Setting**: Services are often provided in natural environments such as the home or a community setting where children without disabilities participate.
- **Plan Details**: It outlines services the child and family will receive, how often, and by whom, and includes a plan for transition to preschool and other future services.
- **Holistic Approach**: The IFSP is broader in scope, addressing not only the child's physical development but also cognitive, communicative, social/emotional, and adaptive development.

IEP:

- **Age Group**: The IEP is for children and youth ages 3 through 21 in the educational system.
- **Education-Centered**: The IEP focuses on the educational needs of the child. It is designed to provide individualized special education and related services in the school environment.
- **Academic Focus**: The plan emphasizes educational goals, including specific learning objectives and how the child's progress will be assessed.
- **Service Setting**: Services are provided within the school setting, including the general education classroom or a special education setting.

- **Plan Details**: It includes the child's present levels of academic achievement, annual academic and functional goals, the special education, and related services to be provided, and how the child will participate in standardized tests and the general education curriculum.
- **Educational Approach**: The IEP focuses more on the educational and academic accommodations, modifications, supports, and services needed to help the child succeed in the learning environment.

Both IFSPs and IEPs are legally binding documents and are based on federal regulations. They require collaborative team efforts, including the child's family, to develop and are reviewed periodically to update the plans according to the child's developmental and educational needs. Transitioning from an IFSP to an IEP typically occurs around the child's third birthday, marking a shift from a family-oriented early intervention service to an educational plan focused on the child's success in the school setting.

Types of assistive technology used in the special education classroom

Assistive technology in the special education classroom encompasses many tools and devices designed to support students with disabilities in their learning process. These technologies can be categorized based on the type of support they provide. The following table describes the main types of assistive technology used in many special education classrooms.

Technology	Examples
Communication devices	**Augmentative and alternative communication (AAC) devices**: These include speech-generating devices, picture boards, or software that help students with speech or language impairments to communicate effectively. **Voice output communication aids (VOCAs)**: Devices that produce spoken language to assist individuals who have difficulty with verbal expression.
Reading and writing aids	**Text-to-speech software**: Converts written text into spoken words, aiding students with reading difficulties, dyslexia, or visual impairments. **Speech-to-text software**: Allows students to dictate their thoughts and have them transcribed, beneficial for students with writing difficulties or physical impairments. **Word prediction software**: Suggests words as the student types, which can help students with learning disabilities or motor challenges in writing.
Hearing aids and audio devices	**FM systems**: Wireless systems that enhance the teacher's voice for students with hearing impairments. **Closed captioning and transcription services**: Provide text alternatives for audio content, aiding students with hearing impairments.
Visual aids	**Screen magnification software**: Enlarges text and images on a computer screen for students with visual impairments. **Screen readers**: Software that reads aloud the content displayed on the screen, essential for students who are blind or have significant visual impairments. **Braille technology**: Devices like braille notetakers and braille printers that facilitate reading and writing for students who are blind.
Mobility aids	**Adaptive keyboards and mice**: Customized keyboards, trackballs, or touchpads to accommodate students with limited mobility or fine motor skills. **Specialized chairs and desks**: Ergonomically designed furniture to support students with physical disabilities.

Technology	Examples
Learning and cognitive aids	**Memory aids**: Tools like electronic organizers or smartphone apps to assist students with memory or attention issues. **Educational software**: Interactive and adaptive learning programs tailored to support students with various learning disabilities.
Behavioral and environmental aids	**Sensory tools**: Items like fidget toys, noise-canceling headphones, or weighted vests to help students with sensory processing issues. **Environmental control devices**: Systems that allow students to manipulate their environment, such as lights or electronic devices, which can be critical for students with severe physical impairments.

Test Tip

The selection of appropriate assistive technology is highly individualized, based on the specific needs and abilities of each student. These technologies aim to increase, maintain, or improve the functional capabilities of students with disabilities, enabling them to access the curriculum, communicate more effectively, and participate more fully in their educational environments.

Culturally responsive transition plans and services

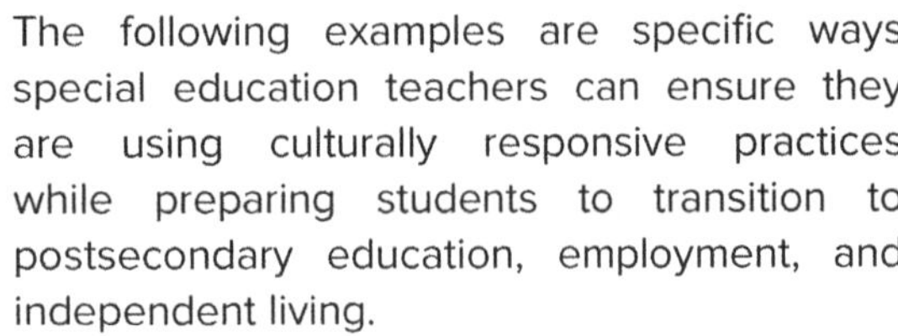

Developing culturally responsive transition plans and services in special education is essential for preparing students with disabilities for postsecondary education, vocational education, integrated employment, and independent living.

Test Tip

According to the Individuals with Disabilities Education Act (IDEA), transition planning must start by the age of 16 (or younger, if deemed appropriate by the IEP team) and should be tailored to each student's unique needs, strengths, preferences, and interests.

The following examples are specific ways special education teachers can ensure they are using culturally responsive practices while preparing students to transition to postsecondary education, employment, and independent living.

Individualized Assessment:

- Holistic evaluation: Conduct comprehensive assessments considering students' academic skills, social-emotional development, cultural background, and personal interests.
- Cultural competence: Ensure assessments and evaluations are culturally sensitive and unbiased.

Student-Centered Planning:

- Student involvement: Actively involve students in the planning process to ensure that their voices and preferences are central.
- Family engagement: Work closely with families, respecting and incorporating their cultural values and expectations into the planning.

Goal-Setting Aligned with Cultural Identity:

- Culturally relevant goals: Set goals that are not only aligned with the student's abilities and interests but also reflect their cultural identity and community values.
- A broad spectrum of opportunities: Consider various postsecondary options, including those highly valued within the student's cultural community.

Collaboration with Community and Cultural Resources:

- Community partnerships: Build partnerships with community organizations, cultural groups, and local businesses that can provide resources, mentorship, and student opportunities.
- Cultural liaisons: Engage representatives who can bridge the gap between school services and the student's community.

Incorporating Cultural Competence in Services:

- Training for educators: Engage in training in cultural competence and sensitivity to ensure that services are delivered in a culturally appropriate manner.
- Adapting services: Modify transition services to respect cultural norms and practices, ensuring they are relevant and accessible to students from diverse backgrounds.

Preparation for Postsecondary and Vocational Pathways:

- Culturally relevant curriculum: Incorporate elements in the curriculum that reflect the student's cultural background, enhancing engagement and relevance.
- Exposure to diverse pathways: Introduce students to a variety of postsecondary and vocational pathways, including those that are esteemed in different cultures.

Support for Integrated Employment

- Culturally diverse work opportunities: Identify employment opportunities that respect and value cultural diversity.
- Workplace skills training: Offer training in skills particularly relevant to the workplaces and industries prevalent within the student's community.

Independent Living Skills:

- Culturally tailored life skills: Teach independent living skills considering the student's cultural background (e.g., community living norms and traditional practices).
- Support networks: Help students build support networks that include members from their cultural community.

Continuous Monitoring and Adjustments:

- Ongoing evaluation: Regularly assess the effectiveness of the transition plan and adjust as needed, ensuring cultural relevance and responsiveness.
- Feedback loops: Create mechanisms for continuous feedback from the student, family, and community members to refine the plan.

Legal Compliance with IDEA:

- IDEA requirements: Ensure that all transition plans and services follow IDEA, providing the necessary resources and accommodations to support each student's unique transition to adulthood.
- Documentation and record-keeping: Keep detailed records of all aspects of the transition plan, including how it addresses cultural needs and preferences.

Expanded Core Curriculum (ECC)

The Expanded Core Curriculum (ECC) is a key concept in special education, particularly for students with visual impairments, including blindness. It is designed to supplement the general education curriculum and includes the teaching of specific skills that students with visual impairments need to learn to access the general curriculum fully and to live independently.

The ECC encompasses nine areas:

1. **Compensatory or functional academic skills**: This includes concept development, spatial understanding, and specialized communication skills like braille or sign language.
2. **Orientation and mobility**: Skills to help students know where they are in space and how to move around safely and effectively.
3. **Social interaction skills**: Teaching students how to interact appropriately with peers and adults.
4. **Independent living skills**: These are daily living skills necessary for personal management, such as cooking, cleaning, and personal finance management.
5. **Recreation and leisure skills**: Encouraging hobbies and activities for enjoyment and relaxation is essential for a balanced life.
6. **Career education**: Preparing students for future employment through career exploration and job readiness skills.
7. **Use of assistive technology**: Training in devices and software that help students access information, such as screen readers or magnification programs.
8. **Sensory efficiency**: Maximizing residual senses like hearing, touch, smell, and taste to compensate for visual impairment.
9. **Self-determination**: Developing the skills needed for students to advocate for themselves, set goals, and take personal responsibility for decisions.

The purpose of the ECC is to provide students with the additional skills they need to access the core curriculum effectively, achieve academic and social success, and become well-rounded, independent individuals. It recognizes that students with visual impairments require direct instruction in certain areas to experience equal educational opportunities as their sighted peers.

Quick Tip

Free appropriate public education (FAPE) is a foundational principle in special education, guaranteed by the Individuals with Disabilities Education Act (IDEA) in the United States. FAPE mandates that children with disabilities are entitled to receive an education that is tailored to their individual needs at no cost to their families. This education must provide significant educational benefits and prepare the child for further education, employment, and independent living. FAPE encompasses special education and related services, such as speech therapy or counseling, provided by a student's Individualized Education Program (IEP). FAPE also underscores the importance of the least restrictive environment (LRE) which ensures that special education students should be educated with their nondisabled peers as much as possible.

Productive Learning Environments

Effective special education teachers plan and implement a productive and supportive learning environment by using routines and procedures and preventive and responsive practices. In addition, teachers must engage in data-driven decisions to plan and implement interventions.

Establish Clear Routines and Procedures

Routines and procedures are pivotal in the special education classroom because they provide structure and predictability, essential for creating a supportive and effective learning environment, especially for students with special needs. The following are methods teachers can use in their classrooms to ensure that special education students are benefiting from routines and procedures.

- **Consistency**: Develop consistent daily routines to help students understand what to expect, reducing anxiety and increasing comfort.
- **Step-by-step instructions**: Break down routines and procedures into clear, manageable steps, especially for complex tasks.
- **Practice and reinforcement**: Regularly practice routines and positively reinforce students for following them correctly.
- **Daily schedules**: Display daily schedules using pictures, symbols, or text, depending on students' reading levels and comprehension abilities.
- **Interactive schedules**: Allow students to interact with the schedule, such as moving a marker to indicate the transition from one activity to the next.
- **Personalized schedules**: Tailor visual schedules to students' needs, particularly those requiring more structure.
- **Defined areas**: Organize the classroom into clearly defined areas for different activities (e.g., reading corner, activity area).
- **Accessibility and safety**: Ensure that the classroom layout is accessible to students with physical disabilities and safe for all students.
- **Sensory considerations**: Be mindful of sensory stimuli in the classroom, such as lighting, noise levels, and seating arrangements.
- **Behavioral expectations**: Clearly state and model positive behavioral expectations.
- **Behavior management strategies**: Implement positive behavior support strategies tailored to individual student needs.
- **Consistent and fair discipline**: Apply discipline consistently and fairly, ensuring that students understand the consequences of their actions.
- **Self-regulation tools**: Teach and provide tools for self-regulation (e.g., calm-down kits, stress balls, relaxation techniques).
- **Promote autonomy**: Gradually encourage students to take more responsibility for their learning and classroom duties.
- **Regular assessment**: Continuously assess the effectiveness of the learning environment and be willing to make changes as needed.
- **Responsive to needs**: Be observant and responsive to students' changing needs, preferences, and behaviors.

Test Tip

Well-established routines and procedures are foundational to the functioning of any classroom. Effective learning depends on the teacher's ability to establish a classroom environment characterized by predictability. Such routines and procedures contribute to sharpened focus, minimized distractions, fostered independence, smoother transitions, and structured interactions. They also play a critical role in managing behaviors, optimizing time use, improving learning outcomes, accommodating the needs of diverse learners, and ensuring consistent practices. These elements are vital for the creation and maintenance of a classroom environment that is both safe and conducive to learning. When presented with options on a test, the mention of routines or procedures often indicates a correct response.

Data-driven decisions

Using data from various sources to plan and implement intervention plans is a key component of effective teaching, especially in special education. Data-driven decision-making allows teachers to tailor interventions to meet the specific needs of each student.

Feedback

Feedback in the special education classroom refers to the information provided by teachers, and sometimes peers, to students about their performance, understanding, and progress in their learning goals. It is crucial in supporting the learning process, particularly for students with diverse learning needs.

In the special education classroom, feedback is not just a tool for academic improvement; it's also crucial for social and behavioral development. It can be used to reinforce positive behaviors, promote self-regulation, and develop social skills. Effective feedback helps create a supportive learning environment where students with special needs feel valued, understood, and motivated to learn. The following are specific ways to use feedback from various sources to help increase student learning outcomes.

Quick Tip

Several key elements characterize effective feedback. Feedback should be specific, meaningful, constructive, positive, timely, individualized, actionable, consistent, goal-oriented, and culturally responsive.

- Collect and analyze feedback from students about their learning experiences, challenges, and preferences. Use this information to adjust teaching methods and materials to better suit their needs.
- Gather insights from parents or guardians about the child's behavior, progress, and concerns at home. Integrate this information into the intervention plan, ensuring consistency between home and school environments.
- Seek input from colleagues and specialists working with the student, such as speech therapists or counselors. Use their observations and suggestions to refine the intervention strategies.

Observations

Observations provide insights into students' learning processes, strengths, challenges, and needs, which might not be evident through traditional assessments. Teachers can use this information to make immediate, informed decisions about instructional strategies and interventions, tailoring their approach to support each student's ongoing learning and development.

Observational data can be used to track progress over time, informing adjustments to teaching methods and learning objectives. This makes observations a dynamic and responsive formative assessment tool, essential for fostering an effective and inclusive learning environment.

- Conduct regular observations of the student in different settings and during various activities.
- Note patterns in behavior, social interactions, and academic performance to identify areas of need.
- Use informal assessments like checklists or anecdotal records during observation to track specific behaviors or skills.

Quick Tip

Observations are an integral part of formative assessment processes. When educators systematically observe students during learning activities, they can collect immediate, qualitative information about their abilities, comprehension, behavior, and social engagement. This assessment method is invaluable for obtaining insights into students' academic progress and social development in real time.

Data Collection

Along with informal assessments, teachers can use formal assessments to collect valuable information regarding student progress:

- Review standardized test scores and skill assessments to gather data on students' academic abilities and developmental levels.
- Compare this data over time to monitor progress and adjust interventions as needed.
- Employ progress monitoring tools to track the student's response to the intervention over time.
- Analyze this data to determine the effectiveness of the intervention and make necessary modifications.

Peer Interactions

Peer interactions provide valuable formative data for special education teachers, offering insights into students' social skills, communication abilities, and behavioral patterns in a group dynamic. Observing how students interact with their peers reveals important aspects of their social and emotional development, such as their ability to share, take turns, resolve conflicts, and express empathy. These interactions also help teachers understand students' abilities to apply social skills learned in a structured setting to more natural social contexts. For special education teachers, this information is crucial for designing targeted interventions that address social skills and behavioral goals. The following is an example of how special education teachers can gather this data.

- Observe and record the student's interactions with peers to assess social skills and challenges.
- Use this data to design interventions that address social and emotional learning.
- If appropriate, gather feedback from peers, especially in inclusive settings, to gain insights into how the student engages with others.
- Incorporate strategies to enhance positive peer interactions and reduce potential social barriers.

Quick Tip

Special education teachers can use a holistic or targeted approach when making data-driven decisions.

- **Holistic**: Combine data from all these sources to get a comprehensive picture of the student's needs.
- **Targeted**: Use the integrated data to develop targeted interventions that address specific areas of need identified through feedback, observations, and data collection.

Peer interactions can highlight areas of strength and interest for each student, which can be leveraged to enhance engagement and learning. By integrating observations of peer interactions into their formative assessment practices, special education teachers can develop a more holistic understanding of each student's needs and progress.

Behavior interventions

Student behavior should be approached the same way student learning is approached. Teachers must observe behavior, collect data on that behavior, and then devise a plan of action. Sending students to detention does not fix a behavior problem. Learning about the behavior and differentiating the approach to the behavior is most effective.

Behavior Tips:

Observe the behavior first. Before a teacher can prescribe punishment or a solution to the behavior, she must first observe the behavior. These observations yield necessary data the teacher should consider before moving forward. Determine the frequency—how often the behavior occurs—and latency—the time between behavior occurrences.

Come up with a plan. Using an evidence-based approach, begin to design a plan of action. Allow the student to be a part of behavior plans. Allowing students to set behavior goals and devise a plan on how to attain them helps students take ownership of the process.

Using positive language, devise an agreement you and the student can live by. Help the student outline a goal. Let the student be part of the construction of the contract. Revisit the contract to celebrate gains and to make new goals.

Positive Behavioral Interventions and Supports (PBIS)

Positive behavioral interventions and supports (PBIS) is a proactive approach in educational settings to foster constructive behaviors in students. This method is grounded in the principles of applied behavior analysis and the prevention approach in psychology. The primary goal of PBIS is to enhance the overall school climate by encouraging positive behavior, reducing disciplinary issues, and improving academic outcomes.

Key characteristics of PBIS

1. **Prevention-oriented**: PBIS focuses on preventing undesirable behaviors before they occur rather than reacting to them afterward. This approach includes setting clear expectations and teaching students the expected behaviors in various school settings.
2. **Data-driven decision-making**: Decisions within a PBIS framework are guided by continuous monitoring and analysis of student behavior data. This data helps in identifying patterns, assessing the effectiveness of interventions, and making informed adjustments to strategies.
3. **Positive reinforcement**: Central to PBIS is using positive reinforcement to encourage desirable behavior. This reinforcement can be in the form of praise, rewards, or privileges, and is more effective when it is immediate and consistent.
4. **Multi-Tiered System of Support (MTSS)**: PBIS typically employs a tiered intervention model. The first level (Tier 1) involves universal strategies for all students to promote a positive school culture. Tier 2 includes targeted interventions for students who are at risk of behavioral issues. Tier 3 offers individualized support for students with chronic and intense behavioral challenges.

Tier 1: Universal Prevention (All)

Tier 1 supports serve as the foundation for behavior and academics. Schools provide these universal supports to all students. For most students, the core program gives them what they need to succeed and prevent future problems.

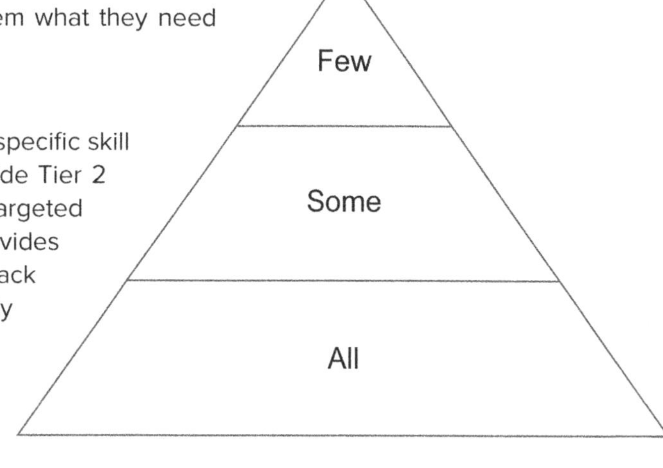

Tier 2: Targeted Prevention (Some)

This level of support focuses on improving specific skill deficits students have. Schools often provide Tier 2 support to groups of students with similar targeted needs. Supporting a group of students provides more opportunities for practice and feedback while keeping the intervention maximally efficient. Students may need some assessment to identify whether they need this level of support and which skills to address. Tier 2 supports help students develop the skills they need to benefit core programs at the school.

Tier 3: Intensive, Individualized Prevention (Few)

Tier 3 supports are the most intensive supports the school offers. These supports are the most resource-intensive due to the individualized approach to developing and carrying out interventions. At this level, schools typically rely on formal assessments to determine a student's need and to develop an individualized support plan. Student plans often include goals related to both academics as well as behavior support.

5. **Collaborative approach**: Implementing PBIS effectively requires collaboration among educators, administrators, and support staff. Involving families and the wider community is essential to creating a consistent and supportive student environment.
6. **Skill development and behavior instruction**: PBIS emphasizes teaching students the skills they need to behave appropriately, much like academic skills are taught. This involves explicit instruction in social, emotional, and behavioral skills.
7. **Respectful and culturally responsive**: It's important that PBIS practices are respectful and culturally responsive, taking into consideration the diverse backgrounds and needs of students.
8. **Individualized consideration**: While PBIS provides a framework, interventions are tailored to meet the unique needs of each student or school environment, recognizing that one size does not fit all in behavior support.

Behavioral Data Collection

Data-driven decision-making is when a teacher collects data, analyzes the data, and then decides on an intervention based on the data. Observing a behavior before deciding how to move forward is data-driven decision-making. Observations, journal entries, surveys, interviews, etc. yield important information teachers can use to effectively apply intervention strategies.

Adolescent Behavior

Adolescence is a time for developing independence. Adolescents typically exercise their independence by questioning and sometimes breaking the rules. During this time, students are trying to develop an identity, gain peer acceptance, and develop competence. The most common function of behavior adolescents display is avoidance coping or avoidance behaviors. Avoidance behaviors are ways of behaving that are motivated by the desire to avoid certain thoughts or feelings. The behaviors include avoiding places or situations such as school or social events.

Most districts have moved from a top-down, punitive system of dealing with behavior to a restorative justice, positive behavior management system. The research shows that positive behavior support yields better results than a system focused on punishments.

Test Tip

Response cost is a behavioral management strategy used in special and general education contexts. It is a form of negative punishment whereby a student forfeits a previously granted reward or privilege due to exhibiting unacceptable behavior. The primary aim of implementing response cost is to reduce the occurrence of undesirable behaviors by introducing a consequence for such actions. It is important for educators to gather observational data to confirm that the application of response cost is justified and tailored to the student's specific situation. Additionally, it should be noted that this approach may not be effective for all students, as responses to this type of intervention can vary.

Functional Curriculum

A functional curriculum in special education refers to a course of study that emphasizes practical life skills and is typically tailored for students with significant cognitive and intellectual disabilities or developmental delays. The primary focus of a functional curriculum is to empower students to achieve as much independence as possible in real-life situations by teaching skills that are immediately applicable to their daily lives.

Core Components of a Functional Curriculum

1. Daily living skills: This includes personal hygiene, dressing, eating, cooking, and managing personal affairs.
2. Community skills: Students learn how to navigate community resources such as public transportation, shopping, using community services like the library, and understanding civic responsibility.
3. Recreational and leisure skills: The curriculum may cover hobbies, sports, and other leisure activities that improve quality of life and provide opportunities for social interaction.
4. Vocational training: Prepares students for the workforce with job readiness skills, vocational skills, and in some cases, specific job training.
5. Social skills: Instruction focuses on communication, interpersonal skills, and appropriate behavior in social settings.
6. Functional academics: This includes teaching academic skills like reading, writing, and math in a context that applies directly to everyday situations, such as reading signs, budgeting, or writing a grocery list.
7. Safety skills: Students learn to recognize and respond to potentially dangerous situations to keep themselves safe.

Rationale Behind a Functional Curriculum

- Individualized education: It acknowledges that traditional academic goals are not always aligned with the needs of all students, particularly those with significant disabilities for whom independent living is a primary objective.
- Real-world application: The functional curriculum is grounded in real-world scenarios, ensuring that the skills taught are not abstract but have direct and immediate application.
- Transition to adulthood: It prepares students for life after school, focusing on transition planning that helps them integrate into their communities and lead fulfilling adult lives.

- Empowerment: By equipping students with functional skills, the curriculum empowers them to be as self-sufficient as possible, enhancing their self-esteem and sense of agency.
- Family and caregiver involvement: Functional curricula often involve families and caregivers to ensure that the skills taught at school are reinforced and utilized at home and in the community.
- Legal compliance: The Individuals with Disabilities Education Act (IDEA) requires that special education services prepare students for further education, employment, and independent living. A functional curriculum directly addresses these requirements by focusing on practical life skills.

By focusing on the individual strengths and needs of each student, a functional curriculum in special education provides a pathway for students to achieve the highest possible level of independence and quality of life.

Transition Planning

Transition planning in special education is a coordinated set of activities designed to prepare students with disabilities for the post-school transition into adulthood. This process aims to facilitate the shift from the school environment to post-secondary life, whether it involves further education, employment, or independent living. Transition planning is mandated by the Individuals with Disabilities Education Act (IDEA) for all students with an individualized education program (IEP).

The individual transition plan (ITP) is part of the IEP, and transition planning can begin as early as 14. By law, special education students must have a transition plan in place by age 16. The plan is in effect until age 22.

The transition IEP is an extension of the IEP that specifically focuses on identifying and achieving post-secondary goals. Here's what it involves:

Transition IEP Components:

- Assessment: The transition planning process begins with transition assessments, which help identify a student's interests, strengths, skills, and needs related to their post-secondary goals.
- Post-secondary goals: These are the long-term goals for life after high school and can include higher education, vocational training, employment, independent living, and community participation. The goals should be based on the student's preferences and interests and should be reviewed and updated annually.
- Transition services: These are a series of coordinated activities that support students in reaching their post-secondary goals. Transition services can include job exploration training, work-based learning experiences, counseling on post-secondary opportunities, instruction in self-advocacy, and developing independent living skills.
- Course of study: The transition IEP outlines an appropriate course of study to help the student acquire the skills and knowledge needed to achieve their post-secondary goals. This might include specific academic courses, vocational education, and other relevant educational experiences.
- Annual IEP goals: The IEP includes annual goals that are directly related to the student's transition services needs. These goals are designed to help students progress toward their post-secondary objectives.
- Agency collaboration: Transition planning may involve collaboration with outside agencies that can provide additional support as the student transitions out of high school. This might include vocational rehabilitation services, mental health services, and developmental disability agencies.
- Student and family involvement: Students and their families play a central role in the transition planning process. They should be actively involved in setting goals, developing the transition plan, and making decisions about the student's future.

Importance of Transition Planning:

- Legal requirement: IDEA requires transition planning to start by age 16, ensuring that students with disabilities have a plan in place for life after high school.
- Promotes independence: Effective transition planning prepares students with disabilities for an independent and fulfilling adult life to the greatest extent possible.
- Enhances outcomes: Research indicates that students with disabilities who have comprehensive transition plans in place are more likely to achieve success after high school in terms of employment, independent living, and community participation.
- Ensures continuity of services: Transition planning helps to identify and establish adult services that the student may need to continue progressing after leaving the school system.

Transition planning is a student-centered process that evolves over the course of the student's secondary education years. It should reflect the student's evolving aspirations, abilities, and needs, to facilitate a smooth and successful transition into adulthood.

Transition goals

The individualized transition plan (ITP) is a section of the IEP that outlines transition goals and services for students with disabilities. The ITP is the template for mapping out short-term to long-term adult outcomes from which annual goals and objectives are defined. The ITP outlines goals for students to work toward to help them move from high school to postsecondary school and career. Because students have varying disabilities, the goals for the ITP vary based on each student. For example, some students' ITP will include a plan for college, while other students' plans may focus on independent living skills like cooking and hygiene.

The ITP must:

1. Address the student's preferences, interests, strengths, and needs
2. Outline parent participation
3. Focus on specific goals
4. Describe activities demonstrating the use of various strategies, community, and adult living experiences
5. Include annual goals
6. Define the responsibilities of parents and students

Quick Tip

IDEA requires all students to have an ITP by the age of 16. However, the transition process starts at age 14. On the exam, you will most likely have more than a few questions about the ITP process. Just like everything else, the ITP is focused on goals that will help students live a full, independent life.

Effective Planning and Instruction and Productive Learning Environments Practice Questions

1. Ms. Hanson is a fifth-grade special education teacher finishing a lesson using informational text. Which of the following approaches indicates that Ms. Hanson uses differentiation in assessment?

   A. Ms. Hanson plans for students to choose how they will show mastery of this skill: a presentation, a short essay, a cooperative learning activity, or drawing a picture.

   B. Students can decide which text they read next: a speech, a newspaper article, or a biography.

   C. Students can choose from various activities to extend the lesson: individualized learning, cooperative learning, or partner learning.

   D. Ms. Hanson will break students up by skill level and use different approaches: 1-1 academic support, targeted reading strategies, or direct instruction.

2. Which of the following is the responsibility of the special education teacher in a general classroom in a full inclusion setting?

   A. Focus on behavior and functional curriculum, while the general education teacher focuses on academics.

   B. Observe general education teachers and apply similar methods in the special education classroom when possible.

   C. Use the least restrictive environment for special education students, while accommodating and modifying based on students' IEPs.

   D. Serve as an assistant to the general education teachers when they need help with special education students' behavior.

3. An English language arts teacher's objective in helping special education students is to encourage them use key vocabulary and relate it to the real world. Which of the following would be most effective? Choose **ALL** that apply.

   ☐ A. Provide the student with a list of vocabulary words to look up in the dictionary and write the definitions of each word.

   ☐ B. Use a word wall to enhance vocabulary knowledge by having students pick words from the wall and analyze them with a partner.

   ☐ C. Pre-teach complex vocabulary before reading an online article that contains the vocabulary.

   ☐ D. Have students quiz each other on vocabulary words using flashcards and memorization techniques.

   ☐ E. Show students how to use the highlight tool while reading an online article to quickly define it while reading.

4. Which of the following is the best rationale for using a task analysis when helping students understand a process for a science lab?

   A. Students will learn to do the tasks of the lesson on their own without explicit instruction and guidance.

   B. Students can work together to complete tasks and rely on one another to help achieve the tasks.

   C. Students can skip tasks on the list that do not apply to them, making the process more streamlined.

   D. Students can succeed by using a task list because it provides explicit and systematic instructions for the lab.

5. A special education teacher communicates behavior expectations when transitioning from math to English language arts. Which of the following approaches would be most effective in helping students meet these expectations?
   A. Clearly and explicitly explain the expectations and allow students to ask questions.
   B. Implement consistent practiced routines and procedures every day in the classroom.
   C. Allow students to discuss the expectations with a partner and ask questions.
   D. Give students examples and non-examples of proper behavior in the classroom.

6. Susan is a special education student with a physical disability that impedes her ability to use her hands. Her IEP outlines the need for assistive technology, specifically an adaptive keyboard and mouse. What can the teacher do to ensure that Susan receives the maximum benefits from this technology?
   A. Provide her with training and equipment for at-home use.
   B. Allow her to use the technology only in accordance with her IEP.
   C. Allow other students to use the technology during cooperative learning.
   D. Attend professional development on how to use the technology.

7. A seventh-grade general education teacher has three special education students in her class who have emotional behavior disturbance (EBD). The students behave appropriately most of the time but do occasionally have outbursts. Which of the following should the teacher do first to help students modify their behavior?
   A. Have them sign behavior contracts at the beginning of the year to get them on the right track before outbursts become problematic.
   B. Observe the behavior outburst, collect anecdotal data, and use that data to plan target interventions for each student.
   C. Implement a system of rewards and consequences for all students in the class so the teacher can address the behavior without singling out each student.
   D. Call the students' parents to report any problematic behavior and work with the parents to intervene when these behaviors occur.

8. Response cost can be classified as a(n):
   A. Benefit
   B. Scaffold
   C. Tiered support
   D. Consequence

9. A special education teacher has a visually impaired student in the classroom. The teacher is focusing on a functional curriculum with this student so she can learn skills to live independently. Which of the following approaches would be most effective?
   A. Expanded core curriculum
   B. Word recognition interventions
   C. Positive behavior interventions and supports
   D. Self-regulation and peer interaction

10. A student who is classified as ADHD on his IEP has trouble concentrating and often wants to get out of his seat. The teacher makes sure all direct instruction is limited to five minutes, but the student still has difficulty staying engaged and still. Which of the following accommodations would be most appropriate for this student during direct instruction?

    A. Have the student work with his peers during direct instruction.

    B. Administer a set of rewards if the student remains seated for direct instruction.

    C. Permit the student to quietly walk to the back of the room and stand during direct instruction.

    D. Have the student sign a behavior contract and agree to remain seated during direct instruction.

Effective Planning and Instruction and Productive Learning Environments Answer Explanations

Number	Answer	Explanation
1.	A	The question stem specifically states differentiated assessment. The only answer choice that outlines a variety of assessments is answer A. Choice B outlines differentiated content. Choice C outlines a differentiated process. Choice D outlines differentiated instruction.
2.	C	The role of the special education teacher is to help students receive the same free, appropriate public education (FAPE). Teachers do this by using the least restrictive environment (LRE). Choice C is the only answer that supports this approach. All the other answer choices go against the FAPE and LRE principles.
3.	B, C & E	Choices B, C, and E are all effective vocabulary instructional techniques. Word walls are interactive and help students with real-world application of complex vocabulary. Pre-teaching vocabulary is a type of explicit instruction that supports vocabulary application while reading. Using technology to highlight complex vocabulary words while reading allows students to understand words in context, a key to real-world application of skills. Choices A and D are not considered best practices in vocabulary instruction.
4.	D	Task analysis, which breaks down instruction into manageable and achievable steps, is crucial for fostering student success. This approach ensures that instruction is consistent, personalized, and systematic, directly contributing to a student's learning achievements. The other answer choices do not properly explain why a task analysis is more important. Choice A is incorrect because students may still need explicit instruction and guidance. Choice B is incorrect because the goal of task analysis is not necessarily cooperative learning. Choice C is incorrect because skipping steps is not an effective approach to a task analysis.
5.	B	The most effective way to ensure students meet behavior expectations, especially when transitioning, is to practice consistent routines and procedures. All the other answer choices are somewhat effective. However, research shows that practicing routines and procedures is the MOST effective when helping students meet classroom expectations.
6.	A	To ensure Susan can engage in writing activities at home, arranging for there to be training and equipment for at-home use is the best way to ensure she receives the maximum benefits of the technology. This way, she'll be able to do her homework and other tasks using the assistive technology. You may be tempted to choose answer D. While professional development for this type of tech would be beneficial, it would not directly impact the student like allowing her to use the tech at home. Choice B is limiting because she may need to use the tech in other areas not specifically stated in the IEP. Choice C is not effective. Other students should not be using the tech unless it is outlined in their IEP.

Number	Answer	Explanation
7.	B	The key word in the question stem is “first.” The first thing teachers should do before planning or intervening is to collect data. Observing the behavior first will allow the teacher to determine when the behavior happens, the frequency of the behavior, and the duration of the behavior. This is important information the teacher can use to then plan for interventions. Choice A is incorrect because it skips the step of data collection. Simply having students sign behavior contracts is not as effective as gathering data and tailoring a plan for each student. Choice C is incorrect because it uses a blanket approach for all students. Choice D is incorrect because calling the parents is a reactive approach and is least effective in this scenario.
8.	D	Response cost is a behavioral management technique used in special education, as well as in general education settings. It is a form of negative punishment where a student loses a previously earned reward or privilege because of undesirable behavior. The goal of response cost is to decrease the frequency of negative behaviors by imposing a cost for those behaviors.
9.	A	The expanded core curriculum (ECC) is a key concept in special education, particularly for students with visual impairments, including blindness. It is designed to supplement the general education curriculum and includes the teaching of specific skills that students with visual impairments need to learn to access the general curriculum fully and to live independently. Choice B is for reading interventions. Choice C is for behavior interventions. Choice D is for social interaction.
10.	C	The most effective answer is to allow the student to quietly go to the back of the room and stand. This will not only satisfy his desire to get up and move around, but it will also reduce interruptions to the learning environment. Other students will not be disrupted. Choices A, B, and D do not accommodate this student and his specific exceptionality.

This page intentionally left blank.

Assessment

This segment of the examination necessitates comprehension of key concepts in two primary domains:

A. Interventions, Eligibility, and Identification

B. Program Planning Based on Data

Examinees should know the various interventions available for students with special needs, the criteria for determining their eligibility for services, and the processes involved in identifying students who require special education.

Furthermore, candidates must be adept at planning educational programs by analyzing and utilizing data. This includes the ability to interpret assessment results and other relevant information to develop effective educational strategies tailored to individual student needs.

Interventions, Eligibility, and Identification

Effective special education teachers use a variety of assessments to measure student progress. In the special education classroom, there are specialized assessments that measure students' abilities and determine if they need special services.

Behavior Assessment System for Children (BASC) or Vineland Adaptive Behavior Scale

This assessment measures behavior and mental health, including how students see themselves and how parents and school staff see the students. These evaluations do not offer a diagnosis but look at life skills, social skills, social concerns, and attention. This assessment may help identify mental health concerns and/or behavioral issues.

Functionality: School Function Assessment (SFA)

The SFA measures a student's functionality in all areas of the school environment. The occupational therapist (OT) administers this assessment. This test evaluates three areas: participation, task support, and activity performance. It is usually used for students in kindergarten through grade 6. It addresses not only classroom access but also playground, lunch, physical education, and other school areas.

The Present Levels of Academic Achievement and Functional Performance (PLAAFP)

The purpose of the PLAAFP is to identify the type and amount of special education a student receives. The PLAAFP must include a statement of the child's present levels of academic achievement and functional performance, including how the disability impacts the individual's involvement and progress in the general education curriculum or participation in age-appropriate activities.

Woodcock-Johnson Psycho-Educational Battery, Third Edition

This assessment provides a comprehensive set of individually administered tests to measure cognitive abilities, scholastic aptitudes, and achievement. This assessment is used to determine if a student has a learning disability.

Functional Behavioral Assessment (FBA)

This assessment is a process for identifying problem behaviors and developing interventions to improve or eliminate those behaviors. For example, a school psychologist may conduct a functional behavior assessment and find that the student uses profanity or pushes other students when lining up for lunch. These behaviors can be identified, and the teacher and school psychologist can choose appropriate interventions to help replace undesirable behaviors with appropriate behaviors.

IQ Tests or Wechsler Intelligence Scale for Children (WISC)

IQ tests are used to determine if a student has a severe intellectual disability. An IQ of 20-35 means that a student has a severe intellectual learning disability. Below is a breakdown of the scores for this assessment.

- **Extremely Low: Below 70**. Students who test in this range may need to be placed in special education courses.
- **Very Low: 70-79.** Students who test in this range may have a learning disability and should review their subtest scores to identify specific areas of cognitive weakness.
- **Low Average: 80-89.** This is slightly lower than the mean score of 100, but still able to perform as expected in the classroom.
- **Average: 90-109**. Most children will score in this range with a mean (averaged) score of 100; the highest possible score on the WPPSI-IV is 160.
- **High Average: 110-119.** This typically indicates a stronger cognitive ability in one or more areas.
- **Very High: 120-129.** A score like this indicates a child is gifted in many areas required for school and testing success.
- **Extremely High: 130+.** Children in this range are usually identified as gifted and talented.

Quick Tip

Intellectual disabilities and learning disabilities are distinct conditions. Intellectual disabilities encompass challenges in everyday life skills, which include social interactions, self-care, and practical daily activities. On the other hand, learning disabilities specifically relate to difficulties in academic areas, such as reading, writing, or mathematics. It is essential to differentiate between these two types of disabilities when taking the exam.

Assessment

Formal vs. Informal Assessments

Formal and informal assessments are two distinct types of evaluation methods used in educational settings, each serving different purposes and providing unique insights into a student's learning and development.

Formal assessments are structured and standardized evaluations that measure a student's performance against a specific set of criteria or standards. These assessments typically include tests and quizzes that are administered under controlled conditions and are scored in a standardized manner. Formal assessments are often used to determine a student's mastery of content, to place students in appropriate educational settings, and to evaluate the effectiveness of educational programs. Examples include statewide achievement tests, standardized tests, and regular classroom exams.

Informal assessments are more flexible and can be adapted to fit the specific context of the classroom. These assessments are typically observational and are used to gather information about a student's learning process, strengths, and areas needing improvement. Informal assessments include teacher observations, classwork, homework assignments, and discussions. This type of assessment is often integrated into the learning process, providing immediate feedback that can be used to adjust teaching strategies and address students' needs in real time. Unlike formal assessments, informal assessments are usually qualitative and provide a more comprehensive picture of a student's overall performance and day-to-day progress. They are particularly useful in identifying specific learning challenges, informing instructional modifications, and fostering a more individualized learning experience.

Test Tip

Summative assessments are used at the end of learning and are outcome-driven. Summative assessments are considered formal assessments.

Formative assessments are used to monitor student progress and modify the learning environment to meet each student's needs. Formative assessments are considered informal assessments.

Progress Monitoring

In the special education classroom, it is imperative that the teacher continuously monitors students' progress. This will help the teacher make decisions that benefit each student based on specific needs. As previously mentioned, this is done in both a formal manner and an informal manner. For example, a teacher might use a quick formative assessment such as an exit ticket to determine if students understand a particular skill or concept. A teacher may also use test scores that measure several concepts to measure progress over time, such as with STAR testing or district quarterly testing. The following are various assessment tools teachers can use to monitor student progress, achievement, and learning gains.

Assessment Type	Definition	Example
Diagnostic	A pre-assessment providing instructors with information about students' prior knowledge, preconceptions, and misconceptions before beginning a learning activity. Diagnostic assessments are considered formative assessments because they inform instruction.	Before starting a science unit, a teacher gives a quick assessment to determine students' prior knowledge of concepts in the text. She uses this information to make instructional decisions moving forward.
Formative	A range of formal and informal assessments or checks conducted by the teacher before, during, and after the learning process to modify instruction.	A teacher is walking around the room, checking on students as they work through math problems and intervening when necessary. The teacher uses this observational data to make instructional decisions.
Summative	An assessment that focuses on outcomes. It is frequently used to measure the effectiveness of a program, lesson, or strategy.	A teacher gives a unit exam to measure outcomes and the effectiveness of instructional strategies.
Performance-Based	An assessment that measures students' ability to apply the skills and knowledge learned from a unit or units of study: The task challenges students to use their higher-order, critical thinking skills to create a product or complete a process.	After reading text about the Civil War, students develop stories about different historical figures in the war. Students then perform these stories in front of the class and answer questions.

Assessment Type	Definition	Example
Portfolio	A purposeful collection of student work that has been selected and organized to show student learning progress over time. Portfolios can contain samples of student work, self-evaluations/reflections, etc.	Over the course of a semester, students collect weekly writing samples and organize them by date in a designated folder. During parent conferences, students show their parents the portfolio and reflect on progress.
Norm-referenced	A norm-referenced test is an assessment designed to compare the performance of a group of test-takers against each other. It ranks individuals to establish a distribution of performance levels across the tested population, typically reported as percentiles, stanines, or standard scores.	The Iowa Tests of Basic Skills (ITBS) is a norm-referenced test designed to assess students' academic skills in areas such as reading, language arts, mathematics, science, and social studies. It compares the performance of individual students and groups of students to a nationally representative sample, providing percentile ranks, stanines, and other statistical measures that indicate how students are performing relative to their peers across the United States.
Criterion-referenced	A criterion-referenced test is designed to assess a test-taker's performance against a fixed set of criteria or learning standards, rather than comparing it to other individuals. These tests measure whether a test-taker has achieved specific skills or knowledge, providing a clear indication of mastery of the content. The results are typically reported as a percentage or a proficiency level, indicating how well the individual met the predetermined criteria.	At the end of the year, all third-grade students take a state-standardized reading exam. The exam measures student proficiency in the state reading standards in English language arts, specially reading. The scores of this exam are used to make instructional decisions for the students for the following year.

Culturally and linguistically appropriate assessments

Identifying and implementing formal and informal assessments that are culturally and linguistically appropriate is crucial in special education to ensure fairness and accuracy in evaluating students from diverse backgrounds. Special education teachers can take the following steps:

1. **Understanding Cultural and Linguistic Diversity:**

   Cultural competence: Develop a deep understanding of the cultural backgrounds and experiences of students. This includes awareness of cultural norms, values, and communication styles.

   Linguistic awareness: Recognize the language proficiencies and needs of students, particularly those who are English language learners (ELLs) or come from homes where a language other than English is spoken.

2. **Selection of Appropriate Assessments:**

   Culturally relevant tools: Choose assessment tools that have been validated for use with students from diverse cultural and linguistic backgrounds. Ensure that the assessments are not biased toward any cultural or linguistic group.

   Language considerations: For linguistically diverse students, consider using assessments in the student's primary language or tools that have been adapted and validated for bilingual or ELL students.

3. **Implementation Strategies:**

   Fair administration: Administer assessments in a manner that is sensitive to the student's cultural and linguistic background. This may include providing instructions in the student's primary language or allowing additional time.

   Professional training: Seek training in culturally responsive assessment practices to ensure a deep understanding of how to administer and interpret results fairly and accurately.

4. **Formal Assessments:**

   Standardized testing with care: When using standardized tests, be cautious of potential cultural or linguistic biases that might affect the student's performance.

   Norm-referenced considerations: Ensure that the normative sample of the assessment is representative of the student's cultural and linguistic background.

5. **Informal Assessments:**

   Observations and interviews: Utilize informal assessments like classroom observations and interviews with students, parents, and teachers, which can provide valuable context and insights.

   Performance-based assessments: Implement performance-based assessments that allow students to demonstrate learning and skills in a practical and culturally relevant context.

6. **Collaboration and Consultation:**

   Work with specialists: Collaborate with bilingual educators, cultural liaisons, and special education specialists to ensure that assessments are appropriate and accurately interpreted.

   Family engagement: Engage with families to understand the student's cultural and linguistic background better and to gain insights that might inform assessment and instruction.

7. **Regular Review and Adjustment:**

   Ongoing evaluation: Continuously evaluate and adjust assessment strategies to ensure they remain relevant and fair for the student's changing needs and abilities.

   Data-driven decision-making: Use assessment data judiciously, considering the cultural and linguistic context of the student when making decisions about eligibility, services, and interventions.

By following these steps, special education teachers can select and implement assessments that are not only valid and reliable but also culturally and linguistically appropriate, ensuring that all students are assessed in a fair, equitable, and meaningful way.

Program Planning Based on Data

As stated previously in this study guide, being a data-driven educator is imperative, especially in the special education classroom.

Interpreting student assessment data for stakeholders:

Explaining the results of student assessments in a way that is comprehensible and useful to various stakeholders, including parents, general education teachers, staff, and specialists (occupational therapists, speech therapists, social workers, etc.) is essential in special education.

It is crucial to ensure that all individuals involved in a student's education have a clear understanding of the student's abilities, progress, and needs. Remember, the student is part of the IEP team, and data communication should include communication with the student.

Quick Tip

The process of discussing assessment results typically takes place during an Individualized Education Program (IEP) meeting, which is a collective effort involving the student who is receiving special education services, their parents or guardians, the special education teacher, specialists, and other pertinent team members. These individuals convene to evaluate and talk about the student's advancement toward their educational objectives. Given that the student is encouraged to engage actively in this conversation, it is paramount that the information shared is delivered in a manner that is both understandable and relatable to them. This approach guarantees that the student can contribute constructively to the dialogue concerning their educational path.

Using assessment data to analyze student progress:

This entails using data from assessments to evaluate how well students are progressing toward their educational goals, to monitor the effectiveness of educational programs, and to make necessary adjustments to instruction.

Regular analysis of assessment data helps in adapting teaching strategies to meet students' evolving needs and in measuring the effectiveness of instructional interventions.

- **Accommodating assessments for individuals with exceptionalities**: This involves adjusting how assessments are administered to cater to the unique abilities and needs of students with disabilities. Frequent breaks, extended testing time, or reading test questions aloud to accommodate learning and physical needs are common assessment accommodations.
- **Modifying assessments as prescribed in the student's IEP**: This refers to altering the content, format, or complexity of assessments based on the specifications in a student's Individualized Education Program (IEP). Using simplified language reduces the complexity of tasks or provides alternate assessment forms.
- **Digital technology tools**: This encompasses the use of various digital technologies, such as virtual classrooms, online programs, and interactive software, to enhance learning and assessment. Digital tools can offer more engaging, diverse, and accessible learning experiences for students with special needs.
- **Error Analysis and progress-monitoring tools**: This involves using tools like exit tickets or checklists to analyze errors and monitor student progress. Error analysis helps in identifying specific areas where students struggle, allowing for targeted interventions, while progress-monitoring tools are used for tracking student improvement over time.
- **Intervention strategies based on data collection for IDEA categories**: This skill involves analyzing evaluation data to identify the specific needs of students eligible for special education services under IDEA, including conditions like dyslexia.

For example, understanding and implementing RTI, a multi-tiered approach to early identification and support of students with learning and behavior needs, is crucial. RTI involves providing interventions at increasing levels of intensity and monitoring progress closely. RTI will be explained more explicitly in the next section of this study guide.

Measurable Goals

Goals and objectives serve different functions in educational planning. Goals are broad milestones that are set to be achieved over an extended period, such as a semester or an academic year. In contrast, objectives are more immediate targets that can often be accomplished within a single class period and are considered steppingstones toward reaching larger goals. Both goals and objectives ought to be quantifiable to track progress effectively. To ensure that goals are measurable and attainable, it is advisable to employ the SMART goal-setting framework, which stands for Specific, Measurable, Achievable, Relevant, and Time-bound. This method aids both educators and students in defining clear and actionable goals.

Classroom Scenario: Strategic Assessment: Integrating Formative and Summative Methods for Student Success

Setting: Spring View Middle School, Special Education Resource Room

Characters:

- Ms. Clarke, a special education teacher
- Ricardo, a student with a specific learning disability (SLD) in written expression
- Emily, a student with mild intellectual disability

Scenario:

Ms. Clarke is well-versed in the nuances of assessment in special education. She knows that to effectively monitor progress and guide instruction, a blend of formative and summative assessments is crucial. Her students, Ricardo and Emily, have diverse needs that require individualized approaches to assessment and goal setting.

Formative Assessments - Monitoring and Classroom Decisions: Throughout her daily instruction, Ms. Clarke employs formative assessments to gauge her students' understanding and adjust her teaching strategies in real time. For Ricardo, this includes short writing prompts at the end of each lesson to check his grasp of the concepts taught. She observes his problem-solving strategies and provides immediate feedback to help him improve his sentence structure and grammar.

For Emily, Ms. Clarke uses questioning techniques during reading sessions to assess comprehension. She listens carefully to Emily's responses, using them to inform her next steps in teaching. She notes which words or concepts Emily struggles with and adapts future lessons to address these gaps.

Summative Assessments - Measuring Learning Outcomes: At the end of each unit, Ms. Clarke implements summative assessments to measure her students' learning outcomes over time. Ricardo completes a multi-paragraph essay demonstrating his ability to organize ideas and use language effectively. Emily works on a book report that assesses her ability to recall key details and summarize a text.

Developing SMART Goals: Using data from both formative and summative assessments, Ms. Clarke sets SMART (specific, measurable, achievable, relevant, time-bound) goals for each student. For Ricardo, a goal is set: "By the end of the semester, Ricardo will write a five-paragraph essay with less than two grammatical errors per paragraph." This goal is specific in its expectations, measurable through writing assessments, achievable with consistent practice, relevant to his learning disability, and time-bound within the semester.

Emily's SMART goal is: "Within the next six weeks, Emily will summarize a grade-level text of at least four paragraphs, verbally identifying the main idea and at least three supporting details." This goal is tailored to her current ability level and designed to push her toward a new milestone in reading comprehension.

Communication and Reassessment: Ms. Clarke communicates these goals to Ricardo, Emily, and their parents, ensuring that everyone involved knows the targets and the strategies in place to achieve them. She continues to use formative assessments to track progress and make instructional adjustments, understanding that assessment is an ongoing process.

Conclusion:

By the end of the term, Ms. Clarke evaluates the effectiveness of her instructional strategies and the achievement of the SMART goals through a final round of summative assessments. The results show significant progress for both Ricardo and Emily, indicating that the targeted goals were appropriate and that the strategies employed were effective. Ms. Clarke prepares to review the outcomes, reflect on the successes and challenges, and set new goals for the upcoming term.

This scenario showcases how a special education teacher can utilize both formative and summative assessments to inform classroom decisions and to set precise, tailored SMART goals that drive student achievement and reflect individual learning paths.

Assessment Practice Questions

1. This year, students will take an exam that compares student performances to one another. Students are taking what type of assessment?

   A. Formative

   B. Norm-referenced

   C. Criterion-referenced

   D. Diagnostic

2. A teacher is administering a functional behavior assessment to a student who is having outbursts during class. Which of the following is the teacher trying to determine by using a functional behavior assessment?

   A. Cognitive disabilities

   B. Effects of consequences

   C. Causes of the behavior

   D. Skills deficits

3. The classification of severe intellectual disability is determined primarily based on:

   A. A score of 20-30 on the WISC test

   B. A score of below level on the BASC

   C. A below average score on the SFA

   D. A below average score on the PLAAFP

4. A teacher notices a student struggling to read a certain part of the text. The teacher wants to understand what specific skill the student lacks so the teacher can address it. What assessment type would be the most effective in this situation?

   A. Summative

   B. Criterion-referenced

   C. Norm-referenced

   D. Diagnostic

5. Which of the following is the most effective way to use a criterion-referenced assessment?

   A. To compare student performances

   B. To drive instructional decisions

   C. To measure student learning at the end of a lesson

   D. To decide where to place students for class ranking

6. A formative assessment is:

   A. Static and used as a preassessment.

   B. Static and used to compare student performances.

   C. Ongoing and used as a final grade for students.

   D. Ongoing and used to determine how to move forward with teaching.

7. Which of the following provides rich qualitative data regarding student behavior?
   A. Diagnostic assessment
   B. Student survey
   C. Anecdotal record
   D. Oral assessment

8. When can teachers provide the accommodation of extra time on a state-standardized criterion-referenced assessment?
   A. If the student has permission from a parent
   B. If a student has permission from the principal
   C. If the student has an IEP with the accommodation outlined in the plan
   D. If the student has a doctor's note outlining test anxiety

9. Which of the following assessments would be most effective in looking over students' progress in writing over a semester?
   A. Portfolio
   B. Criterion-referenced assessment
   C. Norm-referenced test
   D. Screening

10. Which of the following is the most appropriate use of a criterion-referenced test?
    A. To measure a student's mastery of specific knowledge and skills after a unit of study.
    B. To determine a student's reading level to prescribe interventions.
    C. To rank a student's performance against other students who took the same test.
    D. To use a rubric to assess a student's performance on a group project.

Assessment Answer Explanations

Number	Answer	Explanation
1.	B	A norm-referenced assessment yields an estimate of the position of the tested individual in a predefined population with respect to the trait being measured. Use norm-referenced assessments to compare student performances as a percentile ranking.
2.	C	A functional behavioral assessment (FBA) helps to identify the causes of a behavior. This allows teachers to intervene before the behavior starts or set up the learning environment to prevent the behavior.
3.	A	Intellectual disabilities are measured by the Wechsler Intelligence Scale for Children (WISC) test. This is also known as an IQ test. The other assessments do not measure intellectual disabilities.
4.	D	The teacher is trying to diagnose the issue the student is having. Therefore, a diagnostic assessment is appropriate here.
5.	B	The only reason to use any type of assessment is to make instructional decisions in the classroom.
6.	D	Formative assessments are often informal, ongoing checks that help a teacher decide how to move forward in a lesson. Remember formative assessments inform the instruction delivery.
7.	C	For student behavior, observations with anecdotal notes are most effective. The anecdotes provide context and description off the student's behavior. All other answer choices do not address student behavior; rather, they address student learning.
8.	C	The only way a student can receive extra time on a state test is if it is outlined and documented in the IEP.
9.	A	A portfolio showcases students' work over a period of time. In this situation, a portfolio is the most appropriate assessment.
10.	A	Criterion-referenced tests measure students' abilities against a set of standards. These tests are usually administered after students have been exposed to the skills. This type of test can also be classified as a summative assessment because, in this case, it is happening at the end of learning after students acquire the skills or standards. Using the process of elimination choice B is incorrect because it describes a screening test or a formative assessment, depending on the situation. Choice C is incorrect because it describes a norm-referenced assessment. Finally, choice D is incorrect because it describes a measure for a performance-based assessment.

This page intentionally left blank.

Professional Learning, Practice, and Collaboration

This section of the examination comprises two principal areas:

A. Ethical Guidelines, Legal Policies, and Procedures

B. Professionalism and Collaboration

Candidates must grasp the critical elements of the Individuals with Disabilities Education Act (IDEA) and other significant statutes that regulate special education.

Understanding and implementing professional development, practice, and teamwork are crucial for delivering superior educational services to students with disabilities. Continuous professional development is imperative for special education teachers to remain informed about the latest teaching strategies, legal requirements, and research on successful interventions. In application, this means employing high-quality, research-backed instructional techniques and interventions that are customized to suit the varied needs of students with disabilities.

Collaboration is of equal importance and entails working with a multidisciplinary team. This team includes general education teachers, school leaders, specialists, support staff, and families, all working together to formulate an integrated and comprehensive educational strategy. Such a collaborative approach guarantees that every facet of a student's educational journey is considered, cultivating an inclusive setting that nurtures students' development and learning.

Ethical Guidelines, Legal Policies, and Procedures

The guiding legislation for students with disabilities is the Individuals with Disabilities Education Act or IDEA. IDEA is a law that provides free, appropriate public education (FAPE) to eligible children with disabilities nationwide and ensures special education and related services to those children. IDEA has six guiding principles. These are principles to live by if you teach students with special needs.

Quick Tip

Part B of IDEA states that children ages 3 to 21 are eligible for services.

Principle 1: Free Appropriate Public Education (FAPE)

FAPE means that educational services should be provided to students with disabilities at the public's expense, meaning parents should not have to pay for these services. These services must:

- Meet standards established by the state Department of Education
- Be designed to meet the unique needs of each student
- Continue to be provided to students who are suspended or expelled
- Be outlined in a student's IEP

A few aspects of Principle 1 that are very important have to do with an inclusive academic environment. For example, special education programs must:

- Be designed for the student to make progress in the general education curriculum
- Provide a chance for students to meet challenging goals
- Be more than a minimal benefit
- Include related services and supports and provide for participation in extracurricular and other school activities
- Include extended-year services when necessary to provide FAPE.

Principle 2: Appropriate Evaluation

IDEA requires that a student receive an evaluation before receiving special education services to determine whether the student qualifies as a "child with a disability" according to the IDEA definition. If the answer is yes, then determine the educational needs of the student.

The following are important elements of this principle.

- Parents must give permission for evaluation and for services.
- A student must be evaluated in all areas of suspected disability.
- The evaluation should include a variety of tools and strategies to gather functional, developmental, and academic information.
- An evaluation should never be based on a single measure or assessment.
- The instruments and methods used for the evaluation must be technically sound, not culturally discriminatory, and provided in the child's language.
- It should be administered by trained and knowledgeable personnel.
- A new or updated evaluation should be conducted if there is reason to suspect a need or if the parent requests one.
- An evaluation must be conducted within 60 calendar days of the parent giving permission.

According to Principle 2, re-evaluations should occur:

- When conditions warrant new information
- When the parent requests re-evaluation
- Every three years unless both the parent and educators agree it is not necessary

Principle 3: Individualized Education Program (IEP)

An IEP is a written statement for each child with a disability that is developed, reviewed, and revised **at least once a year** by a team including educators, parents, the student whenever appropriate, and others who have knowledge or expertise needed for the development of the student's special education program. The most important part to remember about this principle is the concept of individualization because each student with disabilities has unique needs.

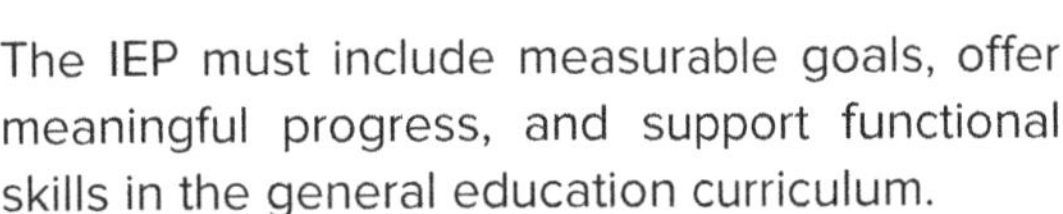

The IEP must include measurable goals, offer meaningful progress, and support functional skills in the general education curriculum.

Quick Tip

Parents and students should be a part of the IEP team and should have meaningful involvement in drafting the goals outlined in the IEP.

Principle 4: Least Restrictive Environment

The IDEA requires that children with disabilities, including children in public or private institutions or other care facilities, be educated with children who are not disabled. This is referred to as the least restrictive environment (LRE) and is an important concept you will see on the exam.

LRE means:

- The child's individual disability-related needs must justify any placement outside the general education classroom.
- Students must have meaningful access to same-age peers without disabilities, when appropriate.
- Schools must consider providing any needed services in the general education classroom and other integrated settings.

- Involvement in music, art, physical education, school trips, clubs, extracurricular and other activities must be accommodated.
- Funding is never an appropriate reason for a more restrictive placement.
- States must maintain a full range of placement options to meet the needs of children who require specialized treatment programs.

Principle 5: Parent and Student Participation in Decision-Making

IDEA ensures parents can participate actively in each step of the special education process. Parents and (whenever appropriate) the student must be meaningfully involved in:

- The development, review, and revision of the IEP
- Educational placement decisions
- Determining what data needs to be collected during evaluation
- Reviewing evaluation data
- Transition planning and services starting by age 14

Principle 6: Procedural Safeguards

Procedural safeguards ensure that the rights of children with disabilities and their parents are protected and that they have access to the information needed to effectively participate in the process. Many of these concepts show up on the exam, so be sure to note the following.

Parents are entitled to notice in writing including:

- Parental rights notice to provide information about special education, procedural safeguards, and student and parent rights
- Notice in writing of IEP meetings
- Prior written notice whenever the school proposes to change or refuses to change the educational programming or educational placement of their child

Parents are entitled to access student records:

- They may review educational records for their child
- They may obtain copies of educational records for their child
- They may place a statement of correction or explanation in the student's record if it contains something they disagree with

Parents have a variety of procedural protections they can invoke when they disagree with educators:

- The resolution facilitator process
- A mediation conference
- A formal written complaint
- A due process hearing

Test Tip

Due process is a significant element of the free, appropriate public education (FAPE) mandate. Therefore, if the term 'due process' appears as an option in a response, it often signifies the correct choice. Due process provides a structured method for parents to address and resolve conflicts with schools regarding educational or disciplinary matters. It grants parents the entitlement to a fair and unbiased hearing officer and allows them to introduce evidence and call witnesses during the due process hearing.

Professional Learning, Practice, and Collaboration

The 13 Disabilities Outlined in IDEA

While there are many ways in which a student can qualify for special education services and an IEP, there are 13 disabilities outlined by IDEA. These 13 disabilities often have other disabilities that fall under them. For example, cerebral palsy falls under orthopedic impairment. The following is a list of the 13 disabilities outlined in IDEA.

1. **Autism** means a developmental disability significantly affecting verbal and nonverbal communication and social interaction, generally evident before age three, that adversely affects a child's educational performance.
2. **Deaf-blindness** means concomitant hearing and visual impairments, the combination of which causes such severe communication and other developmental and educational needs that they cannot be accommodated in special education programs solely for children with deafness or children with blindness.
3. **Deafness** means a hearing impairment that is so severe that the child cannot process linguistic information through hearing, with or without amplification. This can adversely affect a child's educational performance.
4. **Emotional behavior disturbance (EBD)** means a condition exhibiting one or more of the following characteristics over a long period of time and to a marked degree that adversely affects a child's educational performance:
   - An inability to learn that cannot be explained by intellectual, sensory, or health factors.
   - An inability to build or maintain satisfactory interpersonal relationships with peers and teachers. Inappropriate types of behavior or feelings under normal circumstances.
   - A general pervasive mood of unhappiness or depression.
   - A tendency to develop physical symptoms or fears associated with personal or school problems.
5. **Hearing impairment** means an impairment in hearing, whether permanent or fluctuating, that adversely affects a child's educational performance but that is not included under the definition of deafness in this section.
6. **Intellectual disability** means significantly subaverage general intellectual functioning, existing concurrently with deficits in adaptive behavior and manifested during the developmental period, adversely affecting a child's educational performance.
7. **Multiple disabilities** are concomitant impairments, the combination of which causes such severe educational needs that they cannot be accommodated in special education programs solely for one of the impairments. The term does not include deaf-blindness.
8. **Orthopedic impairment** means a severe bodily impairment that adversely affects a child's educational performance.
9. **Other health impairment** means having limited strength, vitality, or alertness, including a heightened alertness to environmental stimuli, that results in limited alertness with respect to the educational environment.
10. **Specific learning disability (SLD)** means a disorder in one or more of the basic psychological processes involved in understanding or using language, spoken or written, that may manifest itself in an imperfect ability to listen, think, speak, read, write, spell, or do mathematical calculations, including conditions such as perceptual disabilities, brain injury, minimal brain dysfunction, dyslexia, and developmental aphasia.
11. **Speech or language impairment** means a communication disorder, such as stuttering, impaired articulation, a language impairment, or a voice impairment, that adversely affects a child's educational performance.

12. **Traumatic brain injury** means an acquired injury to the brain caused by an external physical force, resulting in total or partial functional disability or psychosocial impairment, or both, that adversely affects a child's educational performance.
13. **Visual impairment, including blindness,** means an impairment in vision that, even with correction, adversely affects a child's educational performance. The term includes both partial sight and blindness.

(Authority: 20 U.S.C. 1401(3)(A) and (B); 1401(26))

Test Tip

Be sure you know these 13 main disabilities outlined by IDEA. You may get one or more specific questions about this. For example, while ADHD and cerebral palsy are both conditions where a student will get an IEP, they are not listed. ADHD is covered under other health impairments, and cerebral palsy is covered under orthopedic impairment.

Components of a legally defensible individualized education program

According to IDEA, for an IEP to be defensible, the goals outlined in the IEP must be clear, specific, and measurable. Defensible IEPs contain goals, assessments, services, participation, and a transitional plan. More specifically, an IEP must have the following elements to be considered legally defensible:

- A statement of the child's present levels of academic achievement and functional performance, including how the child's disability affects his or her involvement and progress in the general education curriculum.
- A statement of measurable annual goals, including academic and functional goals.
- A description of how the child's progress toward meeting the annual goals will be measured and when periodic progress reports will be provided.
- A statement of the special education and related services and supplementary aids and services to be provided to the child or on behalf of the child.
- A statement of the program modifications or supports for school personnel will be provided to enable the child to advance appropriately toward attaining the annual goals.
- An explanation of the extent to which the child will not participate in the general education classroom or in extracurricular and nonacademic activities.
- A statement of any individual accommodations that are necessary to measure the academic achievement and functional performance of the child on State and districtwide assessments.
- If the IEP team determines that the child must take an alternate assessment instead of a particular regular State or districtwide assessment of student achievement, the IEP must include a statement of why the child cannot participate in the regular assessment and why the alternate assessment selected is appropriate for the child.
- The projected date for the beginning of the services and modifications, and the anticipated frequency, location, and duration of those services and modifications.

To be eligible for special education and related services, a child must be in the age range of birth to 22 years of age and meet the criteria in two areas outlined in federal law:

1. The child must be identified as a child with a disability in one or more of the 13 categories defined below.
2. The child's disability must adversely affect his or her educational performance.

Children ages 0-3 are found eligible under Part C eligibility criteria of the Individuals with Disabilities Education Act (IDEA), and children ages 3-21 are determined to be eligible under Part B eligibility criteria of IDEA. To determine whether a child is eligible for services, he or she must receive a full and individual initial evaluation.

Major legislation

Family Educational Rights and Privacy Act (FERPA)

FERPA is a federal law that protects the privacy of student education records. The law applies to all schools that receive funds under an applicable program of the US Department of Education.

FERPA gives parents certain rights with respect to their children's education records. These rights transfer to the student when he or she reaches the age of 18 or attends a school beyond the high school level (US Department of Education, 2019).

Every Student Succeeds Act (ESSA)

Advances equity by upholding critical protections for America's disadvantaged and high-need students. Requires all students in America to be taught to high academic standards that will prepare them to succeed in college and careers. Ensures vital information is provided to educators, families, students, and communities through annual statewide assessments that measure students' progress toward those high standards.

No Child Left Behind 2002 (NCLB)

NCLB was signed into law in 2002 and increased the federal role in holding schools accountable for student outcomes.

I. Title I: Improving the academic achievement of the disadvantaged

II. Title II: Preparing, training, and recruiting high-quality teachers and principals

III. Title III: Language instruction for limited English proficient and immigrant students

IV. Title IV: 21st Century Schools

V. Title V: Promoting informed parental choice and innovative programs

VI. Title VI: Flexibility and Accountability

The Consent Decree

Grounded in the 14th Amendment and the result of the League of United Latin American Citizens (LULAC) vs. State Board of Education, the Consent Decree protects English language learners (ELL) and their right to a free, comprehensible education. It addresses the civil and academic rights of ELL students and requires instruction to be delivered in a comprehensible manner so ELLs can fully participate. Since 1975, federal law has required that students with disabilities have access to school and a free, appropriate public education.

Americans with Disabilities Act of 1990 (ADA)

ADA is a civil rights law that prohibits discrimination based on disability. It provides similar protections against discrimination against Americans with disabilities as the Civil Rights Act of 1964 (U.S. Department of Education, 2015).

Section 504 of the Rehabilitation Act of 1973

Section 504 regulations require a school district to provide a free, appropriate public education (FAPE) to each qualified student with a disability who is in the school district's jurisdiction, regardless of the nature or severity of the disability. Under Section 504, FAPE consists of the provision of regular or special education and related aids and services designed to meet the student's individual educational needs as adequately as the needs of nondisabled students are met (US Department of Education, 2015).

Prereferral, referral, identification, and placement

Special education typically involves several key stages: prereferral, referral, identification, and placement. The prereferral, referral, identification, and placement process in special education is crucial for several reasons, which together ensure that students with disabilities receive an appropriate and individualized education that meets their specific needs:

1. **Early Intervention**: The prereferral stage involves identifying students who are struggling in the general education classroom and attempting interventions to support their learning. This early intervention can often address learning difficulties before they become more significant, potentially reducing or eliminating the need for special education services.
2. **Appropriate Evaluation**: The referral and identification process ensures that students suspected of having disabilities are thoroughly evaluated in all areas related to the suspected disability. This comprehensive evaluation is critical to understanding each student's unique needs and strengths, ensuring that any disabilities are accurately identified.
3. **Individualized Education Program (IEP)**: Based on the evaluation results, an Individualized Education Program (IEP) is developed for each eligible student. This document outlines the student's specific learning needs, the services the school will provide, and how progress will be measured. The IEP ensures that education is tailored to the individual, promoting the highest possible educational achievement.
4. **Least Restrictive Environment (LRE)**: The process ensures that students are placed in the least restrictive environment that is appropriate for their needs. This means students should spend as much time as possible with peers who do not have disabilities, in a setting that allows them to achieve their learning goals, thus promoting inclusion and preventing unnecessary segregation.

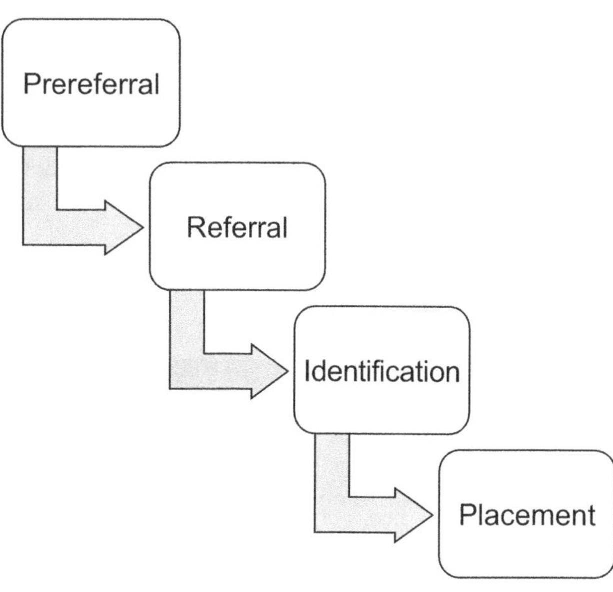

5. **Legal Compliance and Protection**: This structured process ensures that schools comply with federal laws such as the Individuals with Disabilities Education Act (IDEA), which mandates the provision of a free and appropriate public education (FAPE) to children with disabilities. It safeguards the rights of students and families, ensuring that decisions about identification and placement are made objectively and with the student's best interests in mind.
6. **Parental Involvement**: It promotes collaboration between the school and the family. Parents are involved in every step of the process, from initial concerns through the development and implementation of the IEP. This partnership is essential for creating an educational plan that is not only effective but also supports the student's growth and development in and out of school.

Overall, the prereferral, referral, identification, and placement process is fundamental in special education as it ensures that each student's unique learning needs are identified and met with tailored educational strategies, thereby promoting their success and inclusion in the educational system.

Prereferral

- Purpose: The prereferral stage addresses concerns about a student's academic or behavioral performance before formal evaluation for special education services begins.
- Process: Teachers implement various strategies within the general education classroom to support the student. This may include differentiated instruction, peer tutoring, or changes in classroom management strategies.
- Documentation: Progress is closely monitored and documented. If the student does not respond to these interventions, the team may consider a formal referral for special education evaluation.

There are six stages of the prereferral process:

Stage 1: Initial concern regarding a student's progress

Stage 2: Information gathering

Stage 3: Information sharing and team discussion

Stage 4: Discussion of possible strategies

Stage 5: Implementation and monitoring of strategies

Stage 6: Evaluation and decision-making

During the pre-referral stage, it is essential that teachers use response to intervention (RTI) or a multi-tiered system of supports (MTSS). This is when teachers use supports and interventions to prevent students who should not be in special education from being erroneously classified as such.

Most districts have moved to MTSS when addressing the needs of struggling students. The MTSS framework is evidence-based and has had a significant impact on addressing the needs of struggling subgroups of students. Students do not have to be classified as special education to receive MTSS.

- MTSS addresses the academic as well as the social, emotional, and behavioral development of children from early childhood to graduation.
- MTSS provides multiple levels of support for all learners—struggling through advanced.

MTSS Tiered Systems	
Tier 1	This is the type of modification or differentiated instruction ***all*** students get in the form of scaffolding (academic and behavior/social-emotional) and student support. Tier 1 is the basic and general implementation of the core curriculum aligned to the state standards.
Tier 2	This is the type of modification or differentiated instruction ***some*** students receive in addition to Tier 1 instruction. The purpose of Tier 2 instruction and supports is to improve student performance under Tier 1 performance expectations. This is also referred to as accommodations. The standards and expectations remain the same as Tier 1. However, accommodations are used for these students to be successful.
Tier 3	This is the type of modification or differentiated instruction ***few*** students receive and is the most intense service level a school can provide to a student. Typically, Tier 3 services are provided to very small groups and/or individual students. The purpose of Tier 3 services is to help students overcome significant barriers to learning academic and/or behavior skills required for school success.

Quick Tip

It is not the intention of educators and professionals to hastily categorize students as requiring special education solely based on their academic struggles. This is the rationale behind the significance of Response to Intervention (RTI) and Multi-Tiered System of Supports (MTSS) during the pre-referral stage. Teachers are obligated to employ a variety of interventions and support mechanisms, diligently recording their use and effectiveness. Only when these strategies have been fully implemented and documented, and they have not sufficiently addressed the student's needs, should the formal referral process for special education be initiated.

Referral

- Initiation: A formal referral is made when a student continues to struggle despite prereferral interventions. The referral can be made by a teacher, parent, or agency.
- Documentation: The referral typically includes written documentation of the student's academic or behavioral issues, previous interventions, and the student's response to those interventions.

Identification

- Assessment: The identification process involves a comprehensive evaluation to determine if the student has a disability and is eligible for special education services. This evaluation is carried out by a multidisciplinary team and may include intellectual, educational, and psychological assessments.
- Legal framework: Under IDEA (Individuals with Disabilities Education Act), schools must obtain parental consent before conducting these evaluations and must complete the process within a specified time frame.

Placement

- IEP development: If the student is found eligible for services, an Individualized Education Program (IEP) is developed. The IEP outlines the student's specific learning needs, the services the school will provide, and how progress will be measured.
- Determining placement: The IEP team, which includes educators, specialists, administrators, and the student's parents, determines the most appropriate educational placement. The goal is to place the student in the least restrictive environment (LRE) that meets their needs. This means that, to the maximum extent appropriate, students with disabilities are educated with students who are non-disabled, and special classes, separate schooling, or other removal from the regular educational environment occurs only when the nature or severity of the disability is such that education in regular classes with the use of supplementary aids and services cannot be achieved satisfactorily.
- Implementation and monitoring: Once placement is determined, the student's IEP is implemented. Continuous monitoring and regular IEP reviews ensure that the student progresses and that the placement meets their evolving needs.

Throughout these stages, clear communication and collaboration among all parties involved, including parents, educators, and specialists, are key to effectively supporting the student's educational journey. The process is designed to be student-centered and to ensure that each student receives the individualized support necessary to access and progress in the general education curriculum.

Classroom Scenario: Proactive Interventions: Applying MTSS in a General Education Classroom

Setting: Brookside Middle School, a general education seventh-grade classroom.

Characters:

- Mr. Lawrence, a general education teacher trained in a Multi-Tiered System of Supports (MTSS)
- Diego, a student exhibiting behavioral difficulties
- Mrs. O'Neil, the school counselor

Scenario:

Mr. Lawrence's classroom is busy as students work on a group science project. He notices that Diego is becoming increasingly disengaged, frequently interrupting his group, and struggling to follow classroom routines.

As part of the school's MTSS framework, Mr. Lawrence implements Tier 1 strategies to support Diego. He has already established clear classroom expectations and a positive reinforcement system, but he recognizes that Diego may need additional support.

To better understand Diego's behavior, Mr. Lawrence begins collecting data through observation and documentation, noting patterns in Diego's interactions and the contexts in which disruptive behavior occurs. Mr. Lawrence also ensures that Diego has a consistent schedule, providing a structure that is often beneficial for students who are struggling behaviorally.

Seeing minimal progress with these interventions, Mr. Lawrence escalates to Tier 2 supports. He arranges a meeting with Mrs. O'Neil, the school counselor, to discuss Diego's case. Together, they design a check-in/check-out system where Diego can start and end the day with a positive interaction, setting goals, and reflecting on his behavior.

Mr. Lawrence also incorporates social-emotional learning activities into his lessons, providing Diego with strategies to manage his emotions and behavior. He schedules short, frequent breaks for Diego, during which he can engage in a preferred activity after demonstrating positive behavior.

In the meantime, Mr. Lawrence maintains regular communication with Diego's parents, updating them on his progress and seeking their insights. Their involvement is crucial, as they provide additional background and support Diego's behavioral goals at home.

Conclusion:

After several weeks of consistent Tier 2 interventions, Mr. Lawrence reviews the data on Diego's behavior. He notes improvements in Diego's engagement and a decrease in disruptions. The proactive measures taken during the pre-referral phase have helped Diego to better navigate the classroom environment and have prevented the need for more intensive special education services.

This scenario exemplifies how a general education teacher can utilize the MTSS framework to address behavioral challenges proactively. By systematically implementing and monitoring interventions, Mr. Lawrence has supported Diego's success in the general education setting, reflecting the core objectives of MTSS and the pre-referral process in special education.

Reviews and reevaluations

IEPs and special education referrals are not set in stone. Instead, they should be thought of as living processes and documents. Students and parents have the right to IEP reviews and evaluations.

- **Annual IEP Review**: The Individuals with Disabilities Education Act (IDEA) mandates that schools conduct an annual review of a student's IEP. This ensures that the plan remains up to date and addresses the student's current needs and goals.
- **Triennial Evaluation**: Every three years, a comprehensive reevaluation of the student's eligibility for special education services is required under IDEA. This reevaluation may involve assessments, parent input, and reviewing existing data to determine if continued eligibility and services are needed.
- **Additional Reviews as Needed**: An IEP meeting can be called at any time for various reasons, such as concerns about the student's progress, changes in needs, or requests from parents or educators. It's essential to remember that IEPs are not set in stone; they can be modified to better serve the student.

Quick Tip

According to IDEA, the IEP must be updated at least once every 12 months. However, parents may ask for an IEP meeting at any time if they believe it is important to consider changes in your student's IEP.

English language learners in special education

Some students have limited English proficiency and are also classified as having exceptionalities. However, educators must avoid practices that can misdiagnose a language deficiency as a learning disability. Understanding linguistic limitations for English language learners (ELLs) is crucial when classifying students as special education for several key reasons:

1. **Differentiating language proficiency limits from learning disabilities**: ELL students may face challenges in academic performance due to limited English proficiency, which can be mistaken for learning disabilities. It's essential to distinguish whether a student's academic struggles are due to language acquisition issues or if they stem from a genuine learning disability. Misinterpretation can lead to inappropriate classification in special education.
2. **Accurate assessment**: Assessments conducted in a language a student is not fully proficient in can yield unreliable results. Understanding linguistic limitations ensures that evaluations for special education eligibility are fair and accurate. This might involve conducting assessments in the student's primary language or using nonverbal assessment methods.
3. **Cultural and linguistic bias**: Standard assessments can be culturally and linguistically biased, disadvantaging ELLs. Teachers and evaluators need to be aware of these biases to avoid misdiagnosing ELL students with special education needs when, in fact, they are simply navigating the challenges of learning a new language.
4. **Appropriate interventions and support**: Recognizing the difference between language acquisition difficulties and learning disabilities is critical in providing appropriate interventions. ELL students may need language acquisition support, such as English as a Second Language (ESL) programs, rather than special education services. Alternatively, ELL students with genuine learning disabilities require a combination of language support and special education services tailored to their unique needs.
5. **Promoting equity and inclusivity**: Understanding linguistic limitations is part of creating an equitable and inclusive educational environment. It ensures that all students, regardless of their language background, are encouraged to demonstrate their abilities and receive the support they need to thrive academically.
6. **Legal and ethical implications**: Incorrectly classifying ELL students as needing special education can have long-term educational and psychological impacts. It's a legal and ethical imperative to ensure that each student receives the right support to succeed in their educational journey.

Quick Tip

Cultural and linguistic biases can lead to the disproportionate representation of certain groups in special education programs. For example, there have been cases where English language learners (ELLs) are erroneously identified as requiring special education services, an issue often termed as misclassification. Such misclassification occurs when the academic challenges faced by ELL students, commonly stemming from limited proficiency in English, are mistakenly attributed to learning disabilities. To avoid this, it is crucial to discern between the normal challenges of acquiring a new language and the indicators of authentic learning disabilities, which necessitates meticulous and proficient evaluation.

Historical educational foundational theories

Understanding foundational theories in education is crucial for special education teachers as it equips them with the knowledge and perspective needed to navigate the ethical guidelines of their practice. Foundational theories provide a framework for understanding how students learn and develop, informing teachers' approaches to instruction, assessment, and classroom management in ways that respect and uphold the dignity, rights, and potential of every student. This understanding impacts ethical decision-making in several key areas:

1. **Individualized education**: Foundational theories underscore the importance of recognizing and responding to the unique needs of each learner. In special education, this principle is operationalized through the development of Individualized Education Programs (IEPs) and the provision of appropriate accommodations and modifications. Ethically, this approach ensures that every student has access to an equitable education that respects their individual differences and promotes their academic and social development.
2. **Inclusivity and equity**: Educational theories often emphasize the value of inclusivity and equity in teaching practices. Special education teachers, guided by these principles, are better prepared to create inclusive learning environments that support the participation and achievement of students with diverse learning needs. Ethical practice in this context involves actively removing barriers to learning and participation, challenging stereotypes, and biases, and advocating for the rights and inclusion of all students.
3. **Empowerment through education**: Many educational theories highlight the role of education in empowering individuals to lead fulfilling lives. For special education teachers, this translates into a commitment to not only address academic needs but also to support the development of life skills, self-advocacy, and independence. Ethically, this involves respecting students' voices and choices, promoting self-determination, and preparing students for active participation in society.
4. **Confidentiality and professionalism**: Foundational theories in education also touch upon the ethical use of student information and the importance of maintaining confidentiality. Special education teachers are often privy to sensitive information about students' disabilities, health, and personal circumstances. A deep understanding of educational ethics and laws, such as the Individuals with Disabilities Education Act (IDEA) and the Family Educational Rights and Privacy Act (FERPA), guides teachers in protecting student privacy and handling information with the utmost professionalism.
5. **Collaboration and communication**: Educational theories advocate for collaborative relationships between teachers, students, families, and other professionals. In special education, ethical practice involves transparent, respectful, and culturally sensitive communication with families and professionals. This collaboration ensures that educational planning and decision-making are inclusive, responsive to students' needs, and supportive of their best interests.
6. **Reflective practice and continuous learning**: Finally, foundational theories often encourage reflective practice and continuous professional learning. For special education teachers, reflecting on ethical dilemmas and engaging in ongoing professional development are vital for navigating the complexities of their work. This commitment to learning helps teachers stay informed about best practices, legal requirements, and ethical standards, ensuring that their practice evolves to meet the changing needs of their students.

Understanding foundational theories in education empowers special education teachers to navigate the ethical guidelines of their practice with integrity, compassion, and a deep commitment to the well-being and success of all students. This knowledge forms the backbone of ethical decision-making, guiding teachers to act in ways that are just, equitable, and in the best interest of their students.

Foundational Educational Theorists

Educational theorists come from within and outside of structured school settings. Most have backgrounds in psychology. The following is a list of educational theorists and their frameworks.

Jean Piaget. Piaget is widely known for his stages of cognitive development. This is a framework for how students develop intellectually through various stages. Piaget asserted that cognitive development was a reorganization of mental processes resulting from biological maturation and environmental experience (1972).

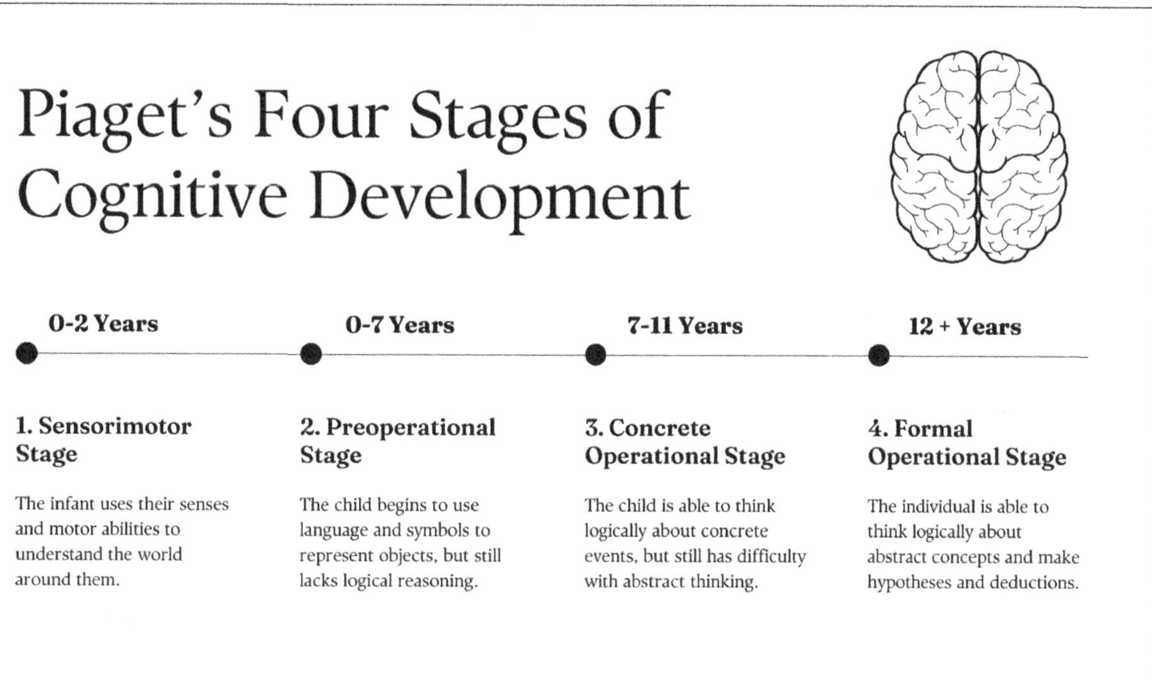

John Dewey - Dewey is one of the most influential theorists in education. Dewey believed that students learn by doing through hands-on, inquiry-based learning. This was revolutionary in the 1900s when schooling consisted mostly of the teacher standing in the front of the room giving students the knowledge. Dewey asserted that it is more effective for students to learn by interacting with their environment, relating the learning to real life, and learning together with the teacher.

Jerome Bruner – Theory of Cognitive Growth

Bruner emphasized the importance of the environment and the experiences provided by parents and teachers in developing children's cognitive processes. Bruner proposed that cognitive processes develop through three stages:

1. **Enactive representation (action-based)**: Knowledge is stored mainly through actions and motor responses, typically seen in infants and toddlers.
2. **Iconic representation (image-based)**: Knowledge is stored primarily in the form of visual images, common in young children.
3. **Symbolic representation (language-based)**: Knowledge is stored in the form of codes and symbols, such as language, which is prevalent in older children and adults.

Bruner also advocated for discovery learning, where students learn through exploration and inquiry, and the concept of the spiral curriculum, where complex subjects are taught at a simplified level initially and then revisited at more complex levels as the learner's cognitive abilities develop. Fundamental concepts of Bruner's philosophy:

- The curriculum should foster the development of problem-solving skills through the processes of inquiry and discovery.
- Subject matter should be represented in terms of the child's way of viewing the world.
- Curriculum should be designed so that the mastery of skills leads to the mastery of still more powerful ones.

B.F. Skinner – Operant Conditioning

Operant conditioning is a method of learning that occurs through rewards and punishments for behavior. Skinner believed that we could control behavior by controlling the consequences of actions. These include:

- Reinforcement (positive and negative): Increases the probability of a behavior being repeated.
- Punishment (positive and negative): Decreases the likelihood of a behavior being repeated.

Questions involving behavior management using rewards and consequences are usually grounded in Skinner's work on operant conditioning.

Erik Erickson - Theory of Psychosocial Development

Like Piaget, Erickson believed that students pass through definitive stages. However, these stages are psychosocial stages. According to Erickson, socialization happens in eight stages:

Key aspects of Erikson's theory relevant to education include:

1. **Trust vs. Mistrust (Infancy)**: In the earliest years, the foundation of learning is established by developing trust in caregivers and the environment. In educational settings, creating a safe and nurturing environment helps infants develop trust in the world around them.
2. **Autonomy vs. Shame and Doubt (Toddlerhood)**: As children enter preschool, fostering autonomy and encouraging exploration are crucial. Educational environments that support choice and self-directed play promote independence while helping children learn to overcome obstacles and build self-esteem.
3. **Initiative vs. Guilt (Early Childhood)**: During the preschool years, children need opportunities to initiate activities and make decisions. An educational approach that encourages curiosity and allows children to take on leadership roles fosters a sense of initiative and reduces feelings of guilt over taking action.
4. **Industry vs. Inferiority (School Age)**: In elementary school, the focus shifts to achieving competence and industry. Providing children with opportunities to achieve, recognizing their accomplishments, and teaching them to persevere in the face of challenges helps them develop a sense of competence and belief in their abilities.
5. **Identity vs. Role Confusion (Adolescence)**: The teenage years are about identity formation. Educationally, this stage calls for opportunities for students to explore different roles, beliefs, and interests. Supportive and diverse educational experiences help adolescents establish a sense of identity and direction.
6. **Intimacy vs. Isolation (Young Adulthood)**: While not always directly related to formal education, this stage emphasizes the importance of forming healthy relationships. Educational settings can support this development by fostering collaborative learning and community engagement.
7. **Generativity vs. Stagnation (Adulthood)**: For adults, the focus in educational contexts might shift towards teaching, mentoring, or contributing to society through one's work. Lifelong learning and professional development opportunities can facilitate generativity.
8. **Ego Integrity vs. Despair (Late Adulthood)**: In this final stage, the emphasis is on reflecting on one's life with a sense of fulfillment. Educational programs that encourage reflection and sharing of life experiences can support positive outcomes in this stage.

Erikson's theory underscores the importance of addressing the psychosocial needs of learners at each developmental stage. It suggests that education should be holistic, supporting not only cognitive development but also social and emotional growth. This approach ensures that educational practices promote resilience and prepare individuals to handle the challenges of each life stage successfully.

Lev Vygotsky – The Zone of Proximal Development

Vygotsky's theories stress the fundamental role of social interaction in the development of cognition. He believed strongly that community plays a central role in making meaning. Vygotsky is most widely known for the Zone of Proximal Development (ZPD), which he asserted is the distance between the actual developmental level as determined by independent problem-solving and the level of potential development as determined through problem-solving under adult guidance or in collaboration with more capable peers (Vygotsky, 1978).

Helping someone move through the Zone of Proximal Development depends on the following:

1. The presence of a more knowledgeable person
2. Social interactions
3. Scaffolding or supportive activities developed by the educator (ZPD is discussed in more detail below)

Albert Bandura – Social Learning Theory

Bandura is best known for his social learning theory on modeled behaviors or observational learning. He believed that students learn from what they observe and that teachers can be proactive about how they demonstrate and promote behaviors. He argues that students are more likely to emulate a behavior if they value the outcome and admire the modeler. His theory builds on the central elements of Vygotsky's learning, emphasizing social learning. Bandura's social learning theory has four stages: attention (observation of modeled behaviors), retention (memory), motor reproduction (practice and replication of behaviors), and motivation (self-efficacy and personal motivation to use new behaviors). (Bandura, 1972)

Abraham Maslow

Maslow's hierarchy of needs is a psychological theory proposed by Abraham Maslow in his 1943 paper "A Theory of Human Motivation" in "Psychological Review." It is often depicted as a pyramid consisting of five levels of human needs, categorized into two main groups: deficiency needs and growth needs. The basic premise is that higher needs in the hierarchy begin to emerge when people feel they have sufficiently satisfied the previous need.

1. **Physiological Needs**: At the base of the pyramid are the physiological needs, which include the most basic requirements for human survival, such as food, water, sleep, and shelter. These needs must be met first before individuals can attend to any other level of the hierarchy.
2. **Safety Needs**: Once physiological needs are met, the need for safety and security becomes predominant. This includes personal security, employment, resources, health, and property.
3. **Love and Belonging Needs**: The next level involves social needs which include emotionally-based relationships in general, such as friendships, romantic attachments, and family. Humans need to feel a sense of belonging and acceptance among social groups, regardless of whether these groups are large or small.
4. **Esteem Needs**: At the fourth level are the esteem needs, which include the need for things that reflect on self-esteem, personal worth, social recognition, and accomplishment.
5. **Self-Actualization Needs**: At the peak of the pyramid is self-actualization. This level relates to what a person's full potential is and the realization of that potential. Maslow describes this level as the desire to accomplish everything that one can, to become the most that one can be.

Above these five basic levels, Maslow later introduced three additional levels: cognitive needs (knowledge and understanding), aesthetic needs (appreciation and search for beauty, balance, form, etc.), and transcendence needs (helping others to achieve self-actualization).

Maslow's hierarchy of needs serves as a framework for understanding human motivation in various fields, including psychology, education, and business. It suggests that the most basic level of needs must be met before individuals can attend to needs higher up in the hierarchy.

Benjamin Bloom – Bloom's Taxonomy

Benjamin Samuel Bloom was an American educational psychologist who made contributions to the classification of educational objectives and the theory of mastery learning. He is widely known for Bloom's Taxonomy—a hierarchical model used to classify educational learning objectives into levels of complexity and specificity. The higher up the pyramid, the more complex the thinking skills. The skills are represented as verbs on the pyramid. When answering questions on the exam about objectives, remember Bloom's Taxonomy.

Create
Analyze
Evaluate
Apply
Compare & Contrast
Categorize
Understand & Identify
Remember & Memorize

IMPORTANT: The figure shown is a modified version of Bloom's Taxonomy. We have modified it to include other skills (verbs) you may see on the exam.

The skills (verbs) at the highest points of the pyramid are *apply*, *analyze*, *evaluate*, and *create*. When you are faced with a critical thinking problem on the test, visualize this pyramid and look for answer choices that reflect the higher portions of the pyramid.

The importance of understanding historical frameworks in education

Historical foundational theories are vital in special education for several reasons, particularly when considering professional collaboration and practice. Understanding foundational theories in education allows the special education teacher to have comprehensive knowledge in the areas of:

1. **Educational strategies**: These theories provide a framework for understanding how students learn and behave. By grounding practice in these theories, special education professionals can develop and choose instructional strategies and interventions that are tailored to the cognitive and developmental levels of their students.
2. **Interdisciplinary applications**: Special education involves collaboration with psychologists, therapists, and other specialists. A shared knowledge base of foundational theories enhances mutual understanding and facilitates more effective team collaboration focused on student-centered strategies.
3. **Behavior management**: Understanding theories such as operant conditioning aids in developing behavior management plans. These plans can include positive reinforcements and appropriate consequences to shape and modify student behavior, which is a common need in special education settings.
4. **Social and emotional learning**: Social learning theory highlights the importance of social interaction in learning. This is particularly relevant in special education, where peer modeling and social skills training are key components of comprehensive educational programs.
5. **Communication with stakeholders**: Foundational theories provide a common language for educators to communicate complex ideas about student learning and behavior to parents and other stakeholders in a clear and understandable way.

6. **Creating inclusive environments**: The theories can guide educators in creating inclusive environments that recognize and accommodate the diverse ways in which students learn and interact with the world. For example, Piaget's stages of cognitive development can help educators understand and respect the intellectual diversity of their students, while Bandura's social learning theory can inform practices that build positive classroom dynamics.
7. **Individualized education program (IEP) development**: A deep understanding of these theories is crucial when developing IEPs. They provide the theoretical basis for setting realistic, developmentally appropriate goals and for choosing the most effective methods to measure student progress.
8. **Reflective practice**: Reflecting on these theories can help educators evaluate and refine their teaching practices, ensuring they are not only evidence-based but also philosophically grounded in a well-rounded understanding of human development and learning.
9. **Professional growth**: Engaging with foundational theories is part of ongoing professional development. It allows educators to critically analyze new trends and approaches within the context of established knowledge, leading to more thoughtful and informed practice.

Classroom Scenario: Cultivating Critical Thinking: Applying Bloom's Taxonomy in Lesson Planning

Setting: Willow Creek High School, 10th Grade Biology Classroom

Characters:

- Ms. Jensen, a biology teacher dedicated to fostering deep understanding
- A diverse group of tenth-grade students

Scenario:

Ms. Jensen stands before her class and explains today's objectives:

- Identify basic parts of the plant involved in photosynthesis.
- Relate the structures of these parts to their function in photosynthesis.
- Evaluate the efficiency of photosynthesis and how it contributes to a plant's growth.

Her goal is not only to have students understand the concept but also to use higher-order thinking skills to apply, analyze, evaluate, and create based on their new knowledge.

Communication of Objectives—Before Learning: Ms. Jensen begins the lesson by clearly articulating her objectives to the class. "Today, we will start by remembering the basics of plant biology and understanding how photosynthesis works. By the end of our lesson, I want you to apply this knowledge to explain why leaves change color in the fall, analyze a plant's growth conditions, evaluate the efficiency of photosynthesis, and create a diagram that depicts the process."

During Learning: As the lesson unfolds, Ms. Jensen guides her students through the various levels of Bloom's Taxonomy:

- **Remember**: She starts with a quick review quiz on plant biology basics.
- **Understand**: She then presents a short video explaining photosynthesis, asking students to paraphrase the process in their own words.
- **Apply**: The students conduct a lab experiment, testing leaves for starch to observe photosynthesis in action.
- **Analyze**: In groups, they compare different plant species to determine how environmental factors affect photosynthesis.
- **Evaluate**: Ms. Jensen poses a question for class discussion: "Which plant adapted best to its environment, and why?"
- **Create**: For the final task, students design a flowchart that illustrates the stages of photosynthesis, integrating creative elements to showcase the cycle.

Communication of Objectives—During Learning: Throughout the class, Ms. Jensen continually refers to the lesson's objectives. She prompts students with questions like, "Have we achieved the first objective, and can we move on to the second?" and "How does photosynthesis contribute to all life on Earth?"

After Learning: As the lesson concludes, Ms. Jensen reviews the day's objectives and activities, connecting each to the corresponding level of Bloom's Taxonomy. She asks students to reflect on their learning by answering closing questions they will revisit the next day.

Conclusion:

Ms. Jensen wraps up the class by emphasizing the importance of pushing beyond rote memorization to deeper cognitive processes. She praises the class for their flowcharts and critical thinking demonstrated in their evaluations. "Today," she says, "you've not only learned about photosynthesis, but you've also practiced how to think like scientists."

This scenario demonstrates how a teacher can effectively use Bloom's Taxonomy to structure lesson objectives and encourage students to engage with content at increasingly complex levels of thinking. By clearly communicating these objectives and their connection to classroom activities, Ms. Jensen ensures that her students know their learning journey and actively participate in their educational experience.

Professionalism and Collaboration

Deepening professional growth is an ongoing process essential for educators, especially those in special education, where student needs can be highly complex and varied. Here's how various strategies contribute to this professional growth:

- **Analyzing student learning** – By closely analyzing student learning and performance, educators can gain a deeper understanding of their students' needs, strengths, and areas for improvement. In addition, using data from student assessments, teachers can make informed decisions about their instructional strategies, adapting and tailoring their approaches to better meet individual student needs.
- **Self-reflecting** – Continuous improvement requires educators to self-reflect. Self-reflection allows educators to consider the effectiveness of their teaching practices critically. It involves thinking about what worked well and what didn't, and why. Reflecting on their teaching experiences helps teachers set personal and professional goals for growth, leading to enhanced teaching practices and student outcomes.
- **Collaborating with other professionals** – Collaboration with colleagues, such as other special education teachers, general education teachers, and specialists (like speech therapists or psychologists), can provide new perspectives and insights and provide space to share expertise. Through collaboration, teachers can learn interdisciplinary strategies and approaches that may be more effective for their students. This also fosters a more cohesive and consistent approach to supporting students across different settings.
- **Professional development –** Engaging in professional development opportunities allows teachers to stay updated with the latest research, tools, and methods in special education. Professional development can range from workshops and seminars to advanced degrees and certifications. These opportunities enable educators to expand their skills and apply new knowledge to their teaching practice.

By incorporating these strategies into their professional practice, special education teachers can continually enhance their skills and effectiveness. This commitment to growth not only benefits their own career but also significantly impacts the learning and success of their students. It ensures that educators are well-equipped to provide high-quality, individualized education and to adapt to the ever-evolving field of special education.

Collaborating with stakeholders

There are also other professionals who work with special education students. Remember that these professionals do much more than what is listed here. However, the following are the main functions of each other these professionals.

- **Paraprofessional** – A special education paraprofessional, under general supervision, aids a classroom teacher and assists in implementing instructional programs, including self-help and behavior management.
- **Occupational Therapist** – An occupational therapist (OT) is a health care professional specializing in occupational therapy and occupational science. OTs help students with intellectual disabilities strengthen their functional skills such as dressing, toileting, and eating.
- **Speech-Language Pathologist** – A speech and language pathologist (SLP) specializes in communication. SLPs work with students on speech sounds, language, social communication, voice, fluency, and feeding and swallowing.
- **School Psychologist** – School psychologists provide direct support and interventions to students, consult with teachers, families, and other school-employed mental health professionals (i.e., school counselors and school social workers) to improve support strategies, work with school administrators to improve school-wide practices and policies, and collaborate with community providers to coordinate needed services. Most often, it is the school psychologist who administers special education screening.
- **Physical Therapist** – Physical therapists assist students in accessing school environments and benefiting from their educational program by helping students with mobility, fine motor skills, and gross motor skills.

Test Tip

You may see the term resource room or resource teacher. In a general education school, a resource room is usually found in the regular mainstream school where children with varied exceptionalities are educated at once.

Collaboration among teachers

Often in a special education classroom and general education classroom, teachers will have the opportunity to work with another professional or teacher in the same room. For example, a teacher and a paraprofessional may work together in a math class. Two teachers may work together in an elementary classroom. Having multiple instructors can be beneficial and create a supportive classroom environment. The following are some examples of coaching approaches.

- **Co-Teaching** – the practice of pairing teachers together in a classroom to share the responsibilities of planning, instructing, and assessing students. Co-teaching is often implemented with general and special education teachers paired together as part of an initiative to create a more inclusive classroom.
- **Station Teaching** – the approach of having an instructor at each center or station. This promotes small group and individualized instruction for specific skills.
- **Alternative Teaching** – a co-teaching model where one teacher works with a small group of students, as the other teacher instructs the large group. This approach allows teachers to maximize the amount of time spent on differentiation and scaffolding techniques.
- **One teach, one assist** – the method where one teacher has the responsibility to deliver the main instruction, while the other teacher walks around the room and assists. The assist teacher may help students get supplies or help clarify if students have questions.

- **One teach, one observe** – this method is often used for data collection. The main teacher instructs the lesson, and the other observes students and collects formative data.
- **Parallel teaching** – this method involves two teachers. The teachers divide the class in half, and each teacher teaches the same thing to each respective half of the class.
- **Team teaching** – this involves two teachers in front of the class sharing the responsibility of whole-group instruction.

Quick Tip

In inclusion settings, an appropriate role for the special education teacher is as a co-teacher with the general education teacher. Both teachers have a level of expertise that allows them to share responsibility for behavior management and the planning and teaching of academic content.

Professional Learning, Practice, and Collaboration Practice Questions

1. According to IDEA, an IEP should be revised:
   A. Every five years
   B. Every three years
   C. Every two years
   D. Every year

2. The least restrictive environment (LRE) means:
   A. Students in wheelchairs should be sat near exits.
   B. When possible, special education students should be educated with nondisabled peers.
   C. IEP teams should determine if a student can be in general education.
   D. Students should receive rewards when they achieve in the general education classroom.

3. Which of the following happens during the prereferral process of an English language learner being considered for special education? Choose **ALL** that apply.
   - ☐ A. Teachers use RTI or MTSS to support the student in the general education classroom and to see if differentiation will help the student.
   - ☐ B. Teachers and specialists determine if the student is experiencing language barriers to avoid misrepresentation.
   - ☐ C. Teachers and specialists gather a team to draft an Individualized Education Program (IEP) for the student.
   - ☐ D. Teachers and specialists monitor the student, gather quantitative and qualitative information, and analyze the information.
   - ☐ E. Teachers and specialists place the student in special education classes temporarily to determine if it will help the student.

4. A seventh-grade special education teacher is using scaffolding techniques to help support students during reading instruction. Which of the following foundational theories in education does this align with?
   A. Social learning theory
   B. Zone of proximal development (ZPD)
   C. Stages of cognitive development
   D. Operant conditioning

5. A teacher uses response cost to reduce the occurrence of a specific, observable behavior in one of her students with EBD. When the student outbursts during direct instruction, the teacher revokes two minutes of the student's playground time. Which of the following foundational theories does this align with?
   A. Social learning theory
   B. Zone of proximal development (ZPD)
   C. Stages of cognitive development
   D. Operant conditioning

6. Julie is a special education student who uses a wheelchair. Julie shows advanced skills in reading and math. Which of the following placements would be most appropriate for Julie?
   A. A self-contained special education classroom where students work on functional skills.
   B. A general education classroom where the student can receive interventions in reading and math
   C. Advanced placement in a general education classroom with a paraprofessional
   D. Spilt time between a self-contained classroom and the general education classroom

7. Which of the following is a key component of the IEP?
   A. Goals
   B. Adaptive technology
   C. Specialist support
   D. Team members

8. Jose is a special education student with ADHD. His parents want to revisit his IEP goals and have requested an additional IEP meeting. Which of the following is true in this situation?
   A. The parents can request an IEP meeting at any time to reevaluate the goals outlined in Jose's IEP.
   B. The parents must wait until the annual IEP meeting to request any changes to Jose's IEP goals.
   C. The parents must contact the state and await approval for an additional IEP meeting.
   D. The parents cannot request a change to Jose's IEP.

9. According to the MTSS framework, these are the interventions given to all students, not just special education students.
   A. Tier I
   B. Tier II
   C. Tier III
   D. Tier IV

10. At what age does transition planning for an individualized transitional plan (ITP) begin?
    A. Starting as early as age 10 and no later than age 14
    B. Starting as early as age 14 and no later than age 16
    C. Starting as early as age 16 and no later than age 18
    D. Starting as early as age 18 and no later than age 21

Professional Learning, Practice, and Collaboration Answer Explanations

Number	Answer	Explanation
1.	D	According to IDEA, IEPs must be revised at least once every year. They may be revised more frequently if requested by parents or teachers.
2.	B	LRE means, whenever possible, special education students should be in general education classrooms with their peers.
3.	A, B & D	The prereferral stage is about information gathering and applying differentiation strategies to possibly avoid designating students as needing special education. The student will also need language evaluation to avoid misrepresenting the ELL as needing special education. Choices C and E are part of the placement stage and not part of the prereferral stage. Finally, teachers do not place students in special education temporarily. Therefore, choice E is incorrect for two reasons.
4.	B	According to Vygotsky, the zone of proximal development (ZPD) is the distance between the actual developmental level determined by independent problem-solving and the level of potential development as determined through problem-solving under adult guidance or in collaboration with more capable peers. Therefore, scaffolding is a strategy aligned with ZPD. Social learning theory is about how students interact with one another. The stages of cognitive development outline processes in the brain based on age. Finally, operant conditioning focuses on how to modify behaviors based on rewards and consequences.
5.	D	Operant conditioning focuses on how to modify behaviors based on rewards and consequences. Therefore, using response cost aligns with this foundational theory. Social learning theory is about how students interact with one another. The stages of cognitive development outline processes in the brain based on age. The zone of proximal development (ZPD) is the distance between the actual developmental level determined by independent problem-solving and the level of potential development as determined through problem-solving under adult guidance or in collaboration with more capable peers.

Number	Answer	Explanation
6.	C	Julie's exceptionality is physical, but her academic performance indicates she is advanced in reading and math. Therefore, she should be given the opportunity to engage in advanced classes with the support of a paraprofessional who can help her with her physical needs. This is the least restrictive environment (LRE). Answer choices A, B, and D are not appropriate for Julie because doing any one of those would hinder her academic performance. A self-contained classroom is for students with severe cognitive, behavioral, or intellectual disabilities. Julie is advanced academically and should be placed in advanced general education classes.
7.	A	The most important part of the IEP is the goals section. Not all special education students will need adaptive technology or specialist support. The IEP team members present is important, but not as important as the goals section. Setting goals for special education students is paramount in delivering free appropriate public education (FAPE).
8.	A	An IEP meeting can be called at any time for various reasons, such as concerns about the student's progress, changes in needs, or requests from parents or educators. It's essential to remember that IEPs are not set in stone; they can be modified to better serve the student. IEPs should be considered living documents that can be modified when appropriate.
9.	A	Tier I modifications or differentiated instruction are given to ***all*** students. Tier I is the basic and general implementation of the core curriculum that is aligned to the state standards. Tier II are given to some students who need more intensive supports. Tier III are given to few students who might need to be in a self-contained classroom. There are no Tier IV interventions.
10.	B	The individual transition plan (ITP) is part of the IEP, and transition planning can begin as early as 14. According to IDEA, special education students must have a transition plan in place by age 16. The plan is in effect until age 22.

Practice Test 1

1. Based on Piaget's Four Stages of Cognitive Development, which of the following behaviors indicates that a child entering the pre-operational stage may be developing atypically?
   A. A failure to apply logical reasoning
   B. An excess of egocentricity
   C. The inability to identify basic objects
   D. The inability to put things in order

2. A middle school teacher has difficulty motivating her special education students to choose a research topic for a class presentation. She decides to offer a variety of topics and presentation formats for students to choose from. What is the teacher trying to foster?
   A. Autonomy
   B. Relatedness
   C. Competence
   D. Self-advocacy

3. An elementary teacher wants to use an extrinsic reward to increase motivation in their special needs students. Which strategy would they most likely use?
   A. Allow the student to dictate the order of their learning schedule for the day.
   B. Plan an event where the student can demonstrate new skills to their parent or guardian.
   C. Explain how hard work can lead to success, such as a higher-paying job.
   D. Give the student ten minutes of extra playtime to meet expectations.

4. Jose is a special education student who frequently interrupts class discussions by calling out without raising his hand and seeking attention from his teacher and peers. Initially, the teacher would respond to the interruptions by stopping the class discussion, acknowledging Jose's comments, and redirecting him to raise his hand before speaking. The teacher then decides to refrain from acknowledging or responding to his outbursts and instead reinforces positive behavior by acknowledging and praising students who raise their hands before speaking. Jose's interruptions gradually decrease in frequency. This is an example of:
   A. Desensitization
   B. Extinction
   C. Group contingency
   D. Premack Principle

5. Which of the following would be an example of manipulating the consequent stimulus?
   A. A teacher arranges the classroom layout so that students are less likely to cause disruptions.
   B. A teacher explains that students will first organize their cubbies, then they will have playtime.
   C. A teacher ignores a student drawing on their desk after being told not to.
   D. A teacher assigns additional cleaning tasks to students who fail to clean their area after an activity.

6. A student in a special education class has difficulty maintaining her balance, particularly when navigating stairs, uneven surfaces, or participating in activities that involve changes in direction. She struggles with tasks that require precise hand movements, such as holding a pencil, using scissors, or buttoning a shirt, and her handwriting is less controlled than her peers. What type of developmental disability does this student most likely have?

   A. ADHD

   B. Autism spectrum disorder

   C. Cerebral palsy

   D. Hearing loss

7. Which of the following is an example of a behavior that might be exhibited by a student with a behavioral disability? Choose **ALL** that apply.

   ☐ A. The student uses limited vocabulary or non-verbal cues to express basic wants.

   ☐ B. The student often acts without considering the consequences, making decisions on the spur of the moment.

   ☐ C. The student requires assistance with activities such as dressing, grooming, and feeding, as well as guidance on hygiene routines.

   ☐ D. The student isolates themself from social interactions and cannot build or maintain satisfactory interpersonal relationships.

   ☐ E. The student displays frequent and intense fluctuations in mood, including periods of extreme depression.

8. Match each student with the correct learning disability.

	Dysgraphia	Dyslexia	Non-Verbal Learning Disability (NVLD)	Dyscalculia
A. The student struggles to understand number relationships, perform mental calculations, and memorize multiplication tables.				
B. The student exhibits significant difficulties with handwriting and fine motor skills and struggles to organize their thoughts on paper.				
C. The student has difficulty decoding and comprehending written language. They frequently reverse letters while reading and have difficulty recognizing sight words.				
D. The student often misunderstands facial expressions and body language, leading to challenges in social interactions and forming friendships.				

9. If there are 3.6 million babies born in the US within one year, approximately what percentage of them will have a disability?

   A. 17%

   B. 20%

   C. 25%

   D. 30%

10. Which of the following factors is a common reason why a student might be mislabeled as special needs?

   A. Lack of parental involvement

   B. Variation in skill development

   C. Language barriers

   D. Unstable living conditions

11. Which of the following students is displaying a comorbid condition?

   A. A student rapidly fluctuates between periods of mania and depression.

   B. A student displays passive-aggressive behavior.

   C. Two siblings are diagnosed with the same learning disability.

   D. A student diagnosed with ADHD also exhibits signs of autism.

12. Which of the following would promote an inclusive environment in special education? Choose **ALL** that apply.

   ☐ A. Praise the student for performing well even though they are disabled.

   ☐ B. Involve parents in public recognition of the student's achievements.

   ☐ C. Provide tips to parents and caregivers that facilitate positive interactions with their child.

   ☐ D. Help students manage their expectations and set simple, realistic goals.

   ☐ E. Facilitate support groups for parents of children with special needs.

13. Which of the following is considered a developmental disability?

   A. A nine-year-old student has a lack of sight in their left eye.

   B. A three-year-old student is hypersensitive to certain textures and materials.

   C. A seven-year-old student has difficulty with some basic math concepts.

   D. A four-year-old has difficulty holding a pencil or using scissors.

14. In what way could a special education teacher implement the theory behind Abraham Maslow's hierarchy of needs in the classroom?

   A. The teacher organizes students into reading groups based on ability.

   B. The teacher communicates with parents to gather information about potential stressors at home.

   C. The teacher challenges students with a high-level activity to raise academic performance.

   D. The teacher reinforces positive student behavior by providing external rewards, such as stickers.

15. Julie is a fifth-grade student who continually gets up to sharpen her pencil during direct instruction. This leads to disruptions and loss of instructional time. Which of the following is an example of a teacher implanting a satiation strategy to eradicate this behavior?

    A. The teacher intentionally ignores Julie's behavior when she gets up to sharpen her pencil. The teacher refrains from providing attention, redirection, or any form of acknowledgment when Julie engages in the behavior.

    B. The teacher gives Julie frequent "pencil sharpening breaks" at the beginning, middle, and end of each class session. The teacher requires Julie to get up and sharpen her pencil during these times, even if Julie doesn't want to.

    C. The teacher places a pencil sharpener directly on Julie's desk. By doing so, the teacher eliminates the need for the student to get up and go to a distant pencil sharpener.

    D. The teacher tells Julie that if she can stay seated for 10 minutes, she can have a brief break to get up and sharpen her pencil.

16. Sophie, a middle school special needs student, has a strong interest in nature. Together with her teacher and other classmates, she works to create an inclusive garden on the school grounds, setting specific goals for the project. As challenges arise, such as needing adaptive tools or addressing specific sensory needs, Sophie works with the teacher and her peers to find creative solutions. What is the student exhibiting?

    A. Self-assessment

    B. Self-regulation

    C. Self-determination

    D. Self-control

17. Max, a 10-year-old student diagnosed with autism spectrum disorder (ASD), is highly sensitive to sensory stimuli. When exposed to unexpected loud sounds, he becomes visibly distressed and exhibits disruptive behaviors, including covering his ears and vocalizing loudly. His teacher begins gradually exposing him to controlled and predictable instances of the trigger stimuli, such as a recorded, low-volume sound resembling the school bell. For each successful exposure to the simulated bell sound without exhibiting disruptive behaviors, Max receives praise, a preferred item, or a short break. Over time, the teacher systematically increases the intensity and unpredictability of the simulated sound. What is this is an example of?

    A. Planned ignoring

    B. Manipulating the consequent stimulus

    C. Extinction

    D. Desensitization

18. Diana is a special education student with emotional behavior disorder (EBD). Whenever she is assigned a writing task, she consistently engages in behaviors designed to avoid the task, such as doodling, daydreaming, and fidgeting. What would be the best approach in this situation?

    A. Call home and discuss possible consequences with Diana's parents.

    B. Provide sentence frames to help Diana organize her writing.

    C. Assign Diana the writing task for homework if she does not complete it during class.

    D. Provide Diana with choices within the writing task to increase her motivation.

19. Jonah is a tenth-grade special education student with a vision impairment disability. He is not completely blind but has limited vision in both eyes. Which of the following preparations should a teacher take when planning a unit on classical literature with Jonah in mind?

A. Allow Jonah to listen to an audio version of the text while following along using a large print version of the text.

B. Have another student read the text aloud to Jonah and have Jonah answer comprehension questions.

C. Provide Jonah with the annotated version of the text so he only has to read a smaller section of the full text.

D. Allow Jonah to watch the movie version of the text and share what he has learned with a partner.

20. A teacher accommodates a student by turning and facing the student while giving instructions. The student most likely has:

A. Dyscalculia

B. ADHD

C. Hearing loss

D. Vision impairment

21. A general education teacher observes that one of her sixth-grade students, who has an IEP, is exhibiting problems with communication, such as substituting, omitting, or repeating sounds or syllables and prolonging sounds. Which of the following would the student benefit from the most?

A. Coordinating with the special education teacher to determine appropriate reading interventions.

B. A request for an interpreter for the student.

C. A meeting with the student's parents to discuss a behavior plan.

D. Gradual increased exposure to social situations.

22. A student with impaired visual-motor integration or dysgraphia would most likely struggle with which activity?

A. Recognizing shapes

B. Handwriting

C. Presenting to the class

D. Comprehending diagrams

23. What is a Functional Behavioral Assessment (FBA) used for?

A. Identifying students who may have a learning or behavioral disability.

B. Ensuring that students with disabilities have access to the general curriculum.

C. Planning a student's special education program based on their individual needs.

D. Verifying that educational services provided to students with disabilities are properly funded.

24. Which of the following goals is most appropriate for a student who has an intellectual disability?

A. Initiate peer interactions during recess

B. Demonstrate appropriate handwashing techniques after using the restroom.

C. Express negative emotions in a healthy manner.

D. Use a daily planner to record assignments and deadlines.

25. Which of the following is a highly effective way to provide classroom accommodations for students with cerebral palsy? Choose **ALL** that apply.

- ☐ A. Create an organized setting with well-defined daily schedules and protocols.
- ☐ B. Implement adapted physical activities that promote motor skill development.
- ☐ C. Ensure that classrooms are wheelchair accessible and have ramps.
- ☐ D. Provide students with a speech-generating device or communication app.
- ☐ E. Utilize color-coded text to emphasize important information in reading materials.

26. An occupational therapist would be most helpful for a student with which disability?

A. Behavioral disability

B. Cerebral palsy

C. Intellectual disability

D. Dyscalculia disability

27. Victor, an eighth-grade student with ADHD, recognizes that he often struggles with focusing during long lectures. During a one-on-one meeting with the teacher, Victor expresses concern about maintaining attention during extended lectures. He suggests alternative strategies that have been helpful in the past, such as taking short breaks, using fidget tools discreetly, or sitting in a specific location in the classroom to minimize distractions. What is the student demonstrating?

A. Competence

B. Self-esteem

C. Desensitization

D. Self-advocacy

28. Which types of support might be needed in a special education class containing several students with severe disabilities? Choose ALL that apply.

- ☐ A. Peer tutoring for advanced concepts.
- ☐ B. The use of cognates in both instructional language and classroom text.
- ☐ C. A communication board consisting of pictures, symbols, or words.
- ☐ D. Text-to-speech software that converts written text into spoken words.
- ☐ E. Curriculum focused on hands-on learning, visual supports, and repetition.

29. A teacher plans accommodations for an upcoming standardized assessment. She will implement frequent breaks for students during the assessment. Which disability do these students most likely have?

A. Attention deficit/hyperactivity disorder (ADHD)

B. Hearing loss

C. Specific learning disability (SLD)

D. Autism spectrum disorder (ASD)

30. Trevor is a fourth-grade special education student with an IEP who encounters challenges in academic tasks, including properly expressing himself during reading comprehension activities. What type of learning disability does this student most likely have?

A. Graphomotor

B. Language-based

C. Non-verbal

D. Intellectual

31. Which type of student is the Expanded Core Curriculum (ECC) designed to aid?

A. A student with hearing loss

B. A student with vision impairment

C. A student with a behavioral disability

D. A student with cerebral palsy

32. Which of the following statements best defines the ecological perspective on autism?

A. Genetic factors are the primary cause of autism.

B. Children with autism need exposure to isolated and controlled social environments.

C. The interactions between individuals and their surroundings play a crucial role.

D. Autism can be prevented through specific dietary interventions.

33. A ninth-grade student is exhibiting the following: inconsistencies in academic performance, inappropriate responses in social situations, memory problems, and deficits in problem-solving and abstract thinking. Which of the following accommodations would be most effective for this student?

A. Set up a rewards system for time spent on task.

B. Allow the student to have frequent breaks.

C. Provide a special keyboard with larger keys.

D. Break down text into smaller segments.

34. Put the following actions for planning instruction in the special education classroom correctly.

I. Plan lessons and activities

II. Identify state-adopted standards

III. Select assessments

IV. Monitor progress

A. II, I, III, IV

B. III, II, I, IV

C. II, III, I, IV

D. III, I, IV, II

35. A seventh-grade science class is conducting a series of experiments that involve the use of proportions and ratios. The science teacher collaborates with the seventh-grade math teacher to ensure her students receive mathematics instruction that integrates these concepts. The teacher is practicing:

   A. Vertical alignment

   B. Horizontal alignment

   C. Content alignment

   D. Subject alignment

36. What components are necessary for a successful and measurable learning objective? Choose **ALL** that apply.

   ☐ A. The skill or behavior to be performed.

   ☐ B. The prerequisite skills students need to complete the task.

   ☐ C. The conditions under which the students will perform.

   ☐ D. The criteria used to measure the objective.

   ☐ E. The most common student misconceptions related to the topic.

37. Which of the following is an example of a goal set for a special needs student that fully aligns with the SMART method?

   A. Over the semester, Mark will improve his ability to solve algebraic equations, a skill relevant to his current math curriculum and abilities.

   B. By the end of the month, Maria will improve her reading comprehension skills by correctly answering questions about a short passage in four out of five attempts, as measured by a formative assessment.

   C. Sarah will try to improve her language skills by writing more accurately over the next few weeks during literary analysis assignments.

   D. Jake will enhance his public speaking skills by confidently delivering a five-minute presentation, using clear enunciation and appropriate body language, during class presentations.

38. Mr. Kim, a second-grade science teacher, wants to implement the station teaching approach in his classroom. How should his classroom be set up?

   A. Mr. Kim creates a section for a hands-on experiment, a reading section, and an exit ticket section in different areas of the room. Both Mr. Kim and groups of students circulate through each area.

   B. Mr. Kim delivers whole-group instruction to the class. Students then conduct a hands-on experiment while an assistant teacher circulates to provide support.

   C. Mr. Kim and an assistant teacher split the class into two groups. Mr. Kim's group is focused on developing research skills for a presentation. The assistant teacher's group is working on a vocabulary card sort. Students rotate through the groups.

   D. Mr. Kim supervises a hands-on activity while an observing teacher uses a checklist or observation sheet to note students' engagement, understanding of the content, and any misconceptions.

39. What is the most effective way to determine students' needs when providing Tier 3 supports related to the Positive Behavioral Interventions and Supports (PBIS) framework?

   A. Create formal assessments

   B. Use observation

   C. Develop an IEP

   D. Read the portfolio

40. Thomas is a sixth-grade student with autism spectrum disorder (ASD). When he successfully follows a visual schedule without exhibiting challenging behaviors, his teacher allows him to erase the whiteboard, an activity he enjoys. The teacher is using which theoretical approach?

A. Cognitivism

B. Behaviorism

C. Social Learning

D. Constructivism

41. Which of the following are key aspects of setting up procedures in the classroom? Choose **ALL** that apply.

☐ A. Allowing students to choose their preferred procedures

☐ B. Communicating procedures to parents

☐ C. Differentiating procedures based on student abilities

☐ D. Establish and practice procedures before learning occurs

☐ E. Practice procedures over and over

42. In a third-grade math class, two teachers split the class into two equal groups, teaching a lesson on fractions to each group. What type of teaching method is this?

A. Team Teaching

B. Parallel Teaching

C. Co-Teaching

D. Alternative Teaching

43. A ninth-grade student with ADHD can easily comprehend classroom texts but struggles to remain engaged when assigned longer texts. Which of the following would be the best learning activity for the student to complete?

A. Chunking

B. Evidence-Based Discussion

C. Reading Response Journal

D. Jigsaw

44. A teacher observes Jessica, a fifth-grade special education student who continuously becomes agitated, yells, and pushes items off her desk. The teacher uses a stopwatch to record the time in between outbursts. What is the teacher trying to determine with this approach?

A. Latency

B. Duration

C. Intensity

D. Frequency

45. What would likely happen if a teacher consistently rewarded positive behaviors with items such as small toys?

A. Students would begin demanding better, more expensive toys.

B. Students would continue to exhibit positive behaviors.

C. Students would trade toys among themselves, leading to disruptions.

D. Students would grow tired of the toys.

46. Mr. Rodriguez, a math teacher, wants to institute a democratic approach to classroom management. Which of the following scenarios should he implement?

A. Dividing the class into small groups where they receive differentiated instruction and increased participation.

B. Explaining a set of classroom rules in detail, ensuring student comprehension and setting clear expectations.

C. A token system designed to reinforce compliance where students earn points for rule adherence.

D. A class discussion on behavioral expectations where students share their ideas and help create a list of shared rules.

47. What is the most important aspect of a rewards-and-consequences system?

A. Giving both rewards and consequences equal weight to each student.

B. Increasing the severity of consequences when behaviors fail to improve.

C. Providing rewards promptly and consistently as students display positive behaviors.

D. Stimulating students' self-determination by allowing them to choose the rewards.

48. A special needs teacher requests that her students engage in reflective journaling to enhance their self-awareness. The teacher is using which theoretical approach?

A. Social Learning

B. Behaviorism

C. Zone of Proximal Development (ZPD)

D. Cognitivism

49. Ms. Jules teaches a ninth-grade social studies inclusion class. She provides accommodations to help her special needs students access the general education curriculum. Which of the following would be an appropriate accommodation? Choose **TWO**.

☐ A. Offer students audio versions of reading materials or assignments.

☐ B. Provide students with graphic organizers to visually organize information during lessons.

☐ C. Reduce the length and complexity of written tasks for students.

☐ D. Adjust the grading scale of the assignments based on students' capabilities.

50. Which of the following accommodations is most likely to appear on the IEP of a student whose only classification is for a non-verbal learning disability?

A. Offer extra time for verbal responses during class time.

B. Incorporate explicit teaching related to interpreting facial expressions and body language.

C. Adjust or waive participation regulations in the classroom.

D. Provide a paraprofessional to facilitate access to the curriculum and ensure individualized assistance.

51. Which of the following techniques are commonly used in task analysis? Choose **ALL** that apply.

- ☐ A. Relatedness
- ☐ B. Chaining
- ☐ C. Kinesthetic learning
- ☐ D. Modeling
- ☐ E. Trial instruction

52. Which of the following is an example of using the response cost intervention method in the classroom?

A. Students gain computer time through good behavior and face deductions for each instance of disruption.

B. Students meet individually with their teacher to discuss their progress toward their IEP goals.

C. Students receive verbal praise when they sit quietly during story time.

D. Students are given a designated space to take a break and regain composure when they exhibit negative behaviors.

53. What is a key approach to developing an Individualized Family Service Plan (IFSP)?

A. Implement a universal approach to developmental milestones for all children with special needs in a school.

B. Outline the unique academic, behavioral, and functional goals for a student within the school setting.

C. Provide assistive technology for students with hearing and visual impairments and a plan to help students access the technology from home.

D. Emphasize services that enhance infant and toddler development within the family's routines and environment.

54. What equipment would be best to use when supporting a student with autism spectrum disorder (ASD) through an emergency safety drill, such as a lockdown or fire drill?

A. A brightly colored vest and a whistle

B. Rewards such as candy or small toys

C. Noise-cancelling headphones and sunglasses

D. Mobility aids such as walkers or wheelchairs

55. Ms. Rodriguez introduces a math lesson by asking students to set personal goals for understanding the new concept. As they work through problems, she prompts them to reflect on their comprehension, discusses challenges, and guides them in adjusting their learning, such as trying different problem-solving strategies. Which instructional approach is the teacher taking in this situation?

A. Cooperative learning

B. Metacognitive

C. Diagnostic Prescriptive

D. Direct instruction

56. Which of the following is an example of the multiple-modality approach in a science classroom?

   A. A teacher incorporates visual aids such as colorful diagrams and charts as well as hands-on experiments and manipulatives.

   B. Students set goals for understanding a complex experiment, monitor their understanding throughout the process, and evaluate the effectiveness of their problem-solving strategies.

   C. A teacher explains key scientific concepts through interactive demonstrations or lectures, providing clear and structured information to the entire class.

   D. Students work in small groups to conduct experiments or analyze data, with each member contributing unique insights and skills.

57. Mr. Patel fosters relatedness in his students by focusing on real-world math applications. He groups students based on their interest in areas such as sports statistics, financial calculations, or architectural design. What type of grouping is Mr. Patel using?

   A. Homogeneous

   B. Heterogeneous

   C. Proficiency-based

   D. Systematic

58. Match each example with the correct form of instruction.

	Experiential and virtual	Independent	Indirect	Direct	Interactive
Modeling learning behaviors such as revising a piece of writing using a document camera.					
Students participate in a virtual lab.					
A student chooses a topic within a class theme of study.					
Whole group math games practicing skip counting, place value, and number fluency.					
Guided reading in cooperative groups.					

59. An eleventh-grade special education teacher conducts a vocabulary review where students revisit and reinforce previously learned words. The teacher is using what type of strategy in this lesson?

    A. Generalization
    B. Differentiation
    C. Modifications
    D. Maintenance

60. A teacher provides one-on-one academic support to a student who is struggling with sight word memorization. When the student shows improvement after one week, the teacher no longer provides the student with specialized attention. What method of instruction was the teaching using?

    A. Supplementary
    B. Modification
    C. Intervention
    D. Accommodation

61. Ms. Kent is a tenth-grade special education teacher working with her students on functional curriculum. Which of the following activities would benefit her students in this area?

    A. A Reader's Theater to improve their reading fluency.
    B. A math activity calculating income and expenses for a monthly budget.
    C. A field trip to a science museum.
    D. A social studies activity comparing primary and secondary sources.

62. Which of the following would be the best assistive technology for a student with an intellectual disability?

    A. A talking calculator
    B. Visual computer cues
    C. Speech-to-text
    D. A recording device

63. Which of the following is **NOT** a required focus of an individualized transition plan (ITP)?

    A. Describe a student's accommodations or modifications.
    B. Address the student's interests, strengths, and needs.
    C. Focus on specific and annual goals.
    D. Define the responsibilities of parents.

64. Which of the following goals would be most appropriate for an Individualized Transition Plan (ITP) for a high school student with autism spectrum disorder (ASD) who wants to work in public relations?

    A. Participate in weekly speech therapy sessions to enhance articulation, voice modulation, and clarity.
    B. Participate in research skills workshops to strengthen abilities in gathering, evaluating, and synthesizing information.
    C. Participate in communication workshops, role-playing scenarios, and networking events.
    D. Focus on developing time management and planning skills, incorporating tools and strategies to effectively manage deadlines.

65. What does the acronym PBIS stand for?

A. Purposeful Behavior Integration Strategies

B. Positive Behavioral Interventions and Support

C. Performance-Based Inclusion Solutions

D. Practical and Balanced Instructional Sequences

66. Which is the best approach for a special needs teacher to provide valuable targeted instruction that focuses on an individual student's knowledge gaps?

A. Have a peer review the student's most recent assignment and point out errors.

B. Schedule a conference with the student's parents to develop a plan for concurrent strategies.

C. Analyze data from both summative and formative assessments.

D. Help the student redefine their personal and academic goals to foster autonomy.

67. A special needs teacher provides targeted instruction to compensate for a specific deficit in some of her students. She regularly incorporates categorization, association, and visualization techniques into her instruction. What deficit is the teacher compensating for?

A. Proprioceptive and vestibular perception

B. Long-term memory

C. Conceptual comprehension

D. Auditory perception

68. What educational technique is most effective in the Zone of Proximal Development (ZPD)?

A. Differentiation

B. Progress monitoring

C. Collaboration

D. Scaffolding

69. Which of the following is an example of a teacher implementing one of the three basic principles of Universal Design for Learning (UDL) in a classroom? Choose **ALL** that apply.

☐ A. The teacher offers alternative ways to present information, such as visual timelines and auditory materials.

☐ B. The teacher gives students the option of creating a traditional written report or a multimedia presentation.

☐ C. The teacher employs well-established teaching methods, leveraging effective lectures and traditional instructional materials.

☐ D. The teacher provides a structured and focused learning environment, promoting discipline and attentiveness.

☐ E. The teacher introduces real-world problem-solving scenarios that relate to students' daily lives.

70. Which is an example of a culturally responsive practice? Choose **ALL** that apply.

☐ A. Build partnerships with local businesses to provide resources and mentorship to special education students.

☐ B. Incorporate elements in the curriculum that reflect students' unique backgrounds.

☐ C. Consider postsecondary options that are highly valued within a student's ethnic community.

☐ D. Ensure that assessments and evaluations are free of bias and mindful of diversity.

☐ E. Teach independent living skills considering the students' traditional practices.

71. What is the purpose of the Present Levels of Academic Achievement and Functional Performance (PLAAFP)?

A. To measure behavior and mental health

B. To measure a student's functionality in all areas of the school environment

C. To identify the type and amount of special education a student receives

D. To identify problem behaviors and develop interventions

72. What three areas does the School Function Assessment (SFA) assess?

A. Participation, task support, and activity performance

B. Motivation, spatial reasoning, and recall

C. Engagement, cognitive ability, and academic performance

D. Communication, behavior, and physical fitness

73. If a student scores between 70-79 on the Wechsler Intelligence Scale for Children (WISC), what is most likely true?

A. They have a severe intellectual disability.

B. They have a learning disability.

C. They are of average ability.

D. They have a moderate developmental delay.

74. What type of assessment is classified as informal?

A. Summative

B. Performance-based

C. Criterion-referenced

D. Formative

75. A teacher administers a performance-based assessment in class. Which of the following is most likely occurring?

A. Over the course of a semester, students collect art samples and organize them by date in a designated folder. During parent conferences, students show their parents the portfolio and reflect on their progress.

B. At the end of the academic year, students take standardized tests that cover the social studies curriculum they have learned.

C. Following a unit on geometry, students collaborate to design and solve complex mathematical problems related to real-world scenarios. They present their solutions in a mathematical exhibition.

D. At the beginning of a language arts course, students complete an assessment that includes grammar exercises, reading comprehension tasks, and writing prompts.

76. What is always a key aspect of an Individualized Education Program (IEP) meeting? Choose **ALL** that apply.

☐ A. Providing positive feedback to the student

☐ B. Setting individual academic goals for the student

☐ C. Interpreting assessment data for stakeholders

☐ D. Making sure data is comprehensible to the student

☐ E. Ensuring language accessibility and support

77. Which of the following is an example of modifying an assessment as prescribed in a student's IEP?

A. Providing frequent breaks, extending testing time, or reading test questions aloud

B. Utilizing virtual classrooms, online programs, and interactive software

C. Implementing the use of exit tickets or checklists

D. Using simplified language, reducing task complexity, or providing alternate assessment forms

78. What type of assessment is classified as formal?

A. Diagnostic

B. Formative

C. Portfolio

D. Criterion-referenced

79. A teacher needs to provide data showing student progress over time, including student self-evaluations and reflections. What assessment type would be the most effective in this situation?

A. Summative

B. Portfolio

C. Diagnostic

D. Performance-based

80. Which of the following is an example of a criterion-referenced test?

A. A state-standardized assessment

B. A writing rubric

C. A student presentation

D. An exit ticket

81. What is a norm-referenced assessment?

A. An exam that places students in appropriate classrooms or grade levels

B. An exam that compares student performances to one another

C. An exam that determines proficiency based on predetermined specifications

D. An exam that informs instruction prior to a learning activity

82. What is the primary reason why a screening assessment would be performed?

A. To evaluate students' physical health

B. To make placement decisions

C. To determine student mastery of advanced concepts

D. To develop an Individualized Education Plan (IEP)

83. When would a summative assessment most likely be used?

A. At the beginning of the year

B. At the beginning of a field trip

C. At the end of a class

D. At the end of a unit

84. When should students be given a rubric?

A. Before an assigned task

B. During an assigned task

C. After an assigned task

D. All the above

85. Ms. Rodriguez is implementing a new art program for her students, and she wants to assess its effectiveness while implementing interventions throughout the process. Which pair of assessments would be most beneficial when measuring the impact of the new art program?

A. Formative and summative

B. Diagnostic and screening

C. Performance-based and rubric

D. Norm-referenced and portfolio

86. The results for this type of assessment are typically communicated as a percentile ranking.

A. Rubric

B. Formative

C. Norm-referenced

D. Diagnostic

87. Which of the following is an example of a stanine score?

A. 72%

B. 16 total correct

C. 61st percentile

D. 7 out of 9

88. A student achieves a raw score of 62 on an assessment. What does this raw score signify?

A. The student's percentile ranking in the assessment

B. The percentage of questions the student answered correctly

C. The student's scale score on the assessment

D. The number of questions the student answered correctly

89. Which type of professional is most likely to administer a Functional Behavioral Assessment (FBA)?

A. A paraprofessional

B. A school psychologist

C. An occupational therapist

D. A general education teacher

90. If a student takes a spelling quiz with ten questions and gets 4 of the questions right, what percentage of the questions did they answer correctly?

A. 4%

B. 40%

C. 6%

D. 60%

91. A ninth-grade student named Sarah has been displaying a range of concerning behaviors both at home and at school. These behaviors include social withdrawal, a decline in academic performance, and frequent expressions of sadness and anxiety. Sarah's teachers, parents, and the school counselor are concerned about her overall well-being and want to understand the underlying factors contributing to her difficulties. Which type of assessment would most likely be administered to Sarah in this scenario?

A. Behavior Assessment System for Children (BASC)

B. Woodcock-Johnson Psycho-Educational Battery

C. Functional Behavioral Assessment (FBA)

D. School Function Assessment (SFA)

92. Which type of professional is most likely to administer a School Function Assessment (SFA)?

A. A speech-language pathologist

B. A school psychologist

C. A school counselor

D. An occupational therapist

93. Which type of assessment is typically used to determine if a student has a learning disability?

A. Present Levels of Academic Achievement and Functional Performance (PLAAFP)

B. Vineland Adaptive Behavior Scale

C. Woodcock-Johnson Psycho-Educational Battery

D. Functional Behavioral Assessment (FBA)

94. Which of the following behaviors might be outlined on a functional behavior assessment (FBA)?

A. Jada often forgets to bring her homework to school.

B. Jada consistently disrupts the class by talking loudly and refusing to follow instructions.

C. Jada has difficulty with time management and often misses deadlines for assignments.

D. Jada finds it challenging to write neatly and handle small objects.

95. A teacher provides a student with the testing accommodation of responding orally to questions. What issue does the student most likely struggle with?

A. Problems remaining on task

B. Limited range of motion in hands

C. Difficulty comprehending text

D. Visual impairment

96. The School Function Assessment (SFA) is typically administered to what grade range?

A. Pre-k-3rd

B. K-6th

C. Pre-K-8th

D. K-12th

97. Which test accommodation would be most appropriate for students who failed to answer more than a third of the questions?

A. Give the student extra time

B. Provide the student with an audio version

C. Provide the student with a screen reader

D. Allow the student to take frequent breaks

98. What does the Least Restrictive Environment principle under IDEA require?

A. Each child with a disability must have an IEP developed, reviewed, and revised at least once a year.

B. A student must be evaluated before providing special education services to determine whether the student qualifies as a "child with a disability."

C. Children with disabilities must be educated with children who are not disabled as much as possible.

D. The rights of children with disabilities and their parents are protected, and they must have access to the information needed to effectively participate in the IEP process.

99. Under IDEA, which principle states that a student with disabilities must continue to receive services even if they are expelled?

A. IEP

B. LRE

C. FAPE

D. IDEA

100. What rights are parents entitled to under IDEA's Procedural Safeguard principle? Choose **ALL** that apply.

☐ A. Written notice of IEP meetings and any changes to the IEP

☐ B. Authority over the teaching methods used in their child's education

☐ C. Access to their child's educational records

☐ D. A due process hearing

☐ E. Full confidentiality regarding their child's educational records

101. Which of the following acts protects public access to student records?

A. FERPA

B. ESSA

C. RTTT

D. ADA

102. According to MTSS, this is the type of modifications or differentiated instruction ***some*** students receive.

A. Tier 1

B. Tier 2

C. Tier 3

D. Tier 4

103. The parents of a child receiving special education services are concerned that their child isn't receiving the proper accommodations. They want the school to make changes to their child's IEP. What should the parents do?

A. Wait until the mandatory annual review of the IEP.

B. Wait until the IEP's triennial evaluation under IDEA.

C. Request an IEP meeting be scheduled.

D. Once an IEP is created, it cannot be changed.

104. A student is in the middle of a key stage of special education. Their teacher has just submitted documentation of the student's academic or behavioral issues, previous interventions, and the student's response to those interventions. Which stage are they in?

A. Pre-referral

B. Referral

C. Identification

D. Placement

105. Dana, a fourth grader with ADHD, has reached the identification stage of the special education process. Based on the list of 13 disabilities outlined by IDEA, which disability would Dana have listed on her IEP?

A. Orthopedic impairment

B. Emotional behavior disturbance (EBD)

C. Specific learning disability

D. Other health impairment

106. What is a key goal of the response to intervention (RTI) or multi-tiered system of supports (MTSS) approach?

A. To ensure that special education students receive the proper placement.

B. To prevent students who should not be in special education from being wrongly classified.

C. To ensure that the rights of children with disabilities and their parents are protected.

D. To prevent children with disabilities from being educated in isolation from children who are not disabled.

107. What law related to English language learners (ELLs) is mandated under the Consent Decree? Choose **ALL** that apply.

- ☐ A. All ELLs must be provided with free, comprehensive special education services.
- ☐ B. All ELLs must be provided with accommodations for both disabilities and language acquisition issues.
- ☐ C. All ELLs must be provided with comprehensible instruction that allows them to fully participate.
- ☐ D. All ELLs must be provided with differentiated instruction based on language proficiency level.

108. Which act, signed into law in 2002, increased the federal role in holding schools accountable for student outcomes by requiring states to establish student academic standards as well as an assessment system to ensure that all students are meeting the academic standards?

A. No Child Left Behind (NCLB)

B. Free Appropriate Public Education (FAPE)

C. Every Student Succeeds Act (ESSA)

D. Family Educational Rights and Privacy Act (FERPA)

109. Which of the following must be included in a legally defensible IEP? Choose **ALL** that apply.

- ☐ A. A statement of measurable annual goals, including academic and functional goals.
- ☐ B. The projected date for the beginning of the services and modifications, and the anticipated frequency, location, and duration.
- ☐ C. A statement of the child's present levels of academic achievement and functional performance.
- ☐ D. An explanation of the extent to which the child will not participate in the general education classroom or in extracurricular and nonacademic activities.
- ☐ E. A statement of any individual accommodations that are necessary to measure the academic achievement and functional performance of the child on State and districtwide assessments.

110. What is the maximum age at which a special education student be finished with TIP (transition planning)?

A. 13

B. 14

C. 15

D. 16

111. Which of the following is an established policy under the Least Restrictive Environment (LRE) principle of IDEA?

A. Students with a disability must never be placed outside the general education classroom.

B. Funding must be considered when applying for a more restrictive placement.

C. States must maintain a full range of placement options to meet the needs of children who require specialized treatment programs.

D. Involvement in music, art, physical education, school trips, clubs, extracurriculars, and other activities must be based on the limitations of the individual child.

112. Which of the following procedural protections can parents of special needs students invoke when they disagree with educators? Choose **ALL** that apply.

- ☐ A. A formal written complaint
- ☐ B. A due process hearing
- ☐ C. A direct appeal to the school board
- ☐ D. The resolution facilitator process
- ☐ E. A mediation conference

113. According to IDEA, children between which ages are eligible for early intervention services?

A. 0 to 2

B. 0 to 6

C. 3 to 6

D. 3 to 12

114. Mrs. Johnson, a general education teacher, is responsible for a diverse group of students, including those with special needs. One of her students, Alex, has been diagnosed with autism spectrum disorder (ASD) and requires additional support in the classroom. Alex is bright and eager to learn, but he benefits from individualized attention and assistance. Which type of support personnel would be most helpful in this scenario?

A. A paraprofessional

B. An occupational therapist

C. A school psychologist

D. A speech and language pathologist

115. Emily is a special needs student who receives the services of a physical therapist twice a week. What issues does Emily most likely struggle with?

A. Challenges in developing and maintaining positive social relationships with peers.

B. Difficulties in processing sensory information, such as sensitivity to touch, sound, or other sensory inputs.

C. Problems forming sentences, using appropriate grammar, or understanding and using vocabulary.

D. Tasks that require precision and control, such as holding a pencil, using scissors, or buttoning a shirt.

116. Which of the following statements about a resource room is correct?

A. A resource room is located within a general education classroom.

B. In a resource room, children with varied exceptionalities are educated at once.

C. A resource room is only accessible in a special education school.

D. A resource room is a place where individualized services are provided to students.

117. A special education teacher is working on increasing his professional growth. He has recently engaged in several professional development opportunities, closely analyzed student learning and performance, and self-reflected on his most recent teaching practices. Which additional strategy would contribute most to his professional growth?

A. Creating a more inclusive classroom environment

B. Implementing differentiated assessment practices

C. Collaboration with other professionals

D. Evaluation of students who might present as special needs

118. Under IDEA, which is legally required for a school to conduct a disability assessment during the identification process? Choose **TWO**.

☐ A. Placing the student in LRE

☐ B. Completing the process within a specified time frame

☐ C. Obtaining parental consent

☐ D. Providing written documentation from the state

119. A teacher has an English language learner (ELL) in the classroom. The teacher decides to conduct assessments in the student's primary language and use nonverbal methods for other assessments. What is the teacher's goal in using this method?

A. To provide accommodations for a student with both language proficiency issues and a disability

B. To avoid a disability misclassification of a student with a language proficiency issue

C. To ensure that the student is provided with modified expectations

D. To prevent the students from losing engagement and intrinsic motivation

120. A special education teacher is using Lev Vygotsky's theory regarding the Zone of Proximal Development (ZPD) to inform many of her approaches in the classroom. What is she most likely doing?

A. Explicit teaching

B. Heterogenous grouping

C. Distance learning

D. Summative assessment

Practice Test 1 – Answer Explanations

Number	Category	Answer	Explanation
1.	I.	C	Piaget's 4 Stages of Cognitive Development include the sensorimotor, pre-operational, concrete operational, and formal operational stages. When children are in the preoperational stage they identify and use symbols for objects but do not have the ability to apply logical reasoning. They know how to play pretend and are egocentric. Choice C shows that a child at this stage may be developing atypically. Choice A is incorrect because logical reasoning is not part of the pre-operational stage; it's part of the concrete and formal operational stages. Choice B is incorrect because children at the pre-operational stage are egocentric; therefore, this would not indicate the child developing atypically. Choice D is a skill indicative of the concrete operational stage.
2.	I.	A	Choice A, autonomy, has to do with students' independence and self-governance. Allowing students to decide how and what they learn, such as giving them research and format options, helps to increase autonomy and intrinsic motivation. Choice B, relatedness, is when students see the value in what they are learning as it pertains to their everyday lives. Choice C, competence, is when students are made to feel that they are equipped to meet the teacher's expectations. Choice D is when students can speak up for themselves and express their needs and wants.
3.	I.	D	Extrinsic motivation refers to behavior that is driven by external rewards. Providing students with a party if they reach their reading goal or allowing students extra playtime (Choice D) are examples of extrinsic motivation. Extrinsic motivation can be helpful in the short term, but it is often unsustainable because once the reward is removed, the student is no longer motivated to achieve. Intrinsic motivation is behavior driven by internal rewards. Choice A is an example of autonomous intrinsic motivation, where students are given choices about their learning to increase their internal motivation. Choice B is an example of competence intrinsic motivation, where students are challenged to demonstrate their abilities. Choice C is an example of relatedness intrinsic motivation, where students can see the value in what they learn daily.

Number	Category	Answer	Explanation
4.	I.	B	Extinction (Choice B) is a technique where the teacher removes the reinforcement for a problem behavior to decrease or eliminate occurrences of these types of negative (or problem) behaviors. Choice A refers to a technique where a person is exposed to small doses of an anxiety-inducing stimulus alongside of a relaxation technique. Choice C refers to a practice where the teacher reinforces the entire class or a smaller group of students for completing tasks, engaging in appropriate classroom behaviors, or exhibiting other targeted behaviors. While the teacher is praising positive behavior in this scenario, they are praising individual behaviors. Choice D is when a teacher explains future events using the structure of "first-then."
5.	I.	D	Manipulating the consequent stimulus is a type of intervention that changes a student's behavior by manipulating conditions that follow such behavior. For example, when a student misbehaves, the student receives timeout or another consequence. This is often referred to as punishment. Choice D fits this type of intervention. Choice A is an example of manipulating the antecedent stimulus, a type of intervention that changes the student's behavior by manipulating conditions that precede such behavior. Choice B is an example of the Premack Principle, when a teacher explains future events using the structure of "first-then." Choice C is an example of planned ignoring, when a teacher identifies undesirable behaviors used for attention and then ignores those behaviors. This reduces undesirable behaviors.
6.	I.	C	Cerebral palsy (CP) is a nondegenerative condition—meaning it does not get worse over time—that affects a person's motor skills and balance. CP is the most common motor disability in childhood. It is estimated that 1 in 345 children are born with CP. Students with ADHD (choice A) may have trouble paying attention, controlling impulsive behaviors (may act without thinking about what the result will be), or be overly active. Students with autism spectrum disorder, or ASD (choice B), can have significant social, communication and behavioral challenges. The learning, thinking, and problem-solving abilities of people with ASD can range from gifted to severely challenged. Students with hearing loss (choice D) can have problems with communication, language, and social skills.

<table>
<tr><th>Number</th><th>Category</th><th>Answer</th><th>Explanation</th></tr>
<tr><td>7.</td><td>I.</td><td>B, D, E</td><td>Choices B, D, and E all describe students exhibiting signs of a behavioral disability (EBD). Students with this type of disability consistently exhibit patterns of behavior that significantly deviate from the norm and impact their ability to function effectively in various settings, such as school or social environments. These behavioral challenges are not typically attributed to intellectual disabilities, sensory impairments, or other medical conditions.

Behavioral disabilities can have various causes, including genetic factors, environmental influences, trauma, or neurological conditions. Choices A and C describe students exhibiting signs of an intellectual disability. This type of disability limits a person's ability to learn at an expected level and function in daily life. Children with an intellectual disability might have a hard time letting others know their wants and needs. They also may not be able to take proper care of themselves. Students with intellectual disabilities often need assistance when learning to speak, walk, dress, or eat.</td></tr>
<tr><td>8.</td><td>I.</td><td>See Table</td><td>
<table>
<tr><th></th><th>Dysgraphia</th><th>Dyslexia</th><th>Non-Verbal Learning Disability (NVLD)</th><th>Dyscalculia</th></tr>
<tr><td>A</td><td></td><td></td><td></td><td>X</td></tr>
<tr><td>B</td><td>X</td><td></td><td></td><td></td></tr>
<tr><td>C</td><td></td><td>X</td><td></td><td></td></tr>
<tr><td>D</td><td></td><td></td><td>X</td><td></td></tr>
</table>
</td></tr>
<tr><td>9.</td><td>I.</td><td>A</td><td>According to the CDC, recent estimates in the United States show that roughly one in six, or 17 percent of children aged 3 through 17 years have one or more developmental disabilities</td></tr>
<tr><td>10.</td><td>I.</td><td>C</td><td>While choices A, B, and D can all contribute to a student's potential mislabeling, choice C is the most common. Often, students who are English language learners (ELLs) are disproportionately represented in special education programs and are labeled learning disabled when they do not have a learning disability, and instead are struggling with the language. Misidentified students are likely to encounter limited access to a rigorous curriculum and diminished expectations. More importantly, mislabeling students creates a false impression of the child's intelligence and academic potential.</td></tr>
</table>

Number	Category	Answer	Explanation
11.	I.	D	When two or more disorders occur at the same time, they are called co-occurring disorders or comorbidity. The most common comorbid relationship is between learning disabilities and attention deficit disorder hyperactivity (ADHD). Choice D correctly describes this phenomenon.
12.	I.	B, C & E	Choices B, C, and E all help to foster optimism in both parents and students. An optimistic perspective will help promote well-being and safeguard parents from the harmful effects of stress and depression usually associated with caring for someone with a disability. Teachers should play a role in this optimism. Things teachers can do are: • Focus on the students' strengths. • Call home with good news. • Celebrate gains with the student and parents. • Help parents with strategies to positively interact with children with special needs. Inadvertently using language that emphasizes the student's disability rather than their accomplishments (choice A) can result in demoralization or embarrassment. Discouraging students from attempting to reach ambitious goals (choice D) fails to provide an optimistic environment. Choices B, C, and E all help to foster optimism in both parents and students.
13.	I.	A	A developmental disability is something a student will not grow out of. Vision impairment (choice A) is a type of developmental disability. Loss of eyesight is not a condition that will correct over time. A developmental delay is something a student can grow out of. Choice B is a type of sensory processing developmental delay. Choice C is a type of academic developmental delay. Choice D is a type of fine motor skills developmental delay.
14.	I.	B	Maslow's Hierarchy of Needs asserts that people are motivated by 5 basic factors: physiological, safety, love, esteem, and self-actualization. Choice B is correct because it focuses on the second tier in the hierarchy—safety, security, family, and health. Choice A is a type of targeted instruction that meets the diverse needs of learners at different proficiency levels but not necessarily part of Maslow's hierarchy of needs. Choice C has to do with differentiated instruction to challenge students who are high achieving. Choice D is an example of a teacher implementing B.F. Skinner's operant conditioning theory. This theory is based upon the idea that learning is a function of change in overt behavior. Using external rewards is a cornerstone of this theory.

Number	Category	Answer	Explanation
15.	I.	B	Satiation is a technique teachers use to overindulge a negative behavior so much that the student becomes bored with the bad behavior and stops doing it. As the student engages in the sharpening routine over time (choice B), the novelty of sharpening the pencil wears off, and the behavior becomes less reinforcing. Choice A is an example of using an extinction strategy, where the teacher removes the reinforcement for a problem behavior to decrease or eliminate occurrences of these types of behaviors. Choice C is an example of manipulating the antecedent stimulus, a type of intervention that changes the student's behavior by manipulating conditions that precede such behavior. Choice D is an example of using the Premack Principle, also known as the first-then principle.
16.	I.	C	Self-determination is the ability to make decisions for oneself and to control one's own future. A student with strong self-determination is motivated by opportunities to collaborate on instructional design, set goals for themselves, and navigate obstacles to succeed. The application of self-determination theory is best understood through intrinsic motivation. Self-assessment (choice A) is a reflection or evaluation of one's own performance. Self-regulation (choice B) and self-control (choice D) relate to the ability of an individual to manage and control their own thoughts, emotions, behaviors, and actions.
17.	I.	D	Desensitization is a technique where a person is exposed to small doses of an anxiety-inducing stimulus alongside of a relaxation technique. This is used in reinforcement theory in which there is a weakening of a response, usually emotional, used to change a behavior. Choice A involves identifying undesirable behaviors used for attention and then ignoring those behaviors. Choice B involves changing a student's behavior by manipulating conditions that follow such behavior (such as punishment). Choice C involves removing the reinforcement for a problem behavior to decrease or eliminate occurrences of these types of negative (or problem) behaviors.
18.	I.	D	An emotional disability is characterized by an inability to learn which cannot be adequately explained by intellectual, sensory or health factors. The best choice in this situation is one that uses good words and practices. Choice D is the best practice because it allows Diana to increase her autonomy. Choice B is a more appropriate intervention for a student with a language barrier. Choices A and C are punitive in nature and are not appropriate.

Number	Category	Answer	Explanation
19.	I.	A	Accommodations for a student with a vision impairment include providing audio versions of text and providing the student with large print. In the question it said that the student is not totally blind, so large print may help the students. Choices B, C, and D do not accommodate for this student's disability. Choice B puts the burden on another student to differentiate instruction. Choice C makes the activity easier and lowers the standard. Choice D is not going to help because watching a movie does not help students who are visually impaired.
20.	I.	C	Hearing loss can affect a child's ability to develop communication, language, and social skills. With mild hearing loss, it helps for a student to see the teacher's lips when the teacher is speaking. Therefore, being sure to face the class when speaking will help students with mild hearing loss understand what is being said. Choice A (dyscalculia) affects a person's ability to understand numbers and learn math facts. People with ADHD (choice B) may have trouble paying attention, controlling impulsive behaviors (may act without thinking about what the result will be), or be overly active. People with vision impairment (Choice D) may have trouble seeing the movements of the teacher's lips. Facing the student would not help in any of these cases.
21.	I.	A	The most effective approach a general education teacher can take when accommodating for special education students is to communicate and collaborate with special education teachers. The special education teacher will most likely have a thorough understanding of this student's exceptionality and effective ways to accommodate them. No other answer choice is as effective as answer choice A.
22.	I.	B	Difficulty coordinating visual information with motor skills is also known as dysgraphia, and it affects fine motor skills needed for handwriting, drawing, or other activities requiring hand-eye coordination.

Number	Category	Answer	Explanation
23.	I.	A	Functional Behavioral Assessment (FBA) is a process for identifying problem behaviors and developing interventions to improve or eliminate those behaviors. Providing students with disabilities access to the general curriculum is mandated under the Individuals with Disabilities in Education ACT (IDEA) (choice B). An Individualized Education Program (IEP) is a written statement for each child with a disability that includes individualized measurable goals and supports for the development of the student's special education program (choice C). Free Appropriate Public Education (FAPE) is a principle that means that educational services should be provided to students with disabilities at the public's expense, meaning parents should not have to pay for these services (choice D).
24.	I.	B	An intellectual disability limits a person's ability to learn at an expected level and function in daily life. Levels of intellectual disability vary greatly in children. Children with an intellectual disability might have a hard time letting others know their wants and needs. They also may not be able to take proper care of themselves. Students with intellectual disabilities often need assistance when learning to speak, walk, dress, or eat. Choice A would be more appropriate for a student with autism spectrum disorder (ASD). Choice C is a relevant goal for a student with behavioral disabilities. Choice D is a relevant goal for a student with ADHD.
25.	I.	B, C, D	Students with cerebral palsy benefit from a classroom environment that prioritizes physical accessibility, individualized instruction, and the use of assistive technology, such as a speech-generating device. Students with autism spectrum disorder (ASD) need a highly structured environment with predictable routines to minimize disruptive and distractive behaviors (choice A). Students with dyslexia, which affects reading and related language-based processing skills, would benefit most from color coded text (choice E).
26.	I.	C	Occupational therapists help students learn skills that will help them in the real world or everyday activities (functional skills). An intellectual disability (choice C) limits a person's ability to learn at an expected level and function in daily life. A student with behavioral issues (choice A) would benefit from interventions with a school psychologist. A student with cerebral palsy (choice B) would benefit from a physical therapy. A student with dyscalculia (choice D) would benefit from intensive math support.

Number	Category	Answer	Explanation
27.	I.	D	Self-advocacy is speaking up for oneself and expressing needs and wants. This is very important in special education because as students get older, they will have to express their needs for accommodations so they can thrive. Choice A is when students feel they are equipped to meet teacher expectations. Choice B is a feeling of pride in oneself. Choice C is a technique where a person is exposed to small doses of an anxiety-inducing stimulus alongside of a relaxation technique.
28.	I.	C, D, E	Choice C is a type of augmentative communication. Choice D is a type of assistive technology. Choice E is a type of functional curriculum. All three are associated with students who have severe disabilities. Choice A is not an appropriate support for students with severe disabilities. Choice B is a support designed to aid English language learners.
29.	I.	A	Attention-deficit/hyperactivity disorder (ADHD) is characterized by difficulty focusing, and frequent breaks (choice A) are an accommodation for students who cannot concentrate for long periods of time.
30.	I.	B	A language-based learning disability, such as dyslexia, affects reading and related language-based processing skills. This student has trouble expressing himself during reading activities. Expressive and receptive vocabulary are both language skills. Choice A (dysgraphia) affects a person's handwriting ability and fine motor skills. Choice C affects the ability to interpret nonverbal cues like facial expressions or body language and may cause poor coordination. Choice D is not a type of learning disability.
31.	I.	B	The Expanded Core Curriculum (ECC) is a framework developed to address the unique educational needs of students with visual impairments or blindness. Traditional academic curricula may not sufficiently cover the essential skills necessary for individuals with visual impairments to thrive in various aspects of life. The ECC was designed to supplement the general curriculum and focus on specific areas that are crucial for the overall development and independence of students with visual impairments.

Number	Category	Answer	Explanation
32.	I.	C	The ecological perspective emphasizes the importance of interactions between the child and the child's environment. Promoting inclusion and providing exposure to diverse social environments is often considered beneficial for children with autism. Encouraging interaction with peers and the broader community helps enhance social skills, communication, and overall well-being. Choice B promotes isolation, which is the opposite of the ecological perspective. While genetics (choice A) play a role in the development of ASD, they are not necessarily the primary factor. Research suggests that a combination of genetic predisposition and various environmental influences contribute to the risk of developing ASD. There is no evidence to support that dietary interventions (choice D) can prevent ASD.
33.	II.	D	Chunking the material into small sections is most appropriate for students who have memory problems, difficulty paying attention, impulsiveness, poor organizational skills, and difficulty reasoning abstractly. Choices A and B are better suited for a student with ADHD. Choice C is better suited for a student with vision impairment.
34.	II.	C	When lesson planning for special education, use backward design. The correct order is: start with the standards, choose the assessments, plan the lessons and activities, monitor the students' progress at key intervals, and adjust short-term objectives accordingly.
35.	II.	B	Horizontal alignment is when content areas are aligned. Effective educators can be sure lessons are horizontally aligned by collaborating with other teachers in professional learning communities (PLCs), researching other content areas that relate to the content being taught, and looking for connections where curriculum can support other content areas. Vertical alignment (choice A) occurs then one skill or grade level builds to the next. Answers C and D are nonsense answers.
36.	II.	A, C, D	Learning objectives are the behaviors or skills students are expected to acquire in a lesson. Objectives contain three main components. 1. The skill or behavior to be performed. 2. The conditions under which the students will perform the skill or behavior. 3. The criteria used to measure the objective. Choice B and E are important aspects of instruction but are not part of the objective.

Number	Category	Answer	Explanation
37.	II.	B	SMART stands for specific, measurable, achievable, relevant, and timely. Choice B contains a specific statement, shows measured progress (four out of five), has a targeted time frame, and shows measured progress (four out of five). It can be inferred that it is also relevant to the student and within the student's abilities. Choice A does not have a way to measure progress using data. Choice C is missing many of the SMART criteria. Choice D contains everything except a clear timeframe.
38.	II.	C	Choice C is the best example of station teaching. In this approach, there is an instructor at each center or station. This promotes small group and individualized instruction for specific skills. While choice A describes a common classroom centers approach, station teaching requires that there be an instructor at each center or station. Choice B describes the one teach, one assist approach, a method where one teacher has the responsibility to deliver main instruction while the other teacher walks around the room and assists. Choice D describes the one teach, one observes method, which is often used for data collection. In this approach, the main teacher instructs the lesson, and the other teacher observes students and collects formative data.
39.	II.	A	Positive Behavioral Interventions and Supports (PBIS) is an evidence-based, three-tiered framework for improving and integrating all the data, systems, and practices affecting student outcomes every day. Tier 3 supports are the most intensive supports the school offers due to the individualized approach of developing and carrying out interventions. At this level, schools typically rely on formal assessments to determine a student's need and to develop an individualized support plan. Student plans often include goals related to both academics as well as behavior support. While observation (choice B) is an important first step in managing student behavior, it is the most important part of tier 3 interventions. Choice C, developing an IEP (Individualized Education Plan), would occur after formal assessment and PBIS. A student portfolio (choice D) is a compilation of academic work and other forms of educational evidence. While it is an important part of tracking students' progress, it is not the correct answer.
40.	II.	B	The teacher is using a system of rewards when the student exhibits a desired behavior. This aligns with classroom management focused on behaviorism. Cognitivism is focused on how the brain works. Social learning theory focuses on how students interact with one another. And constructivism is a learning theory that posits students must engage in the learning to get the most benefits out of the learning.

Number	Category	Answer	Explanation
41.	II.	D, E	Routines and procedures help students understand exactly what is expected every day. In addition, routines provide all students, not just special education students, with stability they crave in the learning environment. Procedures must be practiced repeatedly so students are able to execute procedures for each activity. Procedures should be in place before any teaching or learning occurs. While including students in their own learning is important, procedures are a part of the classroom experience that should be managed and set by the teacher. While it could become necessary later to communicate procedures to parents (for example, if a student is having a hard time following them), it is not a key aspect of initial procedure setup. While classroom accommodations and modifications are sometimes necessary, students would ideally be given the same initial procedures to follow.
42.	II.	B	Parallel Teaching is a method involving two teachers who divide the class in half and teach the same thing to each respective half of the class. Team teaching (choice A) is a method involving two teachers in front of the class sharing the responsibility of whole-group instruction. Co-teaching (choice C) is the practice of pairing teachers together in a classroom to share the responsibilities of planning, instructing, and assessing students. Alternative Teaching (choice D) is a co-teaching model where one teacher works with a small group of students as the other teacher instructs the large group.
43.	II.	A	When students have a hard time with long pieces of text, chunking is usually the best accommodation. Choice B, evidence-based discussion, is when students use examples in the text to support their claims. Reading response journals, choice C, are helpful to encourage students to personally reflect on what they read. This may be helpful for students with ASD who struggle to make personal connections but is not the best accommodation for this student who struggles with lengthy text. Finally, Jigsaw is a whole-group activity and would not be the best approach to differentiate instruction for one student.
44.	II.	A	Latency is the amount of time between behaviors. Duration (choice B) is how long the behavior goes on for. Intensity (choice C) is the strength or concentration of the behavior. The number of times a behavior occurs is the frequency (choice D). Because the teacher is measuring the time in between outbursts, the teacher is determining the latency.

Number	Category	Answer	Explanation
45.	II.	D	While external rewards do work in the short-term, intrinsic rewards (such as students feeling more competent or autonomous) are much more sustainable and yield better results. If you are constantly rewarding good behavior with toys, students will eventually tire of the toys. However, if students feel fulfilled when they exhibit positive behavior, they are more likely to continue that behavior.
46.	II.	D	Using a democratic approach to classroom management is very effective. This means that the teacher involves the students in setting expectations for the class (choice D). Students are more likely to meet expectations they help put in place rather than ones imposed on them top down. Choices A and B do not involve student buy-in or involvement in setting expectations. Choice C focuses on providing external rewards instead of developing intrinsic motivation.
47.	II.	C	Rewards and consequences should be given immediately after the behavior. Otherwise, the effect of the reward or consequence is lost. Choice A is incorrect because students may have different rewards and consequences based off their personalized IEPs. Using positivity to encourage good behaviors is encouraged over a more punitive system (choice B). While it is important to stimulate students' motivation and self-determination, it is not as crucial to the success of this system as is choice C.
48.	II.	D	Cognitivism focuses on intellectual growth and how students learn. This could involve asking students to track their reading progress in a data folder or reflective journaling mentioned in this scenario. Social Learning (choice A) asserts that new behaviors can be acquired by observing and imitating others. Behaviorism (choice B) studies student behavior as a response to stimuli (rewards and consequences). The Zone of Proximal Development (ZPD) (choice C) is the distance between the actual developmental level as determined by independent problem-solving and the level of potential development as determined through problem-solving under adult guidance or in collaboration with more capable peers. This is not related to journaling.

Number	Category	Answer	Explanation
49.	II.	A & B	Accommodations are changes to teaching or testing that remove barriers and provide equal access to learning. Unlike a modification, it doesn't change what a child is learning. It changes how a child is learning. Audio versions of the reading material and visual aids, such as a graphic organizer, can assist students in processing and understanding the content without altering the learning objectives. Choices C and D describe modifications, which are changes to the curriculum and content itself. This involves adjusting the educational expectations and standards to align with the student's individual abilities and learning needs.
50.	II.	B	A non-verbal learning disability affects the ability to interpret nonverbal cues like facial expressions or body language and may cause poor coordination. Therefore, choice B would be most helpful and most likely to appear on the student's IEP.
51.	II.	B, D, E	Task analysis provides consistent, individualized, and systematic instruction for a student's success. It involves instruction that is provided in steps that are easily achievable and that promote student success. Forward chaining, backward chaining, discrete trial instruction, and modeling are all techniques that are most used in task analysis. Relatedness, or making learning relatable and applicable to the real world (choice A) is rooted in inquiry-based learning, which often connects classroom activities to real-world applications. This encourages students to pose questions, investigate, and construct their own understanding, which may not align with the more prescriptive nature of traditional task analysis. While kinesthetic learning (choice C) is recognized as an effective technique for some students, task analysis typically relies on more explicit and communicable methods for breaking down tasks.
52.	II.	A	Response cost is a technique that involves the loss of privileges tied to the occurrence of a specific, observable behavior. Response cost is a behavioral intervention technique used in Applied Behavior Analysis (ABA) therapy to reduce undesirable behaviors and promote positive behavior change in children with autism spectrum disorder (ASD). ABA therapy focuses on using behavioral principles to teach and reinforce desired behaviors while reducing challenging behaviors. Choice A is the only answer choice that executes this intervention.

Number	Category	Answer	Explanation
53.	II.	D	An Individualized Family Service Plan (IFSP) is developed for infants and toddlers (ages birth to three) who have been identified with developmental delays or disabilities. The primary focus is on early intervention services and support for the child's family. Choice D is the only answer choice that mentions family and the infant and toddler stage. None of the other answer choices mention family or the infant or toddler stage of development.
54.	II.	C	Students with autism spectrum disorder (ASD) are often sensitive to loud noises or bright lights. Therefore, choice C would be the best equipment to help them stay calm during a drill. Choice A might exacerbate anxiety during an already stressful situation, potentially leading to increased agitation or difficulty following instructions. Choice B is a form of extrinsic motivation that is most helpful when a student is performing tasks in class. Choice D would be most helpful for a student with cerebral palsy or another disability that affects mobility.
55.	II.	B	The teacher is using a metacognitive approach, which teaches students to think about their thinking and plan, monitor, evaluate, and make changes to their own learning behaviors. Choice A involves students working together in small groups to complete tasks, analyze text, work in labs, etc. The students oversee their learning in this method, and the teacher is a facilitator. Choice C involves identifying the most effective instructional strategies for children who differ on any number of variables believed to be related to academic learning. This requires teachers to analyze formative and summative data and apply particular methods and interventions to meet the needs of a particular student. Choice D is a teacher-directed method that involves the teacher standing in front of the room giving directions or modeling a lesson. This is usually done as a whole-group activity.

Number	Category	Answer	Explanation
56.	II.	A	When teachers use a multiple modality approach, they provide diverse presentations and experiences of the content so that students use different senses and different skills during a single lesson. Often multiple modalities address different learning preferences. In choice A, the teacher is incorporating instruction for both visual and kinesthetic learning styles. Choice B is an example of the metacognitive approach, which teaches students to think about their thinking and plan, monitor, evaluate and make changes to their own learning behaviors. Choice C is an example of direct instruction, which involves the teacher standing in front of the room giving directions or modeling a lesson. Choice D is an example of cooperative learning, where students work together in small groups to complete tasks, analyze text, work in labs, etc.
57.	II.	B	Interest grouping is a type of heterogenous grouping because students with the same interests will have varying levels of academic ability. For example, a high achieving student and a low achieving student may both enjoy football statistics. By grouping them based on interest rather than ability level diversifies the group. Heterogeneous grouping focuses on diversity within the group. The approach in this scenario not only brings together students with diverse mathematical abilities but also allows them to apply mathematical concepts in contexts that align with their personal interests, promoting engagement and a deeper understanding of the subject. Choices A and C groups students together who have the same skill level or who have the same needs. Choice D is a not a type of grouping.

<table>
<tr><th>Number</th><th>Category</th><th>Answer</th><th>Explanation</th></tr>
<tr><td>58.</td><td>II.</td><td colspan="2">
<table>
<tr><th></th><th>Experiential and virtual</th><th>Independent</th><th>Indirect</th><th>Direct</th><th>Interactive</th></tr>
<tr><td>Modeling learning behaviors such as revising a piece of writing using a document camera.</td><td></td><td></td><td></td><td>X</td><td></td></tr>
<tr><td>Students participate in a virtual lab.</td><td>X</td><td></td><td></td><td></td><td></td></tr>
<tr><td>Students choose a topic within a class theme of study.</td><td></td><td>X</td><td></td><td></td><td></td></tr>
<tr><td>Whole group math games practicing skip counting, place value, and number fluency.</td><td></td><td></td><td>X</td><td></td><td></td></tr>
<tr><td>Guided reading in cooperative groups.</td><td></td><td></td><td></td><td></td><td>X</td></tr>
</table>
</td></tr>
<tr><td>59.</td><td>II.</td><td>D</td><td>Maintenance strategies are those that reinforce practice of a skill that students have previously learned. Maintenance helps them retain the skill. Students with learning disabilities require lots of maintenance activities.

Generalization strategies (choice A) are those that help students perform a skill in a variety of settings and situations. This is sometimes referred to as transfer because students can transfer the skill from one activity to another. Differentiation (choice B) aims to meet the individual needs of students by tailoring teaching methods, content, and assessment to accommodate diverse learning styles, abilities, and interests. Modifications (choice C) are changes to the curriculum and learning environment in accordance with a student's IEP. Modifications change the expectations for learning and the level of assessment.</td></tr>
</table>

Number	Category	Answer	Explanation
60.	II.	C	Interventions are used for special education and general education students to meet the needs of every student. They are used to teach the skills kids need to improve a specific area of weakness. Once those skills are gained, interventions are removed. Supplementary curriculum and aids are services and other supports that are provided in regular education classes, other education-related settings, and in extracurricular and nonacademic settings, to enable children with disabilities to be educated with nondisabled children to the maximum extent appropriate. Modifications (choice B) are changes to the curriculum and learning environment in accordance to a student's IEP. Modifications change the expectations for learning and the level of assessment. They remain consistent unless a change is made to the IEP. ...ice D) are formal changes that remove ...dent's disability. Students with an ...on Program (IEP) or a 504 plan have formal ...ded in their plans. They may or may not ...supports throughout their school years.
61.			...is about skills students need to live an ...de of school. Content is selected based ...ded for functioning in current and future ...residential, and vocational environments. ...improving a money management skill ...in the real world. ...e focused on classroom education skills.
62.			...helpful for students with intellectual ...ey can record the lesson or lecture and ...ce and skills they might have missed. ...ice A) are most helpful for students who ...isual computer cues (choice B) are most ...o are hearing impaired. Speech-to-text ...ognition can be helpful for students who ...r hands.

Number	Category	Answer	Explanation
63.	II.	A	Describing accommodations or modifications (choice A) is an aspect of an IEP (Individualized Education Plan) but is not part of the ITP section. The individualized transition plan (ITP) is a section of the IEP that outlines transition goals and services for students with disabilities. The ITP is the template for mapping out short-term to long-term adult outcomes from which annual goals and objectives are defined. The ITP outlines goals for students to work toward that will help them move from high school to postsecondary school and career. An ITP must also describe activities demonstrating use of various strategies, community and adult living experiences.
64.	II.	C	Choice C describes appropriate activities that demonstrate use of various strategies to improve the student's social skills. Also, this answer choice includes role-play, which is an effective approach when working with students with ASD. While choice A is an appropriate goal for a student with ASD, it is more of a short-term goal that would be addressed in an IEP, not a goal for the student to work toward that will help them move from high school to postsecondary school and career (a focus of an ITP). Choice B would be a better ITP goal for a student with a learning disability. Choice D would be a better ITP goal for a student with ADHD.
65.	II.	B	Positive behavioral interventions and support (PBIS) is a set of research-based strategies used to increase quality of life and decrease problem behavior by teaching new skills and making changes in a person's environment. It focuses on the good behaviors and works to eliminate or reduce the bad behaviors.
66.	II.	C	Choice C is correct because special education teachers can use information from multiple assessments to inform their instructional decisions and provide constructive feedback. By analyzing errors and response patterns across various assessments, teachers can identify specific areas where a learner struggles. This allows for targeted instruction that focuses on those identified skills or knowledge gaps. While choices B and D are all helpful strategies, choice C is the best for proving targeted instruction. Choice A is not ideal because while peer support is a valuable strategy for enhancing learning, it is crucial that it is not used as a substitute for direct teacher intervention when a student is struggling.

Number	Category	Answer	Explanation
67.	II.	B	Deficits in memory in special education refer to challenges with the ability to encode, store, and retrieve information. Long-term memory typically manifests as difficulty in storing and retrieving information over longer periods. This might involve struggles in recalling facts, events, or procedures learned in the past. Teaching categorization, association, and visualization techniques is a helpful memory improvement strategy. Proprioceptive and vestibular perception (choice A) involves difficulties in understanding the position and movement of the body, which can affect balance, coordination, and the ability to navigate through space. Conceptual comprehension (choice C) involves trouble grasping abstract concepts, such as time, quantity, or theoretical ideas, which can impact learning in subjects like math and science. Auditory perception (choice D) involves challenges in processing and making sense of auditory information. This can involve problems in distinguishing between sounds, understanding spoken language, or difficulty in filtering out background noise.
68.	II.	D	The Zone of Proximal Development (ZPD) is a term coined by psychologist Lev Vygotsky. It relates to the difference between what a learner can do without help and what they can achieve with guidance and encouragement from a skilled partner. Instructional scaffolding is an educational technique that supports students' learning by providing temporary and adjustable assistance as they acquire new skills or knowledge. Scaffolding is most effective in the ZPD because it is designed to move students progressively toward stronger understanding and, ultimately, greater independence in the learning process. Choice A focuses on implementing instructional strategies that cater to a range of learning styles and abilities. This might include using visual aids, hands-on activities, or technology-assisted instruction. Choice B uses ongoing formative assessments to track student progress toward their goals. It involves adjusting instruction based on assessment data to address areas of need and reinforce strengths. Choice C involves working with teachers in specific content areas to align strategies and reinforce learning across subjects.

PRACTICE TEST

Number	Category	Answer	Explanation
69.	II.	A, B, E	Implementing UDL in educational settings involves a proactive curriculum design that anticipates potential barriers to learning and incorporates a variety of teaching methods, materials, and assessments to meet the diverse needs of all students. It is about designing learning experiences that are accessible and effective for everyone, regardless of ability, disability, age, gender, or cultural and linguistic background. UDL is rooted in three primary principles (what, how, and why). Choice A describes implementation of multiple means of representation (the "what" of learning). This principle emphasizes presenting information and content in various ways to address the diverse needs of learners. Choice B describes implementation of multiple means of action and expression (the "how" of learning). This principle allows learners various ways to express their knowledge. Choice E describes implementation of multiple means of engagement (the "why" of learning). This principle addresses the importance of motivating students. Discussing relatedness to real-world scenarios increases intrinsic motivation. Choices C and D do not focus on either of these three principles.
70.	II.	A, B, C, D, E	Developing culturally responsive transition plans and services in special education is essential for preparing students with disabilities for postsecondary education, vocational education, integrated employment, and independent living. Each answer choice is a specific way that special education teachers can ensure they are using culturally responsive practices.
71.	III.	C	The purpose of the PLAAFP is to identify the type and amount of special education a student receives. The PLAAFP must include a statement of the child's present levels of academic achievement and functional performance, including how the disability impacts the individual's involvement and progress in the general education curriculum or participation in age-appropriate activities. The PLAAFP is a key part of the Individualized Education Program (IEP). The very first PLAAFP for students describes students' skills and abilities based on his initial special education evaluation. Choice A is the purpose of the Behavior Assessment System for Children (BASC) or Vineland Adaptive Behavior Scale. Choice B is the purpose of the Functionality: School Function Assessment (SFA). Choice D is the purpose of the Functional Behavioral Assessment (FBA).

PRACTICE TEST

Number	Category	Answer	Explanation
72.	III.	A	This test evaluates three areas: participation, task support, and activity performance. The occupational therapist (OT) administers this assessment, and it is used for students in kindergarten through grade 6. It addresses not only classroom access but also playground, lunch, physical education, and other school areas. Choices B, C, and D are not areas assessed by this assessment.
73.	III.	B	The Wechsler Intelligence Scale for Children (WISC) is a type of IQ test that compares student performances. A score between 70-79 is considered very low. Students who test in this range may have a learning disability (choice B) and should review their subtest scores to identify specific areas of cognitive weakness. The classification of severe intellectual disability (choice A) is determined primarily based on a score of 20-30. An average score (choice C) ranges between 90-109 on the WISC. The WISC score is not used to assess whether a student has a developmental delay (choice D).
74.	III.	D	Formative assessments are usually referred to as informal assessments because they are flexible and can be adapted to fit the specific context of the classroom. These assessments are typically observational and are used to gather information about a student's learning process, strengths, and areas needing improvement. Informal assessments include teacher observations, classwork, homework assignments, and discussions. This type of assessment is often integrated into the learning process, providing immediate feedback that can be used to adjust teaching strategies and address students' needs in real time.
75.	III.	C	A performance-based assessment measures students' ability to apply the skills and knowledge learned from a unit or units of study. The task challenges students to use their higher-order, critical thinking skills to create a product or complete a process. Choice A is an example of a portfolio, a purposeful collection of student work that has been selected and organized to show student learning progress over time. Choice B is an example of a summative assessment, which focuses on outcomes and is frequently used to measure the effectiveness of a program, lesson, or strategy. Choice D is an example of a diagnostic assessment, a pre-assessment providing instructors with information about students' prior knowledge, preconceptions, and misconceptions before beginning a learning activity.

Number	Category	Answer	Explanation
76.	III.	B, C, D & E	Goal setting is one of the most important aspects of the IEP meeting. In fact, the entire IEP is centered around the goals that the team, which includes the student, establishes. Interpreting assessment data for all stakeholders means that scores and notes from teachers are discussed, and all team members understand them. This is also an important part of the IEP meeting. Making data comprehensible for the student is also imperative because the student is the most important member of the IEP team and needs to understand what the data indicates. Finally, if the student or student's family speaks a language other than English, it is the responsibility of the school to make sure that they provide language accessibility so the student and parents understand everything that happens in the meeting. The only answer that is not a key aspect of the IEP meeting is choice A, critical feedback.
77.	III.	D	Modifying an assessment refers to altering the content, format, or complexity of assessments based on the specifications in a student's Individualized Education Program (IEP). Using simplified language, reducing the complexity of tasks, or providing alternate assessment forms are all examples of this. Choice A lists examples of accommodating assessments for individuals with exceptionalities. Choice B lists examples of digital technology tools that offer more engaging, diverse, and accessible learning experiences for students with special needs. Choice C lists examples of error analysis and progress-monitoring tools: Error analysis helps in identifying specific areas where students struggle, allowing for targeted interventions, while progress-monitoring tools are used for tracking student improvement over time.
78.	III.	D	Criterion-referenced assessments are formal, summative assessments because they measure outcomes. In addition, they are structured and standardized evaluations that measure a student's performance against a specific set of criteria or standards. These assessments are typically administered under controlled conditions and are scored in a standardized manner. Formal assessments are often used to determine a student's mastery of content, to place students in appropriate educational settings, and to evaluate the effectiveness of educational programs. Examples include statewide achievement tests, standardized tests, and final exams. Diagnostic, formative, and portfolio assessments are considered informal assessments and are developed and used by the teacher to monitor progress and make instructional decisions.

Number	Category	Answer	Explanation
79.	III.	B	A portfolio is a purposeful collection of student work that has been selected and organized to show student learning progress over time. Portfolios can contain samples of student work as well as self-evaluations/reflections.
80.	III.	A	Criterion-referenced tests measure student performance against a fixed set of predetermined criteria or learning standards. The most common criterion-reference exams are state standardized assessments. Choice B sets an expectation of the assignment or project that students are graded against. Choice C would most likely be a performance-based assessment. Choice D is a type of quick formative assessment.
81.	III.	B	A norm-referenced assessment yields an estimate of the position of the tested individual in a predefined population with respect to the trait being measured. Norm-referenced assessments compare student performances as a percentile ranking. Choice A is called screening. Students are typically screened throughout the year to determine at what level they are reading. Choice C is an example of a criterion-referenced assessment. Choice D is an example of a diagnostic assessment.
82.	III.	B	A screening assessment is used to place students in appropriate classrooms or grade level. Students are typically screened throughout the year to determine at what level they are reading.
83.	III.	D	A summative assessment focuses on outcomes. It is frequently used to measure the effectiveness of a program, lesson, or strategy. Summative are usually given after a lesson or unit to measure outcomes of the teaching and learning that took place during that unit of study. Choice A is most likely a diagnostic assessment given at the beginning of the year. Choice B is an unlikely scenario for an assessment. Choice C would most likely be an informal formative assessment such as an exit ticket.
84.	III.	D	A rubric is an assessment tool used to measure a student's performance. Rubrics should be given to students before, during, and after the assignment or task. For example, before starting a research paper, the teacher should go over the rubric with students to set expectations and communicate what students must include in the paper. During the writing process, students should use the rubric to be sure they are meeting expectations. Once students complete the research paper, the teacher should use the rubric to score the papers and provide specific and meaningful feedback.

Number	Category	Answer	Explanation
85.	III.	A	Choice A is the nest answer because the question states that the teacher wants to measure effectiveness. Therefore, summative assessment should be one of the assessments used. Measuring effectiveness is measuring outcomes, and summative assessments focus on outcomes. Also, administering formative assessments would help the teacher determine where to implement interventions when needed.
86.	III.	C	Results for norm-referenced tests, an assessment or evaluation that yields an estimate of the position of the tested individual in a predefined population with respect to the trait being measured, are usually communicated as a percentile ranking. A percentile rank tells how well a student performed in comparison to other students who took the same test. The percentile rank value is the percent of students the test taker scored better than on the assessment. A percentile rank of 73 means the student scored better than 73 percent of all the students who took the assessment. The percentile rank does not reflect how well an individual student scored or what they know. It simply compares a student to a much larger group of students to see how their performances compare.
87.	III.	D	Stanine A stanine is a scaled score that is based on a nine-point scale. This simplified scale is a way to easily group students from the lowest performers to the top performers. Stanines are another way to compare groups of students, such as percentile ranks and other types of scaled scores. Choice A is an example of a percentage. Choice B is an example of a raw score. Choice C is an example of percentile ranking.
88.	III.	D	A raw score is the number of questions a student gets correct on the exam. Raw scores are helpful in determining specific academic strengths and weaknesses.
89.	III.	B	School psychologists conduct cognitive assessments that measure a student's intellectual abilities. They are usually the first professionals to evaluate students for special education. A Functional Behavioral Assessment (FBA) is a process for identifying problem behaviors and developing interventions to improve or eliminate those behaviors. For example, a school psychologist may conduct a functional behavior assessment and find that the student uses profanity or pushes other students when lining up for lunch.

Number	Category	Answer	Explanation
90.	III.	B	A percentage is based out of 100 and can translate into how many problems a student answered or did not answer correctly. So if the student got 4 out of 10 correct, their percentage correct is 40 percent.
91.	III.	A	The Behavior Assessment System for Children (BASC) or Vineland Adaptive Behavior Scale measures behavior and mental health, including how students see themselves as well as how parents and school staff see the students. These evaluations do not offer a diagnosis but instead look at life skills, social skills, social concerns, and attention. This assessment may help identify mental-health concerns and/or behavioral issues. Choice B measures cognitive abilities, scholastic aptitudes, and achievement and is used to determine if a student has a learning disability. Choice C is a process for identifying problem behaviors and developing interventions to improve or eliminate those behaviors. The student is not exhibiting disruptive behaviors in this scenario. Choice D measures a student's functionality in all areas of the school environment, including participation, task support, and activity performance. It may be helpful for a student exhibiting the same behaviors as Sarah, but it is usually used for students in kindergarten through grade 6, not high school. The BASC is administered to children up to 21 years, 11 months of age.
92.	III.	D	A School Function Assessment (SFA) measures a student's functionality in all areas of the school environment. The occupational therapist (OT) administers this assessment because an OT is the professional who helps students with functional skills. .
93.	III.	C	The Woodcock-Johnson Psycho-Educational Battery, Third Edition provides a comprehensive set of individually administered tests to measure cognitive abilities, scholastic aptitudes, and achievement. This assessment is used to determine if a student has a learning disability. Choice A is typically used to identify the type and amount of special education a student receives. Choice B (also known as Behavior Assessment System for Children (BASC)), measures behavior and mental health. Choice D focuses on identifying problem behaviors and developing interventions.
94.	III.	B	A functional behavior assessment (FBA) is a process for identifying problem behaviors and developing interventions to improve or eliminate those behaviors. You may be tempted to choose answer D. However, answer D aligns with a functional skills assessment. This scenario is a functional behavior assessment.

Number	Category	Answer	Explanation
95.	III.	B	Speech-to-text, voice recognition, or oral response can be helpful for students who do not have use of their hands. This way the student can demonstrate their learning without having to use their hands to write. A good testing accommodation for choice A might be allowing for frequent breaks. A good modification for choice C might be simplifying the language on the test. A good accommodation for Choice D might be reading the answer options aloud.
96.	III.	B	The School Function Assessment (SFA)is administered to students grades K-6, and it measures a student's functionality in all areas of the school environment. It evaluates three areas: participation, task support, and activity performance.
97.	III.	A	Before the teacher can accurately determine the student's deficit, the teacher needs the student to answer more questions. Allowing the student more time will help the teacher understand the student's skill level. For example, the student may have gotten 10 more questions correct if given extra time. This data would indicate the student has the skill necessary.
98.	IV.	C	The IDEA requires that children with disabilities, including children in public or private institutions or other care facilities, be educated with children who are not disabled. This is referred to as least restrictive environment (LRE). Choice A is IDEA's IEP (Individualized Education Plan) principle. Choice B is IDEA's Appropriate Evaluation principle. Choice D is IDEA's Procedural Safeguards principle.
99.	IV.	C	Free appropriate public education (FAPE) means that educational services should be provided to students with disabilities at the public's expense, meaning parents should not have to pay for these services and that these services continue even if a student is expelled. Choice A stands for Individualized Education Plan. Choice B stands for Least Restrictive Environment. Choice D stands for the Individuals with Disabilities Education Act.
100.	IV.	A, C, D	Choices A, B, C, and D are all listed as parental rights under IDEA's Procedural Safeguard principle. While parents have the right to participate in decisions about their child's education, they do not have the authority to dictate the specific teaching methods or strategies employed by the school (choice B). While parents have a right to access their child's educational records, there are certain limitations to confidentiality, especially in cases where information needs to be shared with relevant school personnel for the benefit of the child's education (choice E).

Number	Category	Answer	Explanation
101.	IV.	A	Family Educational Rights and Privacy Act (FERPA) is a federal law that protects the privacy of student education records. The law applies to all schools that receive funds under an applicable program of the US Department of Education. Every Student Succeeds Act (ESSA) upholds critical protections for America's disadvantaged and high-need students and requires that all students in America be taught to high academic standards that will prepare them to succeed in college and careers (choice B). In Race to the Top (RTTT) (choice C), forty-six states and the District of Columbia submitted comprehensive reform plans to compete in the Race to the Top competition. While 19 states have received funding so far, 34 states modified state education laws or policies to facilitate needed change, and 48 states worked together to create a voluntary set of rigorous college- and career-ready standards (The White House, 2018). The Americans with Disabilities Act of 1990 (ADA) (choice D) is a civil rights law that prohibits discrimination based on disability. It provides similar protections against discrimination against Americans with disabilities as the Civil Rights Act of 1964 (US Department of Education, 2015).
102.	IV.	B	Tier 2 is the type of modifications or differentiated instruction some students receive in addition to Tier 1 instruction. The purpose of Tier 2 instruction and supports is to improve student performance under Tier 1 performance expectations. This is also referred to as accommodations. The standards and expectations remain the same as Tier 1. However, accommodations are used for these students to be successful. Tier 1 (choice A) is the type of modifications or differentiated instruction all students get in the form of instruction. Tier 3 (choice C) is the type of modifications or differentiated instruction few students receive and is the most intense service level a school can provide to a student. There is no Tier 4 (choice D).
103.	IV.	C	The Individuals with Disabilities Education Act (IDEA) mandates that schools conduct an annual review of a student's IEP (choice A). Every three years, a comprehensive reevaluation of the student's eligibility for special education services is required under IDEA (choice B). However, an IEP meeting can be called at any time for various reasons, such as concerns about the student's progress, changes in needs, or requests from parents or educators. This is why choice C is the best answer. Choice D is incorrect because IEPs are not set in stone. They can be modified to better serve the student.

Number	Category	Answer	Explanation
104.	IV.	B	The referral process has two steps. During initiation, a formal referral is made when a student continues to struggle despite prereferral interventions. The referral can be made by a teacher, parent, or agency. During documentation, written documentation of the student's academic or behavioral issues, previous interventions, and the student's response to those interventions is submitted.
105.	IV.	D	Choice D is correct. While ADHD is a condition for which a student will get an IEP, it is not on the official IDEA list. ADHD is covered under other health impairment.
106.	IV.	B	Response to intervention (RTI), or MTSS, is a system designed to identify students at risk for poor academic and behavioral outcomes so the school can develop strategies to help the students succeed. During the pre-referral stage, it is essential that teachers use supports and interventions to prevent students who should not be in special education from being erroneously classified as such. Choice A is part of the placement process for special education students. Choice C is part of IDEA's procedural safeguards policy. Choice D is part of IDEA's LRE (Least Restrictive Environment) policy.
107.	IV.	C & D	Choice C and D both describe comprehensible education for ELLs. Grounded in the 14th Amendment and the result of the League of United Latin American Citizens (LULAC) vs. State Board of Education, the Consent Decree protects English language learners (ELL) and their right to a free, comprehensible education. It addresses the civil and academic rights of ELL students and requires instruction to be delivered in a comprehensible manner so ELLs can fully participate. Since 1975, federal law has required that students with disabilities have access to school and a free appropriate public education. Choices A and B are incorrect because while some students who are ELL need special education services and accommodations, not all ELLs need these services. In fact, educators must be careful not to overclassify ELLs as special education because of language deficits.
108.	IV.	A	NCLB has six "titles," including improving the academic achievement of the disadvantaged, preparing, training, and recruiting high-quality teachers and principals, language instruction for limited English proficient and immigrant students, 21st Century Schools, promoting informed parental choice and innovative programs, and flexibility and accountability. It requires states to establish student academic standards as well as an assessment system to ensure that all students are meeting the academic standards. The assessment system must be statewide, and its purpose is to establish an accountability system.

Number	Category	Answer	Explanation
109.	IV.	A, B, C, D, E	According to IDEA, for an IEP to be defensible, the goals outlined in the IEP must be clear, specific, and measurable. Defensible IEPs contain goals, assessments, services, participation, and a transitional plan. More specifically, an IEP must have the following elements to be considered legally defensible. All these elements must be included in a legally defensible IEP, as well as the following: • A description of how the child's progress toward meeting the annual goals will be measured, and when periodic progress reports will be provided. • A statement of the special education and related services and supplementary aids and services to be provided to the child, or on behalf of the child. • A statement of the program modifications or supports for school personnel that will be provided to enable the child to advance appropriately toward attaining the annual goals. • If the IEP team determines that the child must take an alternate assessment instead of a particular regular State or districtwide assessment of student achievement, the IEP must include a statement of why the child cannot participate in the regular assessment and why the particular alternate assessment selected is appropriate for the child.
110.	IV.	D	According to the Individuals with Disabilities Education Act (IDEA), transition planning must start (and finish) by the age of 16 (or younger, if deemed appropriate by the IEP team) and should be tailored to each student's unique needs, strengths, preferences, and interests.
111.	IV.	C	Choice C explains LRE from IDEA. While this principle strives to avoid placement outside the general education classroom, the policy states that "any placement outside the general education classroom must be justified by the child's individual disability-related needs" (choice A). It also states that "funding is never an appropriate reason for a more restrictive placement" (choice B). Finally, it states that "involvement in music, art, physical education, school trips, clubs, extracurricular and other activities must be accommodated" (choice D).
112.	IV.	A, B, D, E	A direct appeal to the school board (choice C) is considered incorrect in the context of procedural protections for parents of special needs students because the typical dispute resolution procedures as stated by IDEA policy involve more formalized and established processes. While expressing concerns to the school board is a valid form of communication, it is not a recognized legal or procedural step in special education dispute resolution.

Number	Category	Answer	Explanation
113.	IV.	A	Part C of IDEA states that children from birth through two years are eligible for early intervention services.
114.	IV.	A	A special education paraprofessional, under general supervision, aids a classroom teacher and assists in the implementation of instructional programs, including self-help and behavior management. They are typically present in the classroom alongside the general education teacher. An occupational therapist (choice B) helps students strengthen their functional skills such as dressing, toileting, and eating. A school psychologist (choice C) administers special education screening and collaborates with stakeholders. A speech and language pathologist (SLP) specializes in communication. SLPs work with students on speech sounds, language, social communication, voice, fluency, and feeding and swallowing. Choices B, C, and D typically use pull-out methods (outside the classroom) to provide interventions to a special needs student.
115.	IV.	D	Physical therapists specialize in mobility, fine motor skills, and gross motor skills, such as those described in choice D. The struggles described in choice A most likely require the services of a school psychologist. The struggles described in choice B most likely require the services of an occupational therapist. The struggles described in choice C most likely require the services of a speech and language pathologist.
116.	IV.	D	A resource room is a special education room where individualized services and instruction are provided to students (making choice B incorrect). It is found outside of the general education classroom (Making choice A incorrect). In a general education school, a resource room is usually found in the regular mainstream school where children with varied exceptionalities are educated (making choice C incorrect).
117.	IV.	C	Deepening professional growth is an ongoing process essential for educators, especially those in special education, where student needs can be highly complex and varied. Collaboration with colleagues, such as other special education teachers, general education teachers, and specialists (like speech therapists or psychologists) can provide new perspectives and insights and space to share expertise. Through collaboration, teachers can learn interdisciplinary strategies and approaches that may be more effective for their students. This also fosters a more cohesive and consistent approach to supporting students across different settings. Choices A, B, and D are key aspects of instruction, but they are not directly related to professional growth.

Number	Category	Answer	Explanation
118.	IV.	B, C	The identification process involves a comprehensive evaluation to determine if the student has a disability and is eligible for special education services. This evaluation is carried out by a multidisciplinary team and may include intellectual, educational, and psychological assessments. Under IDEA (Individuals with Disabilities Education Act), schools must obtain parental consent before conducting these evaluations and must complete the process within a specified time frame. Choice A is a key aspect of the placement process, not the identification process. Choice D is a key part of the referral process, not the identification process.
119.	IV.	B	Some students have limited English proficiency and are also classified as having exceptionalities. However, educators must avoid practices that can misdiagnose a language deficiency as a learning disability. Understanding linguistic limitations for English language learners (ELLs) is crucial when classifying students as special education. Assessments conducted in a language a student is not fully proficient in can yield unreliable results. Understanding linguistic limitations ensures that evaluations for special education eligibility are fair and accurate. This might involve conducting assessments in the student's primary language or using nonverbal assessment methods. Misclassifying an ELL student can lead to lower expectations and less rigorous standards (choice C).
120.	IV.	B	Heterogeneous grouping is correct because Vygotsky's theories stress the fundamental role of social interaction in the development of cognition. He believed strongly that community plays a central role in making meaning. Vygotsky is most widely known for the Zone of Proximal Development (ZPD), which he asserted is the distance between the actual developmental level as determined by independent problem-solving and the level of potential development as determined through problem-solving under adult guidance or in collaboration with more capable peers (Vygotsky, 1978). Helping someone move through the Zone of Proximal Development depends on the following: 1. The presence of a more knowledgeable person 2. Social interactions 3. Scaffolding or supportive activities developed by the educator (ZPD is discussed in more detail below.) Choice A is related to direct instruction practices. Choice C is related to independent instruction. Choice D is a type of assessment that happens at the end of learning to measure outcomes. Social interaction is particularly relevant in special education, where peer modeling and social skills training are key components of comprehensive educational programs. Choice B, where there is diversity within the group, would be most likely to align with the ZPD.

This page intentionally left blank.

Practice Test 2

1. Choose **TWO** of the following questions that would benefit an IEP team concerned with the etiology of a student's disability.

   - ☐ A. What is the origination or causation of the disability?
   - ☐ B. What linguistic processing difficulties does the student have?
   - ☐ C. What environmental factors may have impacted development?
   - ☐ D. What supports are most effective to help the student meet physical milestones?
   - ☐ E. What supports are most effective to help the student meet cognitive milestones?

2. A student is suffering from atypical development in fine motor skills. Which of the following would be an indication of this condition?

   A. The student walks up and down stairs but has difficulty hopping on one foot.

   B. The student jumps on one foot but has difficulty holding a pencil properly.

   C. The student follows directions but has difficulty with social skills.

   D. The student develops social relationships but has a difficult time behaving in class.

3. A fifth-grade special education teacher has a student with emotional behavior disturbance (EBD). One of the student's IEP goals is to use self-regulation during reading time to sit quietly and engage properly in the lesson. Which of the following approaches would be most effective for the teacher to take when helping this student meet the IPE goal?

   A. Have the student sign a behavior contract that outlines proper behavior during reading time. The teacher administers positive and negative consequences throughout the day following the student's positive or negative behaviors.

   B. The teacher establishes and practices routines and procedures for reading time, observes and collects behavior data regularly on the student, and modifies the learning environment to meet the student's needs.

   C. The teacher has a behavior specialist come in and work with the student on positive behavior supports, allows the student to sit out of reading time when negative behaviors persist, and uses a system of rewards when the student exhibits positive behaviors.

   D. The teacher meets with the student one on one frequently, calls home to report any negative behaviors, and administers a system of rewards when the student exhibits positive behaviors during reading time.

4. A seventh-grade student in a self-contained special education classroom works on time management to reduce frustration and promote independence. Which of the following methods would benefit this student most?

   A. Independent study

   B. Frequent brain breaks

   C. Frequency modulation system

   D. Executive functioning support

5. A fourth-grade general education teacher has several students who have IEPs. The teacher wants to be sure she is meeting the needs of these students. Which of the following would be most effective in achieving this objective?

   A. Collaborate with multidisciplinary teams to determine the least restrictive environment for each student.

   B. Regularly call home and communicate with parents about progress and opportunities for improvement.

   C. Allow the students to be educated in self-contained classrooms rather than the general environment.

   D. Encourage students to work in the general education classroom without accommodations so they can succeed.

6. Which of the following are characteristics of autism spectrum disorder (ASD)? Choose **ALL** that apply.

   ☐ A. Seizures

   ☐ B. Sensory processing disorders

   ☐ C. Neurodevelopmental disorders

   ☐ D. Metabolic disorders

   ☐ E. Traumatic brain injuries

7. A student with autism spectrum disorder (ASD) acts out and becomes overwhelmed when a teacher is going over multi-step processes. Which of the following approaches would be most effective for differentiating for this student?

   A. Allow the student to follow just one or two steps first and then integrate more steps as the student becomes comfortable.

   B. Have the student work with a peer buddy who can demonstrate the steps for the student with ASD.

   C. Provide the student with a visual checklist of the steps of the processes and encourage the student to check off each step once accomplished.

   D. Ask the school occupational therapist to come in and work with the student individually until the student can join the rest of the class.

8. A special education teacher works with students with emotional behavior disturbance (EBD) on self-regulatory behavior. Which of the following approaches would be most effective? Choose **ALL** that apply.

   ☐ A. Encourage regular cooperative learning so students can learn how to interact socially with one another.

   ☐ B. Establish a system of consistent rewards and consequences for good and bad behavior.

   ☐ C. Teach deep breathing, guided imagery, or meditation to help students manage stress and focus.

   ☐ D. Model appropriate behavior, emotional responses, and problem-solving in real time for students to emulate.

   ☐ E. Establish predictable routines and schedules to provide stability and reduce anxiety.

9. Lilly, a sixth-grade student in general education, has an IEP to help teachers differentiate for her exceptionality, dyslexia. Lilly's exceptionality would fall under what type of processing disorder?

   A. Specific learning disability (SLD)

   B. Sensory impairment

   C. Emotional behavior disturbance (EBD)

   D. Intellectual disability

10. Which of the following accurately describes the full inclusion model?

   A. A student with disabilities participates in the same programs and classes as their peers without disabilities, receiving the necessary support within that setting, such as an aide or specialized instructional strategies.

   B. A student spends part of the day in a general education class and part of the day receiving more intensive instruction in a small group setting outside the general classroom, such as a resource room.

   C. A student spends most of the day in special classes with a lower student-to-teacher ratio.

   D. A student attends a specialized school equipped to handle more significant needs that cannot be appropriately met in a traditional school setting.

11. A tenth-grade student with an intellectual disability works with her teacher on functional skills. Which of the following might the student be working on?

   A. Phonics and decoding while reading

   B. Hygiene, using the microwave, and filling out a job application

   C. Self-regulation during the school day to avoid behavior outbursts

   D. Fine motor skills during writing activities

12. Which of the following would be considered a language processing or linguistic exceptionality?

   A. A student requires adaptive equipment and therapies to achieve different levels of mobility and dexterity.

   B. A student has trouble in problem-solving, memory, attention, and the understanding of concepts like cause-and-effect, time, and numbers.

   C. A student experiences difficulties in self-regulation and often disrupts class during reading instruction.

   D. A student experiences delayed speech onset, has a limited vocabulary, struggles with grammar, or uses alternative communication methods.

13. During an IEP meeting, a teacher discusses environmental factors that may affect the special education student. Which of the following would be considered an environmental factor?

   A. Neurochemical imbalances

   B. Socioeconomic status

   C. Metabolic disorders

   D. Genetic disorders

PRACTICE TEST

14. A special education student has difficulty forming and maintaining relationships, responding appropriately to social cues, and expressing or regulating emotions. The student has a(n):

    A. Social/emotional disorder

    B. Language disorder

    C. Environmental disorder

    D. Cognitive disorder

15. What activities can a special education teacher integrate daily to help her students with ADHD?

    A. After whole-group instruction and before transitioning to cooperative groups, students take a five-minute brain break, where they get up and walk around the room, stretch their bodies, and talk with their friends.

    B. Before getting into cooperative groups, students create narratives that describe social situations and appropriate responses to help students navigate interpersonal interactions.

    C. During whole-group instruction, a paraprofessional supports students' cognitive activities that help break down complex information.

    D. Throughout the day, students engage in activities they will need to master to live independently after they graduate.

16. A teacher is reviewing a behavior plan with a student in a special education class. This activity is most effective for:

    A. Neurodevelopmental disorders

    B. Brain injuries

    C. Self-regulation

    D. Comorbid conditions

17. A student is experiencing an intellectual disability, anxiety, and depression. This student is displaying:

    A. Neurodevelopmental disorder

    B. Cognitive disorder

    C. Emotional behavior disturbance (EBD)

    D. Comorbid/cooccurring conditions

18. Conditions like depression, anxiety, and bipolar disorder involve imbalances in brain chemicals and can significantly affect mood, energy levels, concentration, and motivation. These are considered which type of biological factor?

    A. Sensory processing disorders

    B. Neurochemical imbalances

    C. Hormonal imbalances

    D. Metabolic disorders

19. This is an adaptive assistive listening device that enhances the auditory reception of sounds for individuals with hearing impairments, particularly in educational settings.

    A. Sensory implant
    B. Frequency modulation (FM) system
    C. Adaptive keyboard
    D. Self-regulation checklist

20. A teacher considers the complex interplay between a child with exceptionalities and their environment and that a child's development and learning are influenced not only by their individual characteristics but also by the systems and contexts they are part of, such as family, school, community, and society. This teacher is considering:

    A. The least restrictive environment
    B. The adaptive learning environment
    C. The ecological perspective
    D. The interactions between families and communities

21. Students with this exceptionality experience challenges with selective attentiveness and may be easily distracted by background noise, which can interfere with their ability to process auditory information effectively.

    A. Auditory processing disorder
    B. Intellectual disability
    C. Autism spectrum disorder (ASD)
    D. Attention-deficit/hyperactivity disorder (ADHD)

22. The quality of the schools and classrooms, including the availability of specialized support services, class size, educational materials, and teacher expertise, can make a substantial difference in the educational outcomes of students with disabilities. This statement is considering:

    A. Environmental factors
    B. Biological factors
    C. Co-occurring factors
    D. Policy and legislation

23. Which of the following statements best defines the ecological perspective on autism spectrum disorder (ASD)?

    A. Chromosomal abnormalities cause ASD.
    B. Students with ASD benefit from consistent and practiced classroom routines and procedures.
    C. Children with ASD need exposure to higher-order thinking activities to do well in school.
    D. Inclusion settings are less beneficial for students with ASD because they should be in self-contained classrooms.

24. Which of the following scenarios indicates that a fourth-grade student may struggle with an auditory processing disorder?

   A. The student has difficulty interacting appropriately in social settings with peers.

   B. The student has difficulty following verbal instructions even after the teacher repeats them several times.

   C. The student experiences extreme sensitivity to light and sound.

   D. The student has difficulty comprehending the sequence of a story even while using a graphic organizer.

25. Ms. Kaplan wants to accommodate her student, Aden, who has an auditory processing disorder. Which of the following would be most effective for Aden? Choose **ALL** that apply.

   ☐ A. Use nonverbal cues during instruction.

   ☐ B. Allow Aden to use a frequency monitoring (FM) system.

   ☐ C. Allow students to use headphones during read-alouds.

   ☐ D. Provide Aden with written instructions for classroom activities.

   ☐ E. Allow Aden to work with a partner during story time.

26. Ms. Jensen wants to ensure she is creating a culturally inclusive classroom. Which of the following teacher actions should she take to meet this objective?

   A. Allow all students to use assistive instructional technology to enhance classroom instruction.

   B. Encourage English language learners (ELLs) to speak English only during classroom activities to strengthen their language skills.

   C. Facilitate a beginning-of-the-year cultural event where students and parents are invited to share the foods, arts, and crafts of their culture.

   D. Scaffold and differentiate instruction to meet the varied needs of students' culture, language, abilities, exceptionalities, values, and beliefs.

27. A fifth-grade teacher notices that one of her students with a specific learning disability (SLD) struggles to understand the process of class assignments. Which of the following approaches would be most effective in this situation?

   A. Call the student's parents to ensure proper practice happens at home.

   B. Observe the student during class and modify instruction to meet the student's needs.

   C. Increase the student's cooperative learning time.

   D. Have the student sit in the front of the room to mitigate distractions and disruptions.

28. A middle school student with high-functioning ASD is in an inclusion science class. However, the student struggles with appropriate social interactions. Which of the following describes a social skill the student might struggle with?

   A. Maintaining personal space

   B. Organizing steps in a science lab activity

   C. Tolerating loud noises in the learning environment

   D. Making involuntary vocal sounds

29. Creating social stories, which are narratives that describe social situations and appropriate responses to help students navigate interpersonal interactions, would be most beneficial for students with:

A. Auditory processing disorders

B. Visual impairments

C. Autism spectrum disorder (ASD)

D. Intellectual disabilities

30. A teacher gives students who behave properly during reading block five additional minutes on the playground. Which of the following methods is the teacher using?

A. Response cost

B. Positive reinforcement

C. Negative reinforcement

D. Intrinsic motivators

31. A student with emotional behavior disturbance (EBD) will occasionally become overwhelmed and act out. Which of the following would be most effective to help this student calm down while maintaining the learning environment for other students?

A. Stop instruction and tend to the student immediately so the behavior does not increase and further disrupt the class.

B. Send the student to the school counselor to practice mindfulness activities like deep breathing and meditation.

C. Designate a specific area in the classroom where a student can go to regain composure and practice self-regulation strategies.

D. Call the students' parents and ask that they address the situation at home.

32. How can a special education teacher adapt to the learning environment when providing supports in educational settings and other placement options for optimal learning opportunities? Choose **ALL** that apply.

☐ A. Allow students to choose which activities they want to participate in.

☐ B. Consider and address both the health-related and educational needs of students.

☐ C. Collaborate with on-site nursing care for students with medical needs.

☐ D. Determine the least restrictive environment for students.

☐ E. Consider one's cultural beliefs and societal attitudes about students with disabilities.

33. Mr. Gonzalez is a fifth-grade special education teacher with students who have a range of exceptionalities in learning and behavior. Which of the following approaches would be most effective to ensure all students receive proper instruction based on their needs?

A. Analyze errors and response patterns across various assessments and target instruction focusing on those identified skills or knowledge gaps.

B. Reduce the amount of work for each student, identify where students excel, and increase the rigor based on student's individual understanding and needs.

C. Group struggling students together for the grading period and use targeted interventions until those students can rejoin the others who are excelling in their work.

D. Use peer tutoring during instruction where high-achieving students coach low-achieving students until all students reach the same achievement levels.

34. Mr. Green is a special education teacher working with students on how to proceed during school fire drills. After the drills conclude, Mr. Green discusses how students navigated the process. Which of the following is the most effective feedback for this task?

A. "Great job on working through the safety drills!"

B. "You all lined up at the door properly. Now we need to work on the next step in the process."

C. "We need to do a better job lining up and walking through the halls during the fire drill."

D. "Let's go through each step of the drill and see where we met expectations and where we need to continue to practice."

35. A special education teacher works with students who have autism spectrum disorder (ASD) on how to engage with each other socially. She wants her students to use social cues, adhere to personal space, and engage in conversations. Which of the following would be most effective in achieving this objective?

A. Provide a checklist of social behaviors students can use to engage with others socially.

B. Show a video where people engage in positive social behaviors and conversations.

C. Read a story that outlines how to engage in accepted social behaviors.

D. Model and rehearse transition-related social behaviors and use role play to practice.

36. Which of the following statements describes scaffolding accurately?

A. Make assignments easier so struggling students can complete tasks and stay on track with the other students.

B. Break down tasks into smaller, more manageable steps, thereby building the students' skills incrementally.

C. Use various reading materials so each student can find areas of learning that align with their specific interests.

D. Use cooperative learning where students low-achieving students are paired with high-achieving students.

37. Ms. Kepler is a sixth-grade language arts inclusion teacher. She is building a differentiated lesson plan to include activities and assessments for all students at various levels of comprehension. Which of the following should also be included in the plan?

A. Provide a list of targeted vocabulary and their definitions students can use while they read to understand the text.

B. Give students the option to use either screen readers or headphones based on their learning preferences.

C. Various ways to show mastery of their comprehension skills: write an essay, draw a picture, conduct a short presentation, or build a sequence map.

D. A guest speaker to present information to the class in a different format to engage all learners.

38. Jessica is a third-grade student with ADHD. She has an IEP that outlines her accommodations and goals. Which of the following accommodations is likely to be on Jessica's IEP?

A. Extra time on reading assignments and standardized tests

B. Access to a self-contained classroom environment

C. Frequent brain breaks and time to get out of her seat

D. A plan for using the elevator during emergency drills

39. A sixth-grade special education teacher works with students with mild intellectual disabilities on vocabulary while reading an online news article. Which of the following would be most effective in helping these students with vocabulary acquisition?

A. Use context clues to identify meaning while reading the text.

B. Write down complex words and their definitions.

C. Use a word bank worksheet to practice vocabulary before reading.

D. Work with a partner to drill and practice new vocabulary words.

40. A special education teacher is designing lesson plans for the upcoming grading period. Which of the following should be the teacher's first step in this process?

A. Review the state-adopted standards and what mastery of those standards entails.

B. Identify which students will have the most trouble in class and find alternative activities.

C. Find engaging lessons online that will help students understand the lessons.

D. Work with a peer teacher to identify best practices when implementing new concepts.

41. What would be the best approach for a fourth-grade inclusion teacher to ensure that instruction is horizontally aligned?

A. Review the lessons and standards of third grade.

B. Work with other teachers in fourth grade and build interdisciplinary objectives.

C. Ensure that all lessons are easy enough for students with disabilities.

D. Use online lesson plans provided by special education organizations.

42. If a teacher uses backward design to plan lessons, which of the following outlines the most effective way to work through the process?

A. Choose the assessments, plan activities, and determine if the activities and assessments are aligned with the standards.

B. Plan engaging activities, determine if the activities are aligned with the standards, and design assessments that support students.

C. Plan engaging activities, design assessments to test students' skills, and determine if the activities and assessments are aligned with the standards.

D. Identify the standards, choose the assessments, plan activities that align with the standards, and prepare students for the assessments.

43. To help strengthen skills in these areas and compensate for deficits, special educators can use the following approaches. Choose **ALL** that apply.

☐ A. Employ instructional methods like guided reading and questioning techniques to improve comprehension.

☐ B. Use graphic organizers to help students organize and relate information.

☐ C. Teach summarizing and paraphrasing skills to aid in understanding and processing information.

☐ D. Model think-aloud strategies during reading to show students how to use their brains.

☐ E. Lower the standards until students meet expectations.

44. Challenges with manipulating information in the mind that affects the ability to solve problems in one's head, do mental arithmetic, or follow multi-step instructions is what type of memory deficit?

A. Short-term

B. Long-term

C. Working

D. Procedural

45. A student in a sixth-grade math inclusion class suffers from inconsistent retrieval because of a traumatic brain injury (TBI). Which of the following supports would be most effective in helping this student?

A. Encourage the student to use mnemonic devices.

B. Encourage the student to take detailed notes during direct instruction.

C. Encourage the student to work with a partner.

D. Encourage the student to use visual elements in reading.

46. Which of the following would be the most effective approach when administering a functional curriculum to high school special education students focused on the steps in applying for a job?

A. Cueing and prompting

B. Advanced questioning

C. Task analysis

D. Vocabulary drills

47. This is a type of differentiation strategy that involves adjusting the scope and sequence of a lesson to meet the needs of students who struggle.

A. Functional curriculum

B. Collaborative teaching

C. Curriculum modification

D. Individualized education program (IEP)

48. Which of the following would help a teacher regularly monitor student progress and provide feedback? Choose **TWO**.

☐ A. Technology integration

☐ B. Formative assessments

☐ C. Test-taking strategies

☐ D. Individual conferences

☐ E. Peer collaboration

49. A third-grade student is having trouble with abstract concepts in math. Which of the following would help this student bring the abstract to the concrete in math?

A. Technology integration

B. Guided practice

C. Cooperative learning

D. Using manipulatives

50. This is an educational framework that aims to improve and optimize teaching and learning for all people and to guide the creation of inclusive and accessible learning experiences that accommodate individual learning differences.

    A. Free Appropriate Public Education (FAPE)

    B. Universal Design for Learning (UDL)

    C. Individualized Family Service Plans (IFSPs)

    D. Expanded Core Curriculum (ECC)

51. Which of the following would be most effective when working with students to strengthen proprioceptive and vestibular perception?

    A. Use multi-sensory teaching methods, such as visual aids and tactile materials.

    B. Use direct instruction, such as lectures or guest speakers to engage students.

    C. Use technology to help students connect their learning to the real world.

    D. Use small-group instruction and keep distractions to a minimum.

52. Ms. Jensen works with students to strengthen their reading comprehension. Which of the following methods would be most effective to achieve this objective? Choose **ALL** that apply.

    ☐ A. Use read-aloud and think-aloud activities to strengthen metacognition.

    ☐ B. Use graphic organizers to categorize different characters and actions in the text.

    ☐ C. Have students read aloud and determine the correct words read per minute.

    ☐ D. Have students generate questions before, during, and after reading.

    ☐ E. Have students look up difficult words in the glossary before reading.

53. A special education teacher wants to provide support for students while also pushing them toward independence. The teacher does not want students to be over-reliant on support in the classroom. Which of the following would be most effective in helping these students become more competent and confident in their learning?

    A. Provide consistent feedback to students throughout the learning process.

    B. Allow students to work with partners when they feel the content is too complex.

    C. Once students become better at a skill, use the fading technique to remove supports.

    D. Allow students to represent their learning in different ways.

54. Which of the following assistive technology would be on a visually impaired student's IEP?

    A. Frequency monitoring (FM) systems

    B. A screen reader

    C. Augmentative and alternative communication (AAC) devices

    D. Voice output communication aids (VOCAs)

55. Which of the following describes holistic evaluation?

    A. Conduct comprehensive assessments considering students' academic skills, social-emotional development, cultural background, and personal interests.

    B. Set goals that are not only aligned with the student's abilities and interests but also reflect their cultural identity and community values.

    C. Provide training for staff on cultural competence and sensitivity to ensure that services are delivered in a culturally appropriate manner.

    D. Teach independent living skills considering the student's cultural background (e.g., community living norms and traditional practices).

56. This plan outlines goals for students to work toward to help them move from high school to postsecondary school and career.

    A. Individualized Education Plan (IEP)

    B. Universal Design for Learning (UDL)

    C. Individualized Family Service Plan (IFSP)

    D. Individualized Transition Plan (ITP)

57. A teacher wants to be sure to use positive behavior support in her special education classroom. Which of the following is the most important to focus on?

    A. Rewards and consequences

    B. Task analysis

    C. Data analysis and prevention

    D. Transition planning and functional curriculum

58. Maria is a tenth-grade student classified with a specific learning disability (SLD). She receives small group, differentiated instruction focused on math skills needed to perform the order of operations. She struggles with this skill and requires support in this area. The type of instruction Maria receives is:

    A. Cooperative learning approach

    B. Metacognitive approach

    C. Direct instructional approach

    D. Remedial approach

59. Sam is a seventh-grade student who receives special education services under the category of specific learning disability (SLD). Sam's IEP states he should be allowed to use word processing software to complete writing tasks like taking notes and homework assignments. Which of the following actions can the teacher take to ensure Sam successfully uses this assistive technology?

    A. Designate time to go over the technology with the entire class.

    B. Assign keyboarding skills before using the technology.

    C. Have students record direct instruction before taking notes.

    D. Arrange for the student to have access to word processing software at home.

60. Susie is a tenth-grade special education student with difficulty accessing and pulling out information from memory when needed. She also has difficulty recalling previously learned information and applying it to new situations. Susie is most likely displaying a deficit in:

A. Visual perception

B. Retrieval

C. Auditory perception

D. Social comprehension

61. This is a type of behavior management strategy where the teacher takes away privileges when a student displays inappropriate behavior. It is consequence-driven.

A. Positive behavior interventions and supports (PBIS)

B. Response cost

C. Multi-tiered system of supports (MTISS)

D. Functional curriculum

62. Which of the following goals would be best suited for a transition plan for Jenna, who is a tenth-grade special education student? Choose **ALL** that apply.

☐ A. Jenna will successfully fill out three job applications to local businesses in the area.

☐ B. Jenna will increase her correct words per minute by 15 percent in reading class.

☐ C. Jenna will successfully complete her homework assignments for science class.

☐ D. Jenna will work on self-advocacy skills when talking to people in the store.

☐ E. Jenna will engage in cooperative learning in social studies class.

63. Jonathan, a fifth-grade student with muscular dystrophy, suffers from progressive muscle weakness, or a decline in muscle strength. Jonathan receives physical and occupational therapy twice a week based on his IEP requirements. The goals outlined in Jonathan's IEP include improving balance, coordination, posture, and daily living skills. Which of the following is a modification that will most likely help Jonathan in a classroom setting?

A. Allowing Jonathan additional writing time on essays and to take home what he doesn't finish for homework.

B. Providing preferential seating for Jonathan to safely navigate the classroom during safety drills.

C. Reducing the amount of writing Jonathan must do while still meeting the academic standards.

D. Providing Jonathan with a peer buddy who can write for him during longer writing assignments.

64. Which of the following goal statements on an IEP would help ensure the goal is measurable?

A. The student will reduce the number of outbursts by 20 percent based on a tally system.

B. The student will increase his reading score by 15 percent.

C. The student will learn to work together with other students during cooperative learning.

D. The student will self-advocate when working at his job after school.

65. A fifth-grade special education student is having difficulty in word recognition and fluency. Which of the following strategies would be most effective for this student?

A. Repeated reading

B. Questioning

C. Peer-assisted learning

D. Context clues

66. Venn diagrams, story maps, or concept maps are most effective to help students increase:

A. Fluency

B. Comprehension

C. Word recognition

D. Phonics skills

67. Which assistive technology would be most effective for students who cannot use their hands?

A. Screen reader

B. Speech-to-text software

C. Adaptive keyboard

D. Word-processing software

68. Judy is an eighth-grade student with a visual impairment. Which of the following approaches would be most effective in helping Judy access the general curriculum fully so she can live independently?

A. Use an expanded core curriculum in recreation and leisure.

B. Use an FM system when delivering direct instruction.

C. Outline reading comprehension goals in Judy's IEP.

D. Use a holistic evaluation approach when grading Judy's writing.

69. A fifth-grade special education teacher wants to ensure she is using a culturally competent approach to assessment. Which of the following approaches would align with this goal? Choose **ALL** that apply.

☐ A. Actively involve students in the planning process to ensure their voices and preferences are central.

☐ B. Work closely with families, respecting and incorporating their cultural values and expectations into the planning.

☐ C. Conduct comprehensive assessments considering students' academic skills, social-emotional development, cultural background, and personal interests.

☐ D. Call home regularly to communicate with parents when students need support and when they achieve goals.

☐ E. Regularly attend IEP meetings to inform the team of students' progress and additional needs.

70. This is the difference between what a learner can do without help and what they can achieve with guidance and encouragement from a skilled partner. Teachers who are aware of this use proper scaffolding and differentiation techniques.

    A. Expanded core curriculum (ECC)

    B. Universal Design for Learning (UDL)

    C. Zone of Proximal Development (ZPD)

    D. Free Appropriate Public Education (FAPE)

71. A general education math teacher creates a timed assessment on multiplication. The quiz is 10 questions in 10 minutes. The teacher is looking for students to score at 90 percent accuracy. A special education student takes the assessment and gets two correct and six incorrect and leaves two unanswered. What should be the next step in helping the student?

    A. Reteach the material and allow the student to retake the test without being timed.

    B. Assign the same assignment again to the student until he reaches the desired outcome.

    C. Assign extra multiplication homework to remediate the student's skills.

    D. Have a paraprofessional work one on one with the student and allow for a retake.

72. After a student submits her test and the computer grades it, the teacher sees a raw score of 78. What does this mean?

    A. The student scored 78 percent.

    B. The student is in the 78th percentile.

    C. The student answered 78 questions correctly.

    D. The student's scale score is 78.

73. A cognitive assessment is most appropriate for measuring:

    A. Behavior

    B. Functional skills

    C. Social skills

    D. Intellectual ability

74. The Vineland Adaptive Behavior Scale is used to measure:

    A. Physical ability in the real world

    B. Life skills and intellectual ability

    C. The extent of a student's disability

    D. Student behavior in academic settings

75. Which of the following is the most appropriate way to use a summative assessment?

    A. To assign students a percentile ranking

    B. To use as an ongoing measure of students' abilities

    C. To measure student work samples over a period

    D. To measure outcomes after a teacher finishes a unit

76. Which of the following is the primary purpose of a formative assessment?

   A. To progress monitor

   B. To rank students

   C. To measure outcomes

   D. To collect work samples

77. For a student to be classified as having a severe intellectual disability, the student must score at what level on the Wechsler Intelligence Scale for Children (WISC) or IQ test.

   A. Below 120

   B. Below 90

   C. Below 70

   D. Below 30

78. A special education student is taking the Woodcock-Johnson Psycho-Educational Battery, Third Edition. What is this assessment measuring?

   A. A learning disability

   B. An intellectual disability

   C. Social skills

   D. Life skills

79. Julie is a third-grade student with trouble keeping up in the classroom, especially during reading and math time. Julie's parents spoke with the teacher and want to see if Julie has a learning disability. What is the first step the teacher should take?

   A. Formally test the student using Vineland Adaptive Behavior Scale.

   B. Have the school psychologist come in and observe Julie in reading and math.

   C. Recommend the parents meet with the principal to see if special education is an option.

   D. Reduce the amount of reading and math tasks Julie is required to complete in class.

80. Sam has ADHD and a specific learning disability in reading. What would be the most appropriate accommodations to provide Sam during a state standardized assessment? Choose **ALL** that apply.

   ☐ A. Have the proctor read the assessment aloud to Sam.

   ☐ B. Allow Sam to take frequent breaks.

   ☐ C. Allow Sam to have extra time to take the assessment.

   ☐ D. Break the assessment up over several days.

81. Which of the following behaviors might be outlined on a functional behavior assessment (FBA)?

   A. James frequently struggles to remember his multiplication facts.

   B. James has trouble eating with utensils and drinking out of a standard drinking glass.

   C. James can finish his assignments when he is given extra time.

   D. James frequently uses profanity and pushes other students when it's time to line up.

82. An example of proper use of a criterion-referenced exam in an English language arts class would be to:

A. Rank students by percentile

B. Use a rubric to evaluate skills

C. Screen students for class placement

D. Measure students' mastery of the standards

83. Which of the following would be the most appropriate testing accommodation for Juan, who is on grade level but has limited use of his hands?

A. Provide Juan with large print on assessments.

B. Provide Juan with a screen reader for assessments.

C. Allow Juan to respond orally to assessment questions.

D. Allow Juan to have extra time on the assessment.

84. This type of assessment usually provides a score report with scale scores, percentile ranking, and ability levels.

A. State standardized test

B. Rubric

C. Formative assessment

D. Informal assessment

85. A special education teacher wants to collect student writing samples over a semester and have students analyze their performance from the beginning of the semester to the end of the semester. This type of assessment is a:

A. Performance-based assessment

B. Portfolio assessment

C. Norm-referenced assessment

D. Ongoing assessment

86. Which of the following provides rich qualitative data regarding student behavior a teacher can use to provide interventions?

A. Diagnostic assessment

B. Student survey

C. Anecdotal record

D. Oral assessment

87. Ms. Jones is working with her special education students using a new reading program adopted by the district. Which of the following pair of assessments would be most beneficial when measuring the effectiveness of a new reading program?

A. Pretest and summative

B. Pretest and formative

C. Diagnostic and norm-referenced

D. Screening and formative

88. A teacher is analyzing a student's behavior after several intervention strategies. She wants to figure out which intervention diminishes the negative behavior. What can the teacher determine based on the data presented in the graphs below?

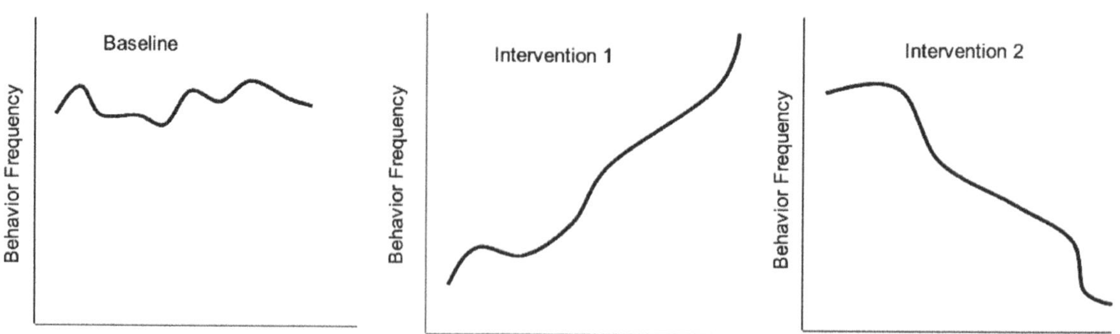

A. A new diagnostic test will need to be administered with better baseline data.

B. Intervention 1 is more effective than intervention 2.

C. Intervention 2 is more effective than intervention 1.

D. Neither intervention 1 nor intervention 2 was effective.

89. Which of the following is an example of a teacher using data to drive instructional decisions in the classroom?

A. A teacher is walking around the room and observing students working on math problems.

B. A teacher conferences with students to discuss feedback on their writing.

C. A teacher uses reading scores to group students temporarily for interventions.

D. A teacher is planning a performance-based assessment.

90. One of the skills outlined in a student's IEP is to participate in group situations actively and appropriately. A teacher has the student actively participate in a cooperative learning exercise. She observes and records the student's efforts in contributing to the group discussion, waiting her turn to speak and sharing relevant information to the discussion. This assessment is:

A. Problem-based

B. Performance-based

C. Project-base

D. Standards-based

91. This test evaluates three areas: participation, task support, and activity performance.

A. Behavior Assessment System for Children (BASC)

B. School Function Assessment (SFA)

C. Woodcock-Johnson Psycho-Educational Battery, Third Edition

D. Vineland Adaptive Behavior Scale

92. A teacher is assessing her students at the beginning of a lesson, throughout the lesson, and at the end of the lesson. Which of the following is the most effective way to use the data she collects from these assessments?

A. To group students by ability level

B. To assign grades for various assignments

C. To make instructional decisions in the classroom

D. To compare with other teachers' data

93. A fifth-grade special education teacher wants to use formative assessments to drive her classroom decisions. Which of the following is the best way to achieve this objective?

A. Work on a unit for two weeks, assess students at the end of the unit, and use those grades to communicate scores with parents.

B. Work on a unit for two weeks, observe student engagement and understanding, and assess students along the way.

C. Administer a pre-test on the unit, work on a unit for two weeks, and assess students with a post-test at the end to determine gains.

D. Administer a pre-test on the unit, decide how to move forward based on the pre-test data, and assess students with a post-test at the end to determine gains.

94. A new special education teacher is trying to decide what reading strategy she will use for the next unit. What would be her best course of action before implementing the strategy?

A. Determine if there is research to support the use of the strategy.

B. Consult with her peer teacher about the strategy.

C. Search online to see if other teachers are using the strategy.

D. Survey the students to see if they want to use the strategy.

95. A teacher wants to see if a new reading curriculum will have a better impact on student reading gains. What should the teacher do?

A. Try the new reading program for a few weeks and continuously collect data on student reading to see if it has a positive impact.

B. Attend professional development on the new program and then decide if it is a good fit for the class.

C. Send an email home to parents to ask for input on the new program.

D. Ask a peer mentor if she uses the program and has seen results.

Use the data from the following chart and information to answer questions 96-98

This is a box and whisker plot that represents the hypothetical scores for letter and word recognition.

The central line in the box represents the median score, while the edges of the box delineate the interquartile range, encompassing the middle 50 percent of scores. The "whiskers" extend to the lowest and highest scores within 1.5 times the interquartile range from the lower and upper quartiles, respectively. Points outside of this range could be considered outliers but are not specifically represented in this plot.

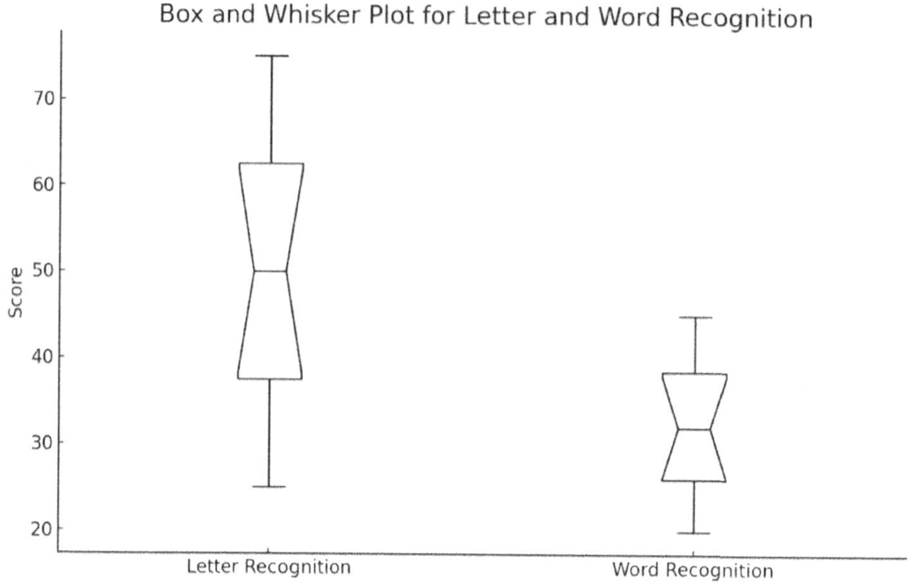

96. Based on the data below, which of the statements is accurate?
    A. Students performed at or above proficiency in both word recognition and letter recognition.
    B. Students performed below proficiency in word recognition and letter recognition.
    C. Students performed at or above proficiency in word recognition; students performed below proficiency in letter recognition.
    D. Students performed at or above proficiency in letter recognition; students performed below proficiency in word recognition.

97. Based on the box and whisker plot for letter recognition, what is the range of scores that fall within the middle 50 percent of students?
    A. 25-75
    B. 40-60
    C. 35-65
    D. 20-45

98. If a student's score for word recognition is 42, which of the following statements is true based on the box and whisker plot?
    A. The student's score is above the median for word recognition.
    B. The student's score is below the median but above the first quartile for word recognition.
    C. The student's score is at the first quartile for word recognition.
    D. The student's score is an outlier.

99. Which of the following is a procedural safeguard according to IDEA?

A. Parents can have their own evaluation done outside of school, and the school has to accept the recommendations.

B. Parents can request special education services regardless of the child's diagnosis or designation.

C. Parents must receive written notice of changes made to their child's IEP.

D. The school must accommodate parents' requests for IEP meetings.

100. This provides students who attend a school that receives federal funds with protection against discrimination based solely on their disability.

A. Federal Education R ights and Privacy Act (FERPA)

B. Procedural Safeguards of IDEA

C. Section 504 of the Rehabilitation Act of 1973

D. No Child Left Behind Act

101. Which **TWO** of the following steps occur during the special education prereferral process?

A. Identify areas where the student struggles and implement tiered interventions like PBIS and MTSS as alternative education strategies.

B. Collect and use data to monitor progress and make academic or behavioral decisions.

C. Conducting intelligence (IQ), behavioral, and achievement assessments to determine placement.

D. Work with the IEP team to plan special education services for the student.

102. According to IDEA, which of the following is true?

A. A student's IEP should be revised once every academic year or when a parent wants a review.

B. A student's IEP should be revised once every academic semester or when a parent wants a review.

C. A student's IEP should be reviewed only as often as the parent wants it to be reviewed.

D. A student's IEP should be reviewed once every three years.

103. Which of the following learning objectives would be considered at the top of Bloom's Taxonomy?

A. Students will identify ways in which photosynthesis contributes to life on Earth.

B. Students will predict what happens in the story and create alternative endings.

C. Students will understand that complete sentences contain both a noun and a verb.

D. Students will categorize rocks based on texture and composition.

104. Ms. Kepler is a special education teacher who is collaborating with professionals in the field. Which of the following professionals would help her engage with students who are working on functional skills?

A. Speech pathologist

B. Paraprofessional

C. Behavioral therapist

D. Occupational therapist

105. Which of the following foundational theories aligns with a teacher modeling appropriate behavior for her students with autism spectrum disorder (ASD)?

A. Operant conditioning

B. Zone of Proximal Development

C. Social Learning Theory

D. Stages of cognitive development

106. Select **ALL** the following that parents are entitled to, according to the procedural safeguards in IDEA.

☐ A. Written notice of any changes in the student's IEP

☐ B. Access to their student's records

☐ C. A due process hearing if their student faces suspension

☐ D. Access to observe their student's classes during the school day

☐ E. Public school funds for private evaluations

107. According to IDEA, a student with the inability to build or maintain satisfactory interpersonal relationships with peers and teachers and who shows inappropriate types of behavior or feelings under normal circumstances is exhibiting:

A. Attention deficit/hyperactivity disorder (ADHD)

B. An intellectual disability

C. Emotional behavior disturbance (EBD)

D. Traumatic brain injury (TBI)

108. Which of the following falls under the Free Appropriate Public Education (FAPE) outlined in IDEA? Choose **ALL** that apply.

☐ A. Curriculum and instruction must meet standards established by the state Department of Education.

☐ B. Instruction must be designed to meet the unique needs of each student.

☐ C. Special education services must continue to be provided to students who are suspended or expelled.

☐ D. Accommodations must be outlined in a student's IEP.

☐ E. Students are eligible for special education services through the age of 23.

109. A comprehensive reevaluation of the student's eligibility for special education services is required under IDEA:

A. Every three years

B. Every two years

C. Every year

D. Every six months

110. An IEP team is meeting to discuss a special education student's placement. Which of the following should the team consider?

A. What grade is the student in?

B. What are the student's interests and goals?

C. What teacher would be best suited for the student?

D. What is the least restrictive environment for the student?

111. A special education teacher is working on a three-year plan for her professional growth. Which **THREE** of the following professional courses would be most beneficial in meeting this objective?

□ A. How to use data to analyze student learning

□ B. A guide to using a grade book

□ C. How to use consequences effectively in the classroom

□ D. A guide to self-reflecting strategies

□ E. Become a peer collaborator in special education

112. Ms. Jensen is planning a parent-teacher conference for Brenden, a student in her special education class. Brenden struggles with acting appropriately during direct instruction and often disrupts the class. Ms. Jensen has tried everything to help Brenden but feels it is time to involve the parents. Which of the following approaches would be most effective to use during the parent-teacher conference?

A. Ms. Jensen should identify specific areas where Brenden is disruptive and show the parents the data she has collected on the student's outbursts.

B. Ms. Jensen should start the meeting with a few positive aspects of Brenden's participation in the class and then move on to opportunities for improvement based on behavior data.

C. Ms. Jensen should suggest that one of Brenden's parents come in and observe his behavior so they can see for themselves what she is dealing with every day.

D. Ms. Jensen should suggest that Brenden receive intensive support in a self-contained classroom where his behavior can be addressed by a professional.

113. This approach provides multiple levels of support for all learners—struggling through advanced and is used during the prereferral process of special education.

A. Least Restrictive Environment (LRE)

B. Free Appropriate Public Education (FAPE)

C. Individualized Education Plan (IEP)

D. Multi-tiered system of supports (MTSS)

114. A teacher is using a behavior system that includes rewards and consequences. For example, when students act appropriately, help clean up, or do something positive, they earn behavior badges. Once they have earned five behavior badges, they can go to the treasure box and pick a small toy. If they misbehave, she removes one of their earned behavior badges. This approach aligns with which foundational theory?

A. Stage of cognitive development

B. Operant conditioning

C. Multi-tiered system of supports

D. Social Learning Theory

115. Allowing students to choose the type of books they read, how they will present what they've learned, and how they will move forward in their education helps increase students':

A. Educational rights

B. Zone of Proximal Development

C. Cognitivism

D. Autonomy

116. According to IDEA, to be eligible for special education and related services, a child must be in the age range of birth to 22 years of age and meet the criteria in the following **TWO** areas outlined in federal law:

☐ A. The child must be identified as a child with a disability in one or more of the 13 categories defined by IDEA.

☐ B. The child must have completed MTSS in the previous grade before entering special education.

☐ C. The child must have both a learning and a behavioral disability.

☐ D. The child must be referred to special education by either a speech or occupational therapist.

☐ E. The child's disability must adversely affect his or her educational performance.

117. Sarah is a general education student who struggles slightly with processing information. Her teacher believes that she just needs extra time on her assignments and tests to be successful in the general education classroom. Which of the following would be the most appropriate approach for the teacher to take to ensure Sarah is receiving properly differentiated instruction while remaining in the general education classroom?

A. A 504 plan

B. An IEP

C. A behavioral plan

D. A co-teaching model

118. A teacher notices one of her special education students is not achieving on her math exams. When she looks over the IEP, she sees that one of the goals of the student's IEP is to meet math proficiency at 80 percent. She determines this goal is too high for the student. She decides to change the goal of the IEP to be more realistic of the student's abilities. What did this teacher fail to consider?

A. The rights of parents to participate in the decision-making process of the IEP.

B. The credibility of the IEP team in its ability to make appropriate goals for the student.

C. The safety of the learning environment.

D. The quality of instruction.

119. Local public schools must provide services designed to help special education students meet their annual goals and progress in the general curriculum at no cost to the parent. This is:

A. Least Restrictive Environment (LRE)

B. Procedural Safeguards

C. Appropriate Evaluation

D. Free Appropriate Public Education (FAPE)

120. A college student is conducting a case study for a master's program in special education. The college student reaches out to a special education teacher for help with the case study. The college student is requesting records of special education students in the school. What should the special education teacher do?

   A. Provide the college student with the records after her identity has been verified.

   B. Provide the records only after documentation has been signed before giving out the records.

   C. Ask the principal to speak with the college student and determine if the records can be given out.

   D. Refuse the college student's request for records on the grounds of FERPA.

Practice Test 2 – Answer Explanations

Number	Answer	Category	Explanation
1.	A & C	I.	Etiology is the study of causation or origination. This can include a wide range of factors, such as genetic, neurobiological, environmental, and psychological causes that contribute to developing a condition or behavior. Choices B, D, and E refer to typical milestone development and not etiology.
2.	B	I.	Fine motor skills involve the coordination of small muscles, typically in the hands and fingers, with the eyes to execute precise movements, such as writing, buttoning a shirt, or manipulating small objects. Choice A outlines gross motor skills, which involve large muscles in the body. Choices C and D outline social and behavioral skills, not motor skills.
3.	B	I.	Practice routines and procedures are beneficial for all students, especially for students who have EBD. In addition, Choice B outlines a data collection plan, which is also important in helping the student meet behavior goals. Finally, modifying the learning environment to meet the student's needs is essential in differentiation and accommodation for students with exceptionalities. Choice A has no plan for data collection and instead jumps right to a behavior contract, which may or may not work. Choice C relies on a specialist to differentiate instruction, which is usually not the correct answer on this exam—differentiation should come from the classroom teacher. Finally, choice D relies on calling parents for negative behavior and a system of extrinsic rewards or punishments, which is not the most effective approach.
4.	D	I.	Reducing frustration and promoting independence is part of executive functioning. Remember, functional curriculum and activities focus on tasks needed for everyday life. Therefore, choice D is correct. Choice A, independent study, would not reduce frustration and might even increase frustration for this student. Choice B, using frequent brain breaks, is a modification that benefits students with ADHD. Choice C, frequency modulation (FM) systems are assistive listening devices that enhance the auditory reception of sounds for individuals with hearing impairments

Number	Answer	Category	Explanation
5.	A	I.	Choice A has the term least restrictive environment (LRE) which is considered a good term on this exam. LRE is mandated by the Individuals with Disabilities in Education ACT (IDEA) and requires teachers to help students receive a free and appropriate public education in the general classroom with their non-disabled peers as much as possible. This is an inclusion model and is the most effective. Also, collaborating with multidisciplinary teams is most effective because it will help the teacher determine the support the students need to achieve in the general education classroom. Choice B is usually not the correct answer on this test because it relies on parents to accommodate for students, which should be done in the classroom. Choice C is the opposite of LRE and should be avoided as much as possible. Choice D ignores the need to differentiate for special education students.
6.	B & C	I.	Individuals with ASD often experience sensory processing disorders and may be sensitive to noise and light. In addition, students with ASD can also experience neurodevelopmental disorders which can impact social interactions. Seizures can be a condition associated with epilepsy. Metabolic disorders are usually associated with diabetes. Traumatic brain injuries can be congenital or acquired and are not indicative of ASD.
7.	C.	I.	Visual timetables, charts, and checklists help students understand and anticipate upcoming transitions or activities and can reduce anxiety, especially in those with ASD. Choice A lowers the standard and is not most effective. Choice B puts the burden of the peer buddy to differentiate, which is the role of the teacher. Choice D outlines a practice that is the opposite of the least restrictive environment (LRE).
8.	C, D & E	I.	Self-regulation is when students can identify when they are getting angry or anxious and then practice techniques to avoid outburst or destructive behavior. Deep breathing techniques, guided imagery, and meditation are all effective in helping students self-regulate their behavior. Modeling appropriate behavior is also effective because it helps students see what appropriate behavior looks like. Finally, establishing predictable routines and procedures reduces stress and helps students self-regulate. Encouraging cooperative learning will not help students self-regulate and may exacerbate anxiety. A system of rewards is an extrinsic approach because the rewards come from the teacher, which is the opposite of self-regulation.

Number	Answer	Category	Explanation
9.	A	I.	Specific learning disabilities (SLD), such as dyslexia, can affect the processing of written and sometimes spoken information, making it difficult for students to decode text, spell, or comprehend complex sentences. Sensory impairments are usually associated with hearing loss or impairment. EBD is a behavior disability and not a language processing disability. Finally, an intellectual disability affects functional skills, such as those used in hygiene and employment.
10.	A.	I.	A. Full inclusion: A student with disabilities participates in the same programs and classes as their peers without disabilities, receiving the necessary support within that setting, such as an aide or specialized instructional strategies. B. Resource room: A student spends part of the day in a general education class and part of the day receiving more intensive instruction in a small group setting outside the general classroom, such as a resource room. C. Special classes: For students whose needs cannot be met in the general education classroom, even with supports, special classes with a lower student-to-teacher ratio may be provided for a portion or the entire day. D. Special schools: Some students may attend specialized schools that are equipped to handle more significant needs that cannot be appropriately met in a traditional school setting.
11.	B	I.	Functional skills are those used in everyday life that help and individually live independently. A functional curriculum is one that focuses on real-world skills with the goal or helping special education students live independently after high school.
12.	D	I.	Linguistic or language-based exceptionalities involve difficulties processing linguistic information, which may manifest as challenges in understanding or producing spoken or written language. Choice A outlines a physical exceptionality. Choice B outlines a cognitive exceptionality. Choice C outline a behavioral exceptionality.
13.	B	I.	Environmental factors are factors that, through their absence or presence, limit functioning and create disability. These factors can include a physical environment that is not accessible, like steps into a building or an inaccessible transportation system. Choices A, C, and D are all biological factors, which are internal processes such as genetic, neurological, chemical, physiological, and physical conditions.

Number	Answer	Category	Explanation
14.	A	I.	Social/emotional exceptionalities involve challenges in managing emotions, behaviors, and interactions with others. These can manifest as difficulty in forming and maintaining relationships, responding appropriately to social cues, and expressing or regulating emotions.
15.	A	I.	Students with ADHD need frequent breaks and opportunities to move around the room. Brain breaks can be very beneficial for these students. Choice B is appropriate for students with emotional disorders. Choice C is appropriate for students with cognitive disorders. Choice D is appropriate for students with intellectual disabilities.
16.	C	I.	Self-regulation refers to an individual's ability to manage their emotions, behavior, and body movement in response to a situation and to control their impulses. Therefore, a behavior plan aligns with self-regulation.
17.	D	I.	Co-occurring or comorbid conditions refer to two or more disorders or disabilities in the same individual. The student in the scenario is experiencing an intellectual disability, anxiety, and depression.
18.	B	I.	Neurochemical disorders affect mood and energy levels. They involve imbalances in brain chemicals and result in anxiety and depression. Sensory processing disorders affect how students interact with their environment and can lead to difficulties in concentration. Hormonal imbalances affect the body's hormone levels and can influence energy, growth, and metabolism. Finally, metabolic disorders are conditions like such as phenylketonuria (PKU) or diabetes.
19.	B	I.	Frequency modulation systems (FM systems) are assistive listening devices that enhance the auditory reception of sounds for individuals with hearing impairments, particularly in educational settings. An FM system typically consists of a transmitter microphone used by the speaker (often the teacher) and a receiver worn by the student. The transmitter captures the speaker's voice and sends it directly to the receiver, which can be tuned to a specific frequency. The receiver transmits the sound to the student's hearing aids, cochlear implants, or headphones.

Number	Answer	Category	Explanation
20.	C	I.	The ecological perspective in special education is a framework that considers the complex interplay between a child with exceptionalities and their environment, and that is what is described in this scenario.
21.	D	I.	Students with ADHD often have challenges with selective attention and may be easily distracted by background noise, which can interfere with their ability to process auditory information effectively.
22.	A	I.	The quality of the schools and classrooms, including the availability of specialized support services, class size, educational materials, and teacher expertise, can make a substantial difference in the educational outcomes of students with disabilities and is considered a type of environmental factor.
23.	B	I.	The ecological perspective emphasizes the importance of interactions between the child and the child's environment. The environment encompasses the behavior setting, patterns of behavior across settings, and the child's community and culture. Choice A emphasizes the environment. Choice A is incorrect because it erroneously explains a genetic factor not an ecological factor. Choice C may benefit some students with ASD, but not every student with ASD is the same. Choice D is incorrect because it is the opposite of the least restrictive environment.
24.	B	I.	Students with auditory processing disorder experience difficulties with following verbal directions in a classroom. Choices A and C are indicative of autism spectrum disorder. Choice D describes a linguistic or language disorder.
25.	A, B & D	I.	Nonverbal cues and written instructions are helpful for students with auditory disorders because they can see what they cannot hear. In addition, using a frequency monitoring (FM) system would help Aden. Choice C, headphone, will not help Aden because he is hearing impaired. Finally, choice E, working with a partner, will not necessarily help Aden understand the story.

PRACTICE TEST

Number	Answer	Category	Explanation
26.	D	I.	In a culturally inclusive classroom, student learning, cultural competence, and social-emotional development are central. Teachers achieve this by differentiating instruction to meet students where they are academically, emotionally, and physically. Choice A is incorrect because not every student needs assistive technology. Choice B is incorrect because English-only practices are not culturally responsive. Choice C is incorrect because organizing a one-time cultural event does not necessarily ensure that the classroom will be culturally responsive.
27.	B	I.	Choice B is the best answer because it describes data-driven decision-making, which is paramount for effective teaching. Observing the student provides the teacher with necessary data to make instructional decisions. Choices A, C, and D do little to help the student. Also, calling parents is usually the incorrect answer for questions like this.
28.	A	I.	The scenario describes difficulty in appropriate social interactions. The only answer choice that describes social interaction is choice A.
29.	C	I.	Students with ASD often struggle with social interactions. Therefore, creating social stories would benefit these students most. Students with hearing and visual impairments do not necessarily have difficulty with social interactions. Students with intellectual disabilities struggle with functional skills.
30.	B	I.	Positive reinforcement is a reward system to encourage and reinforce self-regulatory behaviors, which is what is described in the scenario. Choices A and C are the same. Response cost or taking away a privilege for inappropriate behavior is a negative reinforcement. Intrinsic motivators do not rely on extrinsic rewards like extra time on the playground and instead rely on feeling good about oneself when engaging in appropriate behavior.
31.	C	I.	The only effective approach to this situation is to allow the student a safe place to self-regulate. The other answer choices either disrupt the learning environment or rely on outside personnel and parents to fix the problem.

Number	Answer	Category	Explanation
32.	B, C, D & E	I.	Choices B, C, D, and E all describe a teacher who is adapting the learning environment. In addition, choice E considers the teacher's own bias, which is important in creating optimal learning environments for students with disabilities. Choice A is not effective and promotes exclusion from activites.
33.	A	II.	Choice A details data-driven decisions, which is the most effective way to differentiate instruction based on students' needs. Analyzing errors and using targeted interventions is considered a best practice in special and general education. Choice B reduces the standards, which is not effective. Choice C outlines homogeneous grouping incorrectly. Students should not stay in homogenous groups for an entire nine weeks. Instead, homogeneous groups should be used temporarily for targeted instruction. Choice D puts the burden of differentiating instruction on high-achieving students, which is inappropriate for this scenario.
34.	D	II.	Feedback should be specific and meaningful. Choice D achieves this because students will examine specific areas where they did the procedures properly and areas where they can improve. Going through each step allows students to see details about the process. This also details what students did right and where they can improve. While saying, "Good job!" is positive, it is not specific or meaningful. Choice B is close to the correct answer but is not as effective as choice D. Choice C is somewhat specific but only focuses on one step and only focuses on the negative aspects of what students did.
35.	D	II.	The most effective way to help students understand proper social behaviors is for the teacher to model or demonstrate those interactions and to have students engage in practicing acceptable social behaviors. This is much more effective than following a checklist, watching a video, or reading a story.
36.	B	II.	Think of scaffolding instruction the same as scaffolding on a building. We do not lower the building to we can work on the roof. Instead, we build structures to move up the building. For instruction, we do not lower the standard. Instead, we build supports needed for students to meet the standard. Therefore, choice B is the best answer. Choice A lowers the standard. Choice C is interest-based instruction and not specific to scaffolding for skill levels. Choice D requires other students to do the job of scaffolding, which should be done by the teacher.

Number	Answer	Category	Explanation
37.	C	II.	Choice C outlines differentiated product or assessment. If the teacher is most concerned with mastery of skills, students can show mastery in a variety of ways. Choice A focuses only on vocabulary and is not effective in helping students with comprehension in a differentiated manner. Choice B may seem like differentiation but only gives students two options: screen readers or headphones. Some students may not need either. Choice D is not differentiation and simply changes on method of direct instruction from the teacher to a guest speaker.
38.	C	II.	Students with ADHD need frequent breaks and designated time to get up and move around. Therefore, choice C is the best answer. Choice A is an accommodation given to students with learning disabilities. Choice B is an accommodation given to students who cannot function safely in the general classroom environment. Choice D is an accommodation given to students who use a wheelchair and need a safe way to exit the building.
39.	A	II.	The most effective way to teach vocabulary is in context. This means that students apply context clues to figure out words while reading. Students used other words, pictures, and sentence structure to identify meaning. This approach is much more beneficial to language acquisition than writing definitions, using worksheets, or drill and practice. In fact, when you see answer choices like B, C, and D, they are usually the wrong answers.
40.	A	II.	The most important aspect of any lesson plan is standards alignment. Therefore, the first step teachers should take when lesson planning is to review the state-adopted standards. All planning, assessments and activities should follow those standards. While the other answer choices may seem like logical things to do when lesson planning, none are as important as standards alignment.
41.	B	II.	Horizontal alignment occurs when lessons are aligned to other academic disciplines and content areas. In this example, the fourth-grade teacher can work with other fourth-grade teachers to ensure lessons have interdisciplinary objectives. Choice A describes vertical alignment. Choices C and D are not effective ways to plan lessons.

Number	Answer	Category	Explanation
42.	D	II.	Backward design is a method of planning instruction that follows these steps: 1. Review the state-adopted standards. 2. Identify the assessments needed to determine mastery. 3. Design lessons and activities.
43.	A, B, C, & D	II.	All the methods listed are considered best practices except choice E. Choice E, lowering the standards, is not best practice. Instead, teachers should keep standards high and use scaffolds and interventions to help students master the standards.
44.	C	II.	Working memory deficits presents challenges with manipulating information in the mind. This affects the ability to solve problems in one's head, do mental arithmetic, or follow multi-step instructions. You may be tempted to choose procedural. However, procedural affects just the step-by-step processes in the brain, and the question outlines other issues beyond that.
45.	A	II.	Mnemonic devices are memory aids that can help students recall information by associating it with something more memorable. This will also help with retrieving information in a structured format.
46.	C	II.	A functional curriculum's primary focus of a functional curriculum is to empower students to achieve as much independence as possible in real-life situations by teaching skills that are immediately applicable to their daily lives. Therefore, a task analysis would be most beneficial because this activity focuses on steps to applying for a job. A task analysis helps students break down each task and complete each step.
47.	C	II.	Curriculum modification is when a teacher adjusts the scope and sequence of the curriculum to align with the student's abilities and goals. This may involve simplifying content, reducing the number of concepts taught at one time, or providing alternative assignments that better suit the student's learning style. A functional curriculum (choice A) focuses on skills students need in the real world. Collaborative teaching (choice B) is when two or more teachers work together to deliver a lesson. Finally, an IEP is a plan designed by the IEP team that outlines students' exceptionalities, goals, and modifications.

Number	Answer	Category	Explanation
48.	B & D	II.	Formative assessments are the best tool for teachers to use to monitor student progress. These come in the form of observations, quizzes, and quick checks. They are ongoing and provide valuable data teachers can use to differentiate instruction. Once teachers look over the formative data, they can engage students in individual conferences to provide feedback and set goals. Technology, test-taking strategies, and peer collaboration do little to help teachers monitor progress and provide feedback.
49.	D	II.	Incorporating hands-on learning tools like counters, number lines, and geometric shapes make abstract concepts more concrete and is the most effective approach for this scenario.
50.	B	II.	Universal Design for Learning (UDL) involves a proactive curriculum design that anticipates potential barriers to learning and incorporates a variety of teaching methods, materials, and assessments to meet the diverse needs of all students. It is about designing learning experiences that are accessible and effective for everyone, regardless of ability, disability, age, gender, or cultural and linguistic background. Free Appropriate Public Education (FAPE) is part of the Individuals with Disabilities Act (IDEA) and requires that educational services be provided to students with disabilities at the public's expense, meaning parents should not have to pay for these services. Individualized Family Service Plans (IFSPs) are part of students' IEPs and outline assistive technology and services students might need in the home as well as school. Expanded Core Curriculum (ECC) is a key concept in special education, particularly for students with visual impairments, including blindness. It is designed to supplement the general education curriculum and includes the teaching of specific skills that students with visual impairments need to learn to access the general curriculum fully and to live independently.
51.	A	II.	Proprioceptive and vestibular perception is understanding the position and movement of the body. Deficits in this area can affect balance, coordination, and the ability to navigate through space. To help strengthen skills in these areas and compensate for deficits, special educators can use multi-sensory teaching methods, such as visual aids, tactile materials, and auditory input, to enhance perception.

Number	Answer	Category	Explanation
52.	A, B & D	II.	Metacognition is thinking about thinking and is a necessary component of reading comprehension. Read aloud think aloud is a way to strengthen metacognition. Graphic organizers can help enhance reading comprehension because it takes abstract concepts and makes them concrete and visual representations. Question generation is also directly related to reading comprehension and higher-order thinking skills. Choice C is a fluency strategy and not directly linked to comprehension. Choice E is an ineffective vocabulary strategy. Looking words up and writing definitions is typically not the correct answer on the exam.
53.	C	II.	Choice C focuses on the gradual removal of support. As students become more competent and confident, the scaffolding is gradually removed. This process is often called "fading" and is crucial to encourage independence and prevent over-reliance on support. Choice A is an effective technique, but it is not specific in helping students become more independent in their learning. Choice B outlines cooperative learning and not independence. Choice D outlines differentiated instruction, specifically differentiated product and not independent learning.
54.	B	II.	Screen readers are assistive technology that read aloud the content displayed on the screen. This technology is essential for students who are blind or have significant visual impairments. FM systems, choice A, are used for students with auditory impairments. Choices C and D are assistive technologies that help students with language impairments.
55.	A	II.	A holistic approach considers the entirety of the student's output rather than isolating specific elements. Therefore, choice A is the best answer. Choice B outlines goal setting and not assessment. Choice C outlines professional development for the teacher. Choice D focuses on independent living and functional curriculum.
56.	D	II.	The ITP outlines goals for students to work toward to help them move from high school to postsecondary school and career. Because students have varying disabilities, the goals for the ITP vary based on each student. For example, some students' ITP will include a plan for college, while other students' plans may focus on independent living skills like cooking and hygiene.

Number	Answer	Category	Explanation
57.	C	II.	PBIS focuses on preventing undesirable behaviors before they occur rather than reacting to them afterward. This approach includes setting clear expectations and teaching students the expected behaviors in various school settings. In addition, decisions within a PBIS framework are guided by continuous monitoring and analysis of student behavior data. This data helps in identifying patterns, assessing the effectiveness of interventions, and making informed adjustments to strategies.
58.	D	II.	Remedial instruction is one-on-one or small-group instruction that focuses on the needs of the individual student. Since Maria struggles with math skills, she would benefit from a remedial, focused approach described in the scenario.
59.	D	II.	For Sam to be successful in using this assistive technology, he should have access to the tech at home. There will be times when he must complete assignments for homework. Therefore, he should receive the same access at home as he does in school. Choice A is incorrect because the whole class is not using word processing software. This is an accommodation for Sam. Choice B is incorrect because it is not necessary for Sam to learn keyboarding skills, and this may hinder his access to the assistive technology. Choice C is not related to the scenario.
60.	B	II.	Deficits in retrieval, within the context of special education, refer to difficulties in accessing and pulling out information from memory when needed. Retrieval is a critical part of the learning process, as it allows students to recall previously learned information to apply to new situations or to demonstrate understanding. It may also include difficulty in recalling information without cues or prompts, inability to access specific information even though it has been studied, and delayed recall of information.
61.	B	II.	Response cost is a behavioral management technique used in special education, as well as in general education settings. It is a negative punishment where a student loses a previously earned reward or privilege because of undesirable behavior. The goal of response cost is to decrease the frequency of negative behaviors by imposing a cost for those behaviors. Choice A and C are not consequence-driven and instead are prevention-driven. Choice D is not related to behavior.

Number	Answer	Category	Explanation
62.	A & D	II.	Transition planning in special education is a coordinated set of activities designed to prepare students with disabilities for the post-school transition into adulthood. This process aims to facilitate the shift from the school environment to post-secondary life, whether it involves further education, employment, or independent living. Choices A and D involve goals for outside of school. Choices B, C, and E are goals focused on the school environment.
63.	C	II.	Jonathan will have a difficult time writing because of his muscular dystrophy. Reducing the amount of writing is the best accommodation listed. In addition, the teacher is ensuring he is still meeting academic standards. You may be tempted to choose A, but allowing additional time may not be a suitable accommodation because he will still have a difficult time completing writing assignments. Choice B is not related to academics and is focused on safety drills. Finally, choice D is not an appropriate accommodation for Jonathan or the peer buddy.
64.	A	II.	The only answer choice that provides a way to measure the goals is answer A with a tally system. The other choices do not provide a way to measure the goal. Remember, goals should be SMART—specific, measurable, attainable, relevant, and time-bound.
65.	A	II.	Repeated reading is the best way to help with fluency and word recognition. When students read and reread text, they become comfortable and increase their fluency. Choice B is a comprehension strategy. Choice C is a cooperative learning strategy. Choice D is a vocabulary strategy.
66.	B	II.	Graphic organizers are used before, during, and after reading to help students organize information, which is essential in reading comprehension.
67.	B	II.	Students with severe physical disabilities would benefit from speech-to-text software. This allows students to dictate their thoughts and have them transcribed on the screen. This is especially beneficial for students with writing difficulties or physical impairments. Choice A, screen reader, is best for students with visual impariments. Choices C and D would be helpful for students with limited mobility. However, the scenario in the question says the students have no mobility in their hands.

Number	Answer	Category	Explanation
68.	A	II.	The Expanded Core Curriculum (ECC) is a key concept in special education, particularly for students with visual impairments, including blindness. It is designed to supplement the general education curriculum and includes the teaching of specific skills that students with visual impairments need to learn to access the general curriculum fully and to live independently. Choices B, C, and D are focused on school-related skills. However, the question asks for an approach that will help Judy live independently.
69.	A, B & C	II.	Choices A, B, and C all outline specific ways special education teachers can ensure they are using culturally responsive practices while preparing students to transition to postsecondary education, employment, and independent living. Choices D and E are effective approaches but not necessarily focused on cultural competence.
70.	C	II.	Scaffolding is particularly effective in the zone of proximal development (ZPD), a term coined by psychologist Lev Vygotsky. The ZPD is the difference between what a learner can do without help and what they can achieve with guidance and encouragement from a skilled partner or teacher.
71.	A	III.	The student needs more support because of the low score. However, the student also did not answer two of the questions, indicating that the student ran out of time. To accurately measure this student's skills, reteaching the material and allowing for the test to be untimed is most appropriate in this situation.
72.	C	III.	A raw score measures how many questions the test taker got correct. You may be tempted to choose answer A. However, we do not know how many total questions there are, so 78 percent cannot be the answer. If there were 100 questions, then the raw score and percentage would be 78. However, this student could have scored a 78/80, which is 98 percent or a 78/120, which is 65 percent.
73.	D	III.	Cognitive means intellectual or having to do with the brain. A common cognitive assessment is an intellectual quotient (IQ) test.
74.	B	III.	Intellectual ability is not just a measure of how a person scores on an academic assessment. Intellectual ability has to do with life skills, social concerns, social skills, and ability. The Vineland Adaptive Behavior Scale test measures intellectual ability in these areas.

Number	Answer	Category	Explanation
75.	D	III.	Summative assessments happen at the end of learning and measure outcomes. Answer A describes a norm-referenced assessment. Answer B describes a formative assessment. Answer C describes a portfolio (also considered formative) assessment.
76.	A	III.	Formative assessments are ongoing and help a teacher to measure progress and adjust instruction when needed.
77.	C	III.	Below 70 on an IQ test is considered having a severe intellectual disability.
78.	A	III.	The Woodcock-Johnson Psycho-Educational Battery, Third Edition provides a comprehensive set of individually administered tests to measure cognitive abilities, scholastic aptitudes, and achievement. It is important to remember that an intellectual disability and learning disability are two different conditions.
79.	B	III.	Because it is early, observation by the school psychologist is the best first step. Formal testing outlined in answer A is jumping ahead. Answer C, meeting with the principal, is not appropriate. Finally, simply reducing the amount of reading and math tasks is not effective in this situation.
80.	B, C & D	III.	These three accommodations are appropriate for Sam's situation. However, on a state assessment, those accommodations must be listed on the IEP. Teachers cannot just provide accommodations on a state test as they see fit. Reading the test aloud to Sam does nothing to help him considering his disabilities.
81.	D	III.	A functional behavior assessment (FBA) is a process for identifying problem behaviors and developing interventions to improve or eliminate those behaviors. You may be tempted to choose answer B. However, answer B aligns with a functional skills assessment. This scenario is a functional behavior assessment.
82.	D	III.	Criterion-referenced exams measure students' knowledge against a criterion. The most common and arguably important criteria is the state standards. State standardized assessments are considered criterion-referenced tests.
83.	C	III.	The best accommodation for this situation is to allow Juan to respond orally; this way he can demonstrate his learning without having to use his hands to write. Juan does not need large print or a screen reader because he not visually impaired. Also, Juan is on-grade level, so he does not need extra time, which eliminates answer D.

Number	Answer	Category	Explanation
84.	A	III.	A state-standardized test is a formal assessment that usually provides data on scale scores, achievement levels, and percentile ranking. Even if you do not know a lot about scale scores or percentile rankings, you can use process of elimination to get the correct answer. The elements described in the question are formal, so we can eliminate answer D immediately. A rubric is used to grade essay writing or projects and does not fit here, eliminating answer B. Finally, a formative assessment is a type of informal check like an observation or a quick assessment, so we can eliminate that.
85.	B	III.	Because the teacher is collecting specific student artifacts over time, this is a portfolio assessment.
86.	C	III.	For student behavior, observations with anecdotal notes are most effective. The anecdotes provide context and description off the student's behavior. All other answer choices do not address student behavior; rather, they address student learning.
87.	A	III.	Summative data measures progress when the lesson, strategy, or unit is finished. Determining the effectiveness of a reading program requires student scores at the beginning (pretest) and at the end after the reading program was administered (post-test or summative). Formative assessments are ongoing, during the teaching, so formative assessments would not be helpful in evaluating the effectiveness of a program. Therefore, answer choices B and D are not appropriate in this situation. A norm-referenced test does not give specific information about skills learned, so answer choice C also does not fit this situation.
88.	C	III.	In this case, the frequency of behavior goes up with intervention 1. The frequency of behavior goes down with intervention 2. Therefore, intervention 2 is more effective than intervention 1.
89.	C	III.	In every answer choice, the teacher is administering an assessment of some kind. However, only in answer choice C does she make a decision—grouping and interventions.
90.	B	III.	A performance-based assessment measures a student's ability to apply knowledge or skills to perform a task in a relevant situation. In this case, the student is using appropriate behavior in a group setting. Answer choice B is the best answer here.

Number	Answer	Category	Explanation
91.	B	III.	The skills listed in the question are functional skills. Therefore, the SFA is the best assessment for this situation. The SFA addresses not only classroom access but also playground, lunch, physical education, and other school areas.
92.	C	III.	There are various types of assessments teachers will use throughout the day, week, unit, semester, and school year. The reason for all assessments should be to make effective decisions in the classroom. That is always going to be the best answer on this test.
93.	B	III.	Formative assessments are informal checks that help teachers make immediate and impactful decisions in the classroom. They are ongoing. Answer choices A, C, and D are all summative assessments because they reference student outcomes—grades and gains—after a post assessment. Formative assessments are ongoing; summative assessments happen at the end of learning to determine outcomes.
94.	A	III.	The first and most important thing she should do is determine if the strategy is researched-based. That will determine if the strategy is effective and worth the time of using it. Remember, evidence-based and research-based are good words on this exam. This is one of those questions where all four answers could be beneficial in this situation. Because she is a new teacher, it makes sense that she would consult her peer teacher. In addition, using the Internet to see how other teachers feel about the strategy is something teachers do all the time. Finally, surveying students is also a good way to decide whether to use the strategy. However, the question asks what the best course of action is ***before*** implementing the strategy. That's why choice A is the best answer.
95.	A	III.	Data-driven decision-making is an important part of special education and a consistent theme throughout the exam. Above everything else, teachers should use data to determine if strategies, programs, and approaches are working in the classroom.
96.	D	III.	The box and whisker plot for 'Letter Recognition' shows scores distributed around the grade level, suggesting that the student is meeting expectations in this area. The box and whisker plot for 'Word Recognition' shows lower scores, indicating that the student is below grade level for this skill.

Number	Answer	Category	Explanation
97.	B	III.	The middle 50 percent of scores, also known as the interquartile range (IQR), is represented by the box in a box and whisker plot. For letter recognition, the lower edge of the box (the first quartile) is at 40, and the upper edge of the box (the third quartile) is at 60, which makes the IQR 40-60.
98.	A	III.	The median scores for word recognition is between 25 and 38, approximately. Therefore, if the student scored 42, the student is above the average for word recognition. In addition, a score of 42 reaches into the top "whiskers" of the chart and indicates the student is scoring in the top quartile of students.
99.	C	IV.	The procedural safeguard is a part of IDEA that lays out the process and the steps that schools go through during evaluation. According to this rule, the school must give the parents written notice before it makes any changes to the IEP. None of the other answer choices are listed in the procedural safeguards of IDEA.
100.	C	IV.	The promise of Section 504 of the Rehabilitation Act of 1973 is that a qualified individual cannot be denied participation in programs or services because of a disability if the school receives federal funds. Choice A, FERPA, has to do with student privacy not disabilities or discrimination. Choice B is a part of the Individuals with Disabilities in Education Act, but procedural safeguards protect the rights of children with disabilities and their parents. These safeguards include the right to participate in all meetings, to examine all educational records, and to obtain an independent educational evaluation (IEE) of the child. Choice D, NCLB, was an accountability law that established standards-based education and is not specific to students with disabilities.
101.	A & B	IV.	The *prereferral* process happens *before* the student is referred to special education classes. It is important that the teacher and other staff members try to meet the needs of the student in the general curriculum first. They do this by using tiered support systems like PBIS or MTSS. In addition, the teacher should use data to monitor progress of these interventions and make decisions based on the data. Choices C and D are part of the referral process and come after the teacher has exhausted tiered systems of supports and decides that the student may be a candidate for special education.

Number	Answer	Category	Explanation
102.	A	IV.	According to IDEA, IEPs should be revised and new goals should be drafted once every academic school year. However, a parent can request that an IEP be revised even if it has not been a full year.
103.	B	IV.	According to Bloom's Taxonomy, *create* is at the top of the pyramid. In choice B, students are creating their own ending based on predication. This is a higher-order skill. Choice A contains the verb *identify*, which is a low-level skill. Choice C contains the verb *understand*, which is a low-level skill. Choice D contains the verb categorize, which is a mid-level skill. However, it is not as advanced as *create* in choice B.
104.	D	IV.	An occupational therapist (OT) is a health care professional specializing in occupational therapy and occupational science. OTs help students strengthen their functional skills such as dressing, toileting, and eating.
105.	C	IV.	Bandura is best known for his social learning theory on modeled behaviors or observational learning. He believed that students learn from what they observe and that teachers can be proactive about how they demonstrate and promote behaviors. He argues that students are more likely to emulate a behavior if they value the outcome and admire the modeler. Choice A has to do with behavior and rewards. Choice B has to do with scaffolding. Choice D has to do with students' cognitive abilities.
106.	A, B &C	IV.	Procedural safeguards ensure that the rights of children with disabilities and their parents are protected and that they have access to the information needed to effectively participate in the process. This includes written notice of changes in the student's IEP, access to the student's records, and a due process hearing if the student faces disciplinary action at school. Choice D and E are not protections under the procedural safeguards of IDEA. Parents do not have access to observe classes. That would be very disruptive. Also, if parents want a private evaluation, they must pay for that themselves.

Number	Answer	Category	Explanation
107.	C	IV.	Emotional behavior disturbance (EBD) means a condition exhibiting one or more of the following characteristics over a long period of time and to a marked degree that adversely affects a child's educational performance: • An inability to learn that cannot be explained by intellectual, sensory, or health factors. • An inability to build or maintain satisfactory interpersonal relationships with peers and teachers and shows inappropriate types of behavior or feelings under normal circumstances. • A general pervasive mood of unhappiness or depression. • A tendency to develop physical symptoms or fears associated with personal or school problems
108.	A, B, C & D	IV.	All the services outlined in the answer choices fall under FAPE and IDEA except choice E. Special education is provided to students from age 3-21 per part B of IDEA.
109.	A	IV.	Every three years, a comprehensive reevaluation of the student's eligibility for special education services is required under IDEA. This reevaluation may involve assessments, parent input, and reviewing existing data to determine if continued eligibility and services are needed. This is called a triennial evaluation. A student's IEP should be reviewed and revised every academic year.
110.	D	IV.	The IEP team, which includes educators, specialists, administrators, and the student's parents, determines the most appropriate educational placement. The goal is to place the student in the least restrictive environment (LRE) that meets their needs. This means that, to the maximum extent appropriate, students with disabilities are educated with students who are non-disabled, and special classes, separate schooling, or other removal from the regular educational environment occurs only when the nature or severity of the disability is such that education in regular classes with the use of supplementary aids and services cannot be achieved satisfactorily.
111.	A, D & E	IV.	To increase professional growth, the teacher can learn to analyze data to evaluate student learning. That is data-driven instruction. Self-reflection is also an effective way to grow professionally. Peer collaboration is also a huge part of special education. Choice B would not necessarily be effective because using a grade book is not something that will advance her professional growth. Choice C focuses on consequences in the classroom and is limited in its scope of impact for professional growth.

Number	Answer	Category	Explanation
112.	B	IV.	When conducting a parent-teacher conference, it is important to start with positive things the student does. Then the teacher can show the parents behavior data to support her concern about his outbursts. Choice B does this. Choice A launches right into Brenden's negative behaviors and does not mention positive behaviors. Choice C puts the burden on his parents and is not appropriate. Suggesting a self-contained classroom is also not appropriate as the IEP team must agree on this. Ms. Jensen alone cannot make this decision.
113.	D	IV	During the pre-referral stage, it is essential that teachers use multi-tiered system of supports (MTSS). This is also referred to as response to intervention (RTI).This is when teachers use supports and interventions to prevent students who should not be in special education from being erroneously classified as such. This method also provides the necessary supports for struggling students.
114.	B	IV.	Operant conditioning is a method of learning that occurs through rewards and punishments for behavior. Skinner believed that we could control behavior by controlling the consequences of actions. These include: • Reinforcement (positive and negative): Increases the probability of a behavior being repeated. • Punishment (positive and negative): Decreases the likelihood of a behavior being repeated.
115.	D	IV.	Autonomy has to do with students' independence and self-governance. Allowing students to decide how and what they learn helps to increase autonomy and increase motivation. Students should be permitted to self-select books and work on things that interest them.
116.	A & E	IV.	To be eligible for special education and related services, a child must be in the age range of birth to 22 years of age and meet the criteria in two areas outlined in federal law: 1. The child must be identified as a child with a disability in one or more of the 13 categories defined in by IDEA. 2. The child's disability must adversely affect his or her educational performance.
117.	A	IV.	A 504 plan would be most appropriate for this student because a 504 plan is governed by section 504 of the Americans with Disabilities Act (ADA) and is less formal than an IEP. The 504 is intended for general education students, and an IEP is for special education students.

Number	Answer	Category	Explanation
118.	A	IV.	Parents and students have the right, under the law, to be actively involved with the IEP process and decisions made by the IEP team. A teacher should NEVER make changes to an IEP. Rather, she should share observations and data during the IEP meeting so the team can make decisions collectively. The team includes the parents and the student.
119.	D	IV.	Under Free Appropriate Public Education (FAPE), students who live in Florida, who are at least three years old and less than 22 years old, who meet the eligibility criteria and who have not yet graduated from high school with a standard diploma are entitled to receive free exceptional education services from the local school district.
120.	D	IV.	Under the Family Education Rights and Privacy Act (FERPA), student records are protected, and only the parents or legal guardians of students should get access to student records. The request should be refused on the grounds of FERPA.

Good Words List

We want you to *Think Like a Test Maker™* and pass your exam quickly and efficiently. To do this, we recommend identifying *good words* in the answer choices to determine correct and incorrect answers. Good words are terms and phrases from the test specifications and standards highlighting best practices. If you see these words in answer choices on the exam, slow down and look closer. There is a good possibility these words are in the correct answer choices. We have also included a list of *bad words* and phrases to avoid. These are typically not the correct answer choices on the exam.

Good Words and Phrases

Accommodations. Modifying instruction or using supports to help special education students achieve. Accommodations do NOT involve lowering the standard or delaying learning.

Action research. Evaluating data in the classroom to identify issues and implementing effective and quick actions to solve problems.

Allocating resources. Portioning resources so all students have equal opportunity and time while balancing curriculum and instruction.

Assessments. Using formative and summative data to monitor progress and measure outcomes.

Authentic instruction. Providing students with meaningful, relevant, and useful learning experiences and activities.

Balanced literacy. Reading and writing instruction that uses a variety of literary genres including literary and informational texts.

Bilingual instruction. Helping students use elements of their first language to support learning in English.

Celebrate culture. Finding materials and resources to celebrate the different cultures represented in your classroom.

Classroom management. A variety of skills and techniques that teachers use to keep students organized, orderly, focused, attentive, on task, and academically productive during class.

Collaborative learning. Strategies that are student-centered and self-directed rather than led by the teacher. Collaboration can also be working with colleagues or stakeholders to improve, create, or produce something.

Comprehensible education. Making information and lessons understandable to students by accommodating and using ancillary materials to help with language barriers.

Graphic Organizers. Visual representations of content. Especially useful for illustrating concepts like cause and effect, problem and solution, compare and contrast, etc.

Consent Decree. Protects students' rights to a free, comprehensible education. It addresses the civil and academic rights of English language learners (ELLs) and requires instruction to be delivered in a comprehensible manner, so all students can fully participate.

Critical thinking. Higher-order thinking skills that involve evaluating, analyzing, creating, and applying knowledge.

Cultural responsiveness. Instruction as a pedagogy that empowers students intellectually, socially, and emotionally by celebrating and learning about other cultures. This includes recognizing the importance of including students' cultural references in all aspects of learning and designing a productive learning environment.

Data-driven decisions. Using scores, writing samples, observations, and other qualitative and quantitative data to make instructional decisions.

Developmentally appropriate instruction (DAP). Choosing text, tools, and appropriate activities for the student's grade level.

Differentiated instruction. Providing all learners in a diverse classroom with different methods to understand instruction.

Diversity as an asset. Seeing diversity in the classroom as an opportunity to learn new things through the perspectives of others.

Evidenced-based. Providing instruction using materials with the best scientific evidence available.

Follow the IEP. A student's individualized education program (IEP) is a legal document. Teachers must always follow the IEP.

High Expectations for ALL Learners. Holding all students to high academic standards regardless of the student's achievement level, ethnicity, language, or socioeconomic status.

Horizontal Alignment. Organization and coordination of standards and learning goals across content areas in the same grade level.

Inclusion. Providing students with resources and experiences representing their culture and ethnicity and including special education students in general education activities.

Informal Learning. Supporting students with self-directed, collaborative learning outside of the classroom.

Interdisciplinary Activities. Activities that connect two or more content areas promote relevance and critical thinking.

Intrinsic Motivation. Answers that promote autonomy, relatedness, and competence are ways to apply intrinsic motivation. Be on the lookout for these answer choices.

Least Restrictive Environment (LRE). Educating special education students with their non-disabled peers.

Metacognition. The awareness and understanding of one's own thought processes, including the ability to monitor, regulate, and direct oneself to optimize learning. It encompasses the knowledge about when and how to use strategies for learning or problem-solving.Top of Form

Modeling. Demonstrating the application of a skill or knowledge.

Modifications. Changes to the curriculum and learning environment based on a student's IEP. Modifications change the expectations for learning and the level of assessment.

Outcomes. The results of a program, strategy, or resources implemented in the classroom.

Performance assessment. An activity assigned to students to assess their mastery of multiple learning goals aligned to standards.

Prior knowledge. What students know about a topic from their previous experiences and learning.

Progress monitor. Keeping track of student or whole class learning in real-time. Quantifiable measures of progress, conferring, observing, exit tickets, and student self-assessments.

Relevance, real-world, and relatable. Be sure to choose answers that promote real-world application and make learning relatable to students' lives.

Reliable. Consistent. Producing consistent results under similar conditions. Assessments should be reliable.

Remediation. Correcting or changing something to make it better.

Rigorous. A word used to describe a curriculum that is challenging and requires students to use higher-order thinking skills.

Routines/Procedures. Creating habits in the classroom helps students know what to expect every day. This type of predictability is especially helpful for students with autism spectrum disorder (ASD).

RTI/MTSS. A method of providing interventions before students are labeled as needing special education. These are used in the prereferral phase of special education.

Scaffolding. Using supports to help students achieve a standard they would not achieve on their own.

Setting Clear Expectations. This is a proactive approach to communicating how students should behave in class. This practice sets students up for success.

Specific and meaningful feedback. More than just a grade at the top of a paper, effective feedback includes positive aspects and how students can apply those positive aspects to improve. In addition, feedback should contain specific things the student should do to improve.

Standards-aligned. Ensuring that curriculum and instruction are aligned to the state-adopted standards.

Student-centered/learner-centered. A variety of educational programs, learning experiences, instructional approaches, and academic support strategies that address students' distinct learning needs, interests, or cultural backgrounds.

Vertical alignment. Organization of standards and learning goals across grade levels. Structure for which learning and understanding are built from grade level to grade level.

Wait time. The time between a question and when a student is called on or a response to a student's reply.

Bad Words and Phrases

Avoid answer choices with these words or phrases.

Bias. Inserting personal beliefs, stereotypes, and assumptions in the learning process. This can also include learning materials developed from the perspective of the dominant culture that excludes minority perspectives.

Call the parents, principal, district, etc. You are expected to effectively manage your classroom without deferring responsibilities to others. In real life, teachers will often need to call the parents or principal. But on this exam, avoid answer choices that defer responsibilities to someone other than the teacher.

Exclusion. Anything that excludes a student or keeps a student away from peers is the wrong answer.

Extra homework. On this exam, students should get all the instruction they need in class. In real life, we all assign homework. However, on this exam, extra homework is not the correct answer choice.

Hiring a contractor or external vendor. Anytime the answer choice includes using an outside resource like a contractor or a vendor to provide instruction or classroom management, this is typically not the correct answer choice. You are expected to be able to manage your own classroom using your own skills and capabilities.

Homework. Assigning homework is not a preferred strategy on this exam, especially when students struggle with the material.

Punitive solutions. Avoid answer choices that sound like punishments. For this exam, teachers are expected to implement positive behavior support methods to avoid any answer choices that sound punitive.

Student aides. While cooperative and social learning are very effective, avoid answer choices where the teacher uses a student to do important work like differentiating, translating, or scaffolding. Using students as translators or support for special education or ELL students can burden students with responsibilities they are ill-equipped to handle.

This page intentionally left blank.

Bibliography

Center for Disease Control (2018). 1 in 4 US adults live with a disability: Cognitive disability most common in younger adults; mobility disability most common for others. Retrieved from https://www.cdc.gov/media/releases/2018/p0816-disability.html

DiPasquale, G. (n.d.). Comorbidity: Learning Disabilities Association of Ontario. Retrieved from https://www.ldao.ca/introduction-to-ldsadhd/articles/about-lds/considering-coexisting-conditions-or-comorbidity-2/

Erbeli, F., Hart, S. A., & Taylor, J. (2019). Genetic and Environmental Influences on Achievement Outcomes Based on Family History of Learning Disabilities Status. *Journal of learning disabilities*, *52*(2), 135–145. https://doi.org/10.1177/0022219418775116

Federal Interagency Forum on Child and Family Statistics. (2009). *America's children: Key national indicators of well-being*. Washington, D.C.: U.S. Government Printing Office.

Georgia Department of Education (2011). *Special Education Supplement Glossary*. Retrieved from https://www.gadoe.org/Curriculum-Instruction-and-Assessment/Special-Education-Services/Documents/Supplement%20-%20Glossary.pdf

Gordillo, W., (2015). Top 10 trends in special education. Retrieved from https://www.scilearn.com/blog/2015-special-education-trends

Hansen S, Lignugaris/Kraft B. Effects of a dependent group contingency on the verbal interactions of middle school student with emotional disturbance. Behavioral Disorders. 2005;30:169–184.

Harry, B., Klinger, J.K., Sturges, K.M., & Moore, R. (2002). Of rocks and soft places: Using qualitative methods to investigate disproportionality. In D. J. Losen, & G. Orfi eld (Eds.), Racial inequity in special education. Cambridge, MA: Harvard Education Press.

Hurst, S. (2014). What's the difference between RTI and MTSS? Reading Horizons. Retrieved from https://www.readinghorizons.com/blog/what-is-the-difference-between-rti-and-mtss

IDEA Partnership (n.d.) Functional behavior assessment. Retrieved from http://www.ideapartnership.org/documents/ASD-Collection/asd-dg_Brief_FBA.pdf

Long, E. J., Long, J. N., & Whitson, S. (2009). The angry smile: the psychology of passive aggressive behavior in families, schools and workplaces (2nd ed.). Austin: PRO.ED, Inc.

National Research Council. (2002). Minority students in special and gifted education. Committee on Minority Representation in Special Education, M. Suzanne Donovan and Christopher T. Cross, (Eds.) Division of Behavioral and Social Sciences and Education. Washington, DC: National Academy Press.

Rubin, I. L., & Crocker, A. C. (1989). *Developmental disabilities: Delivery of medical care for children and adults*. Philadelphia: Lea & Febiger.

The Center on Positive Behavior Interventions and Supports (PBIS) (n.d.). *Tiered Framework*. Retrieved from https://www.pbis.org/pbis/tiered-framework

The Division on Career Development and Transition of the Council for Exceptional Children (2018). *Appendix A: National secondary transition technical assistance center (NSTTAC) age-appropriate transition assessment article.* Retrieved from https://www.iidc.indiana.edu/styles/iidc/defiles/INSTRC/TransitionAssessment/7%20Transition%20Assessment%20Resource%20Guide%20-%20Appendices%20A%20&%20B.pdf

The Global Educator Institute (2015). *7 critical areas for arranging your special education classroom.* Retrieved from http://geiendorsed.com/blog/learning-environment/7-critical-areas-for-arranging-your-special-education-classroom/

The U.S. Department of Education (2015). Disabilities discrimination: Overview of the laws. Office for Civil Rights. Retrieved from https://www2.ed.gov/about/offices/list/ocr/disabilityoverview.html

The U.S. Department of Education (2021). Every Student Succeeds Act (ESSA). Retrieved from https://www.ed.gov/essa

The U.S. Department of Education (2021). No Child Left Behind (NCLB). Retrieved from https://www.ed.gov/nclb

Made in the USA
Middletown, DE
13 November 2024

64537480R00126